Creating
Small Scale
Social Programs

SAGE HUMAN SERVICES GUIDES

A series of books edited by ARMAND LAUFFER and CHARLES D. GARVIN. Published in cooperation with the University of Michigan School of Social Work and other organizations.

Creating Small Scale Social Programs

Planning, Implementation, and Evaluation

Barbara Schram

SHSG SAGE HUMAN SERVICES GUIDES 72

Published in cooperation with the University of Michigan School of Social Work

SAGE Publications
International Educational and Professional Publisher
Thousand Oaks   London   New Delhi

For information:

SAGE Publications, Inc.
2455 Teller Road
Thousand Oaks, California 91320
E-mail: order@sagepub.com

SAGE Publications Ltd.
6 Bonhill Street
London EC2A 4PU
United Kingdom

SAGE Publications India Pvt. Ltd.
M-32 Market
Greater Kailash I
New Delhi 110 048 India

Printed in the United States of America

Library of Congress Cataloging-in-Publication Data

Schram, Barbara, 1934-
    Creating Small Scale Social programs: Planning,
    implementation, and evaluation / by Barbara Schram.
      p. cm. — (Sage human services guides; v. 72)
    Includes bibliographical references and index.
    ISBN 0-8039-7434-5 (cloth). — ISBN 0-8039-7435-3 (pbk.)
    1. Human services—United States—Planning. I. Title.
II. Series.
HV91.S2948 1997
361'.0068—dc21   97-4906

97 98 99 00 01 02 03 10 9 8 7 6 5 4 3 2 1

Acquiring Editor: Jim Nageotte
Editorial Assistant: Kathleen Derby
Production Editor: Michèle Lingre
Production Assistant: Lynn Miyata
Typesetter/Designer: Rebecca Evans
Indexer: Cristina Haley

CONTENTS

INTRODUCTION

If you are the kind of person whose typical response to a new challenge at work is "That's not my job!" (or as Alfred E. Newman would put it, "What? Me, worry?"), then this book is not for you. But then, chances are you would not be reading this book, would you? If you get turned on by improving things at work, starting up new projects, figuring out how to serve clients better, and seeing changes you initiated take hold, however, then this book may be just what you have been looking for.

In it, you will meet agency staffers and students who, like you, are engaged in teaching, counseling, organizing—that is, in some aspect of program implementation. Also like you, they all have the potential for influencing those programs—improving or expanding them—and in starting up new activities that take those programs to the next step.

Taking the next step and bringing others along with you is what this book is all about. It deals with program design and implementation, not large-scale, multidimensional programs that require a great deal of time and lots of dollar resources but rather those small-scale programs that take imagination, elbow grease, and know-how. Know-how is what Barbara Schram has and shares with you.

Schram writes like a novelist, but she thinks like a seasoned pro who knows what to do to make life better for workers and clients in a social agency and how to do it. She shares that know-how with you by demonstrating how others do it. What is the "it"? It is figuring out what needs doing and why, who cares, who can make things happen, and what resources it is going to take to do it. It is also how best to proceed and to assess how well we are doing what we set out to do. That is it in plain

English. In jargon, we might have used terms like *goals, missions, needs, strategies, procedures, tasks, stakeholders, monitoring, and evaluation.*

She writes like most of us speak. If she uses jargon, she explains what it means. Also, she backs up what she says with tons of experience—her own and that of the thousands of human service workers whose practices have been studied and catalogued. That is why you are likely to find this book useful—directly useful—in your work. It shows you what others have done and do and suggests ways for you to engage in program design. You are likely to find it full of down-to-earth and practical suggestions for how to get things done that often get left undone or that get done poorly. That—and the fact that it is a fun read—is why the book is likely to be so frequently selected for classroom teaching and agency in-service training. I have certainly enjoyed reading it and think you will too.

Armand Lauffer

Director of Project STAR
The University of Michigan
Ann Arbor, MI 48109-1285

1

AN OVERVIEW OF PLANNING
THE SMALL-SCALE PROGRAM

The future never just happens. It has to be created.
—Will and Ariel Durant, Historians

Today we suffer from an almost universal idolatry of giantism. It is
therefore necessary to insist on the virtue of smallness, when appropriate.
—E. G. Schumacher (1975, p. 217)

WHAT IS PROGRAM PLANNING
IN THE HUMAN SERVICES?

Social planning and the planning of social programs will always be
necessary in our society because the major forces shaping our lives are
essentially unplanned. New technology and the movement to or from a
global economy will uproot a workforce with the attendant family upheaval. Gentrification will destroy small apartments that have been home
to an economically stressed population, whereas war, floods, and dramatic
changes in social values will create new needs (Dyckman, 1983).

In the next several chapters, we will be traveling down a long, sometimes rocky and often exhilarating path, watching as several social programs are planned, implemented, and evaluated. We will start the journey
with some definitions. All successful planning can be thought of as a
process that creates concrete realities out of our dreams, vague desires,
and painful crises. The planner attempts to bring rational means to play
in the improvement of those conditions he or she finds in the community.

1

In all probability, however, the process will never be completely rational because the constituents or consumers of the program, the agency and the planners themselves, will be making uneasy choices and trade-offs at every stage of the planning process. Also, all the systems in their environment will place demands on them and place constraints on the ultimate shape of the plan (Ecklein & Lauffer, 1972). Publicly oriented planners need to worry not only about efficiency but also about social justice and decent outcomes.

The social planning we are concerned with has as its primary focus reducing or even eliminating the impact that social problems have on people's lives. It aims at improving the well-being of a targeted group by eliminating those barriers that keep individuals from obtaining the social goods and services they need to survive and thrive. Sometimes, social planning aims at expanding the boundaries of opportunity for that targeted population in new and imaginative ways.

Many social planners work at the administrative level of public and non-profit agencies, legislative bodies, and community or service coordinating councils. You do not have to have the title of "social planner" or be employed in a complex agency, however, to engage in planning a social program.

Every staff member or volunteer in a social agency can engage in program planning aimed at filling a social need. Program planning is that complex of activities that produces a specific product or event specifically tailored to meet those social needs. For example, a wilderness program in a residential program for troubled teenagers is composed of a complex of activities that has been designed and perhaps revised several times to create a safe but challenging series of events. It is likely to follow a certain set of procedures and be repeated over time. A farewell party to honor a long-time volunteer in a hospital recreation program is likely to be a onetime event. Both these programs have a limited audience; they are localized small-scale planning projects rather than citywide or national ones.

Organizing these types of programs falls within the mission of most social agency staff and volunteers. Doing them with confidence and panache is what this book is about.

Although much of the vocabulary and many of the techniques I will describe have been borrowed from the business world, I will try to never lose sight of the very human side of planning. This is not always easy to do. As volunteer efforts become institutionalized, they often develop into bureaucracies that dull imagination and the human spirit. Successful small-scale programs that once bore the personal stamp of their founding clients and staff often expand into major enterprises. Although I will suggest many aids to the rational planning process, I do not believe that people can be managed scientifically. I encourage the student of planning to combine a logical planning model with passion, gut reaction, and intuition (Aldridge, Macy, & Walz, 1982).

Planning even the smallest and most seemingly benign event can suddenly catapult the planners out of their systematic processes and into a political maelstrom. I use the term *political* in its most generic sense. Politics is not a mystical process reserved for the movers and shakers of the society. Rather, politics—which exists in all social groups—is simply a system for allocating resources. Someone decides who gets what, where, when, and how.

For every problem a planner decides to tackle, hundreds will be left untouched. For every consumer group included in the plan, many others will be deemed ineligible. Planners do not work on a neutral stage, an ideally liberal setting in which all affected interests have a voice; they work with political institutions, on political issues, and on problems whose most technical components may be celebrated by some and contested by others (see Forester, 1989; Gummer, 1990).

In this book, I will illustrate small-scale planning techniques with examples drawn from Let Infants and Families Thrive (LIFT) House, a community residence for young mothers who were previously homeless. In every activity they mount, volunteers, staff members, and residents of the house are constantly reminded that the question of how many resources should be allotted to young single mothers is controversial. It is hotly debated in the neighborhood bar as well as in the halls of Congress.

Because of the inevitability of conflicts surrounding planning decisions, there will be times when planners need to utilize techniques usually associated with community-organizing practice. This overlap is inevitable. A well-crafted program plan will remain on paper if support for it cannot be marshaled and opposition overcome. The reverse is also true. The most promising grassroots program for social change can lose momentum if its organizers lack the skills to conduct an awards ceremony to acknowledge dedicated volunteers or orchestrate a press conference explaining their opposition to a piece of legislation.

HOW DOES PLANNING THE SMALL-SCALE PROGRAM DIFFER FROM SOCIAL PLANNING OR STRATEGIC PLANNING?

This book is about designing programs tailored to meet a specific social need and then organizing the relevant community and human resources to implement it. It is planning with a small p, however, on the microlevel of the community, within one of the multitude of agencies and volunteer groups that comprise the human service network. Most of the programs I use to illustrate the planning model will, at least initially, be limited in duration. Some are onetime events that may or may not be repeated. Most will have small budgets, often supplemented by donations. Many will be coordinated by a small group of volunteer or frontline staff.

Small-scale planning is specific, detail and activity oriented, and attempts to implement the long-range goals or strategic plan of its parent organization (if there is one). Those long-range goals are usually established by the members of the board of directors or a government bureau. After articulating long-range goals, they continue to adjust them, trying to predict the organization's future needs and setting a direction in light of those forecasts. As you will see when you read about the LIFT House programs, each is supposed to emerge from and support those long-range goals. Abels and Murphy (1981, p. 118) suggest that a useful distinction between small-scale planning and long-range or strategic planning lies in the questions that each asks.

The strategic plan asks the question: *"What long-run strategies are required to move our service organization to fulfill this set of goals?"* The small-scale plan asks: *"In light of our overall plan, what activities should be done? What resources are required and available to do them and who will take what action, when and how?"*

Although the programs I will be describing are small in scale, they will often have significant impact. Many innovative programs started out as just such modest efforts. Some energetic person puts a tentative toe in the water, gathers a few neighbors, and organizes a support group for adoptive parents like himself or herself. Another convinces his or her friends to run a fund-raiser for the family of a paralyzed teenager. Perhaps these programs will be onetime-only events. Perhaps they will be repeated and expand, first throughout the community and then, like Alcoholics Anonymous, throughout the world.

Small-scale programs have the advantage of flexibility. They can slowly introduce people to a new concept or way of doing business in a manner that is not too threatening. Researchers who study organizational change suggest that "Innovations that are amenable to trial on a partial basis will have a higher adoption rate than innovations that necessitate total adoption without an anticipatory trial" (Rothman, Erlich, & Teresa, 1976, p. 22).

Small-scale programs take the same careful planning as their larger cousins. Small grants often require as much effort to propose, justify, and evaluate as their larger counterparts. Many of the techniques employed to plan small programs and special events in social agencies are the same ones used by planners operating on a larger scale or at a higher level of authority.

PLANNING IS BOTH AN ORDINARY
AND A VERY SPECIALIZED PROCESS

Planning is both an ordinary and a very specialized process. All of us have been planning programs throughout our lives. As children, we had to decide what TV shows we wanted to watch and then figure out how we could finish our homework in time to return to the TV set. We had to convince our parents that our plan made sense. If our plan to juggle homework and TV failed, it was quickly evaluated by the teacher the next day.

At some point during middle school, we had to construct a project for the science fair. Perhaps we decided to build a papier mâché volcano. We gathered a shoe box, paints, glue, and a bunch of scrap materials. We had to start work on it far enough in advance to have it ready on the appointed day. All our powers of persuasion were mobilized to convince a parent or sibling to act as our "consultant." We had to figure out the chemical mix that would create smoke and a big bang. Finally, we had to arrange a method to transport it to school and present it in a way that would engage the viewers and evaluators.

In later years, we probably sent for college catalogs, wrote an admission essay lauding our accomplishments, and sifted through the small print of financial aid forms. Perhaps we have had to implement a plan to close down a home and move to another city for a new job. Perhaps we have dealt with the complexity of planning a dream vacation to an exotic destination where planes are frequently late and you cannot drink the water.

Each occupational role requires some systematic thinking about the elements or steps in accomplishing a task in a logical sequence. Every new job plunges us into a political milieu, competing for coveted resources.

Some of us genuinely enjoy the challenge of fitting all the pieces together, and others dread it. Many new social service workers expect to focus primarily on interaction with people in need, avoiding the minutiae of regulations, budgets, and proposals. That narrow vision of the professional role, however, is no longer possible. Most agency workers are now required to be generalists, equally as competent in reading a budget as they are at "reading" a client's body language. As far back as 1978, a survey of 167 executives of social agencies in Los Angeles, California, found that staff were involved in program planning activities in 49% of their agencies (Jansson & Taylor, 1978). This trend has continued to grow for the following reasons:

- The line has blurred between the job descriptions of various human service roles. Robert Weinbach (1994) asserts that even caseworkers, therapists, or social workers, who spend most of their day in direct services, are still required to spend a considerable amount of time on program planning management functions. It is not true that managers manage, supervisors supervise, and caseworkers are left alone to see clients. Deinstitutionalization has spurred growth in the number of small decentralized agencies. The smaller the agency, the more likely it is that everyone on staff will pitch in when an event is being planned.

- Programs to prevent the emergence of social problems have steadily grown in importance. Even large, highly compartmentalized agencies now incorporate preventive program work into the job descriptions of the clinical staff. Instead of waiting for people infected with HIV to come and ask for assistance, they are sending staff out into the community to conduct workshops and public forums in male-female relationships and safe sex. Instead of simply working with court-mandated clients on domestic abuse after it occurs, they are organizing conflict resolution programs in schools for young children in the hope of avoiding violence later. Most child welfare advocates recognize that money and effort spent up front on parenting education might avoid the wasteful expenditure of money and human potential spent on placing children in foster care further down the line.

- Varying the tasks of workers has been recognized as burnout prevention. Agencies have realized that by varying a social service professional's job tasks within the agency, especially if they are highly stressful, worker burnout and worker turnover can be minimized. Finding innovative ways of delivering services is a constructive response to the demoralization that can ensue when the agency is forced to downsize and public support for its work seems to be eroding. Downsizing can mobilize workers to innovate new ways of tapping the potential of nontraditional volunteers and forging cooperative relationships among community resources.

Finally, direct practice workers often get promoted to management with little formal training in the requisite skills. Although the language of planning and administration, often lifted whole from an MBA program, may be off-putting, the techniques can be creatively adapted to our milieu. Mastering the skills of creating a small program also makes us more systematic workers when we are implementing the more traditional direct service interventions.

EXAMPLES OF PLANNING TASKS
IN SOCIAL SERVICE AGENCIES

A counselor in a community mental health center might be asked to take the lead or join an interdisciplinary team that is organizing one of the following:

- Compiling a directory of resources for children with learning disabilities
- Planning a staff retreat to cope with projected budget cuts
- Creating a seminar for professionals for a new approach to treating eating disorders
- Writing a proposal to a foundation to obtain funds for a summer program for teenagers who have problems with violence
- Preparing a support session for parents coping with the aftermath of the sudden death of a neighborhood child
- Establishing a child care corner in the agency's waiting room
- Mounting an open house for the agency's newly renovated facility
- Recruiting and orienting volunteers to assist in the transport of elderly or sick clients
- Organizing an information hotline for people who have questions about sexual identity

When given one of these assignments for the first time, the social agency worker is likely to fall back on those planning skills useful in private life. Just as an interview with a client is far more structured and self-conscious than a casual conversation with a friend, however, so too is planning in the social services far more systematic than the planning skills used in private life.

The ramifications of professional planning tasks are likely to be felt by a wide range of people who might not survive a bungled effort. Professional planners also never have the luxury of working alone. They are always interacting with colleagues, clients, the sponsoring organization, and the public. That adds dynamism to planning, but it challenges us to sculpt a smoothly running series of events out of the maelstrom of often conflicting viewpoints, levels of insight, and communication skills.

When program planning, we will also use many of the same techniques we employ when caregiving and counseling. Of course, these techniques will also need to be recalibrated somewhat. The content of our intervention might be different and our stance may need readjusting, but the tasks and the sequence in which we use them should be familiar ones.

I review those tasks in the following section.

TASKS PERFORMED IN ALL HUMAN
SERVICE INTERVENTIONS

The tasks performed in all human service interventions include the following (adapted from Pincus & Minahan, 1983):

Collecting data
Storing and sharing information
Negotiating contracts
Building relationships
Designing action plans
Implementing plans
Monitoring and evaluating

COLLECTING DATA

Many planners try to build their interventions on as solid a base of relevant information as possible. Sometimes we rely on interviewing skills to elicit pertinent information. We also collect data, however, by reviewing agency records of past services, entitlements or grants applied for and received, results of physical exams, psychological tests, research reports, conference papers, surveys, journal articles, and newspaper clippings.

We usually receive some type of referral statement from the client, worker, or group concerned with the problem. Sometimes, to collect data we visit and observe clients in action in homes, communities, other agencies, or groups.

STORING AND SHARING INFORMATION

All the preparatory data that is gathered will need to be put into a format that is easy to store and retrieve. Process recordings or minutes and notations on file cards or in a computer or tape recorder are all systems for storing and sharing information. We update and share our data via case conferences and other professional activities.

Often, we pass along the information accumulated to the media or as communications to the legislature or courts. We disseminate the information we have accumulated by preparing and distributing reports, resource directories, professional articles, or manuals or by making a video or tape recording, as appropriate to the situation. Both the written format and the computer networks are major methods of dissemination.

NEGOTIATING CONTRACTS

For an intervention to proceed with a probability of success, those involved will need to share a reasonably similar level of commitment and agree on a method of working together. Those who have a stake in the outcome should be aware of, and supportive of, the goals of the intervention. Through negotiating contracts, we try to increase the clarity of mutual expectations and the "rules of the road" that will govern our working together. The process of refining our commitment and methods is likely to be ongoing throughout the intervention.

BUILDING RELATIONSHIPS

In every human service intervention, relationship building is critically important. Without developing trust, respect, and some capacity to deal with and resolve conflicts, a planning process can run into all kinds of snags and blockages. Respectful and supportive relationships between and among clients and workers provide the mortar that holds all the building blocks of an intervention together. This is equally true when the worker is counseling a client or planning a program with a variety of other interested parties.

DESIGNING ACTION PLANS

The action plans that workers and clients design to guide the course of their future work often have much in common, even if they have different titles and degrees of formality. An individual education plan lists the specific objectives and items of work to be done with a learning disabled student in a school. An individual service plan charts the goals that will be worked on with an adult who is developmentally delayed or has a severe mood disorder. The worker undertaking a planning assignment is guided by an agency proposal, mission statement, work plan, or all three.

These action plans specify the hoped-for outcomes of the intervention and the activities or resources that will be employed within a specified period of time. They also describe the way the work will be monitored, evaluated, and readjusted.

IMPLEMENTING PLANS

Before a plan is put into action, workers often help to make the choice among alternative pathways. By anticipating stumbling blocks and figuring out how to get around them, they can offer emotional support, share their knowledge of theory and resources, and provide a reality check. They can also encourage and perhaps help to pick up the pieces if the plan falls apart.

MONITORING AND EVALUATING

Because interventions and relationships are dynamic, they need to be consistently monitored and evaluated so adjustments can be made. Social service knowledge and skills grow through a combination of action followed by evaluative reflection.

Attitude surveys or other test measures, as well as the opinions of outside "experts," provide the evaluative data on which to judge the progress of interventions. Each evaluation sets the stage for the next and, it is hoped, more successful action plan.

WHERE DO PROGRAM IDEAS COME FROM?

Ideas for new or expanded programs emerge from a surprising variety of sources. They bubble up from the bottom, fueled by the discontents and frustrations of workers, clients, or the general public. Sometimes, these discontents grow to massive proportions until there is enough momentum to create a new or expanded program. Less frequently, but just as significantly, ideas are generated at the top of a bureaucracy or hierarchy. Perhaps administrators have noticed, even before the general public, that a need exists and they may respond by redirecting their agency priorities or sponsoring a new initiative.

PROGRAM IDEAS OFTEN GROW OUT OF
DISCONTENTS AND COMPLAINTS

Although the expression is trite, "necessity" is indeed "the mother of invention." An urgent problem, however, might be publicly acknowledged only when many voices shout: "Something is seriously wrong and if we don't fix it, even worse things will happen!"

The often raucous public protests of the group ACT-UP have been credited by many with accelerating the cumbersome testing protocols for new AIDS medications. Cloward and Piven, in *Regulating the Poor* (1971), a classic review of the history of welfare reform in the United States, suggested that the periods of the most progressive social reform have usually been preceded by widespread strikes and riots that threatened the equilibrium of the whole country.

You can hear problems defined and program ideas proposed on park benches in school yards, at church meetings, and at the corner bar when people complain about their life situations. Systematic needs assessment can turn these vague rumblings of discontent into a coherent profile of what is wrong in a community and what programs might be useful.

Landmark federal legislation, such as Public Education Law 94.142—the act that mandated the mainstreaming of handicapped children into public school classrooms (wherever possible)—grew out of the accumulated years of anguish of parents who had been forced to send their children away to distant institutions or leave them at home unschooled. Those complaints, coupled with the research and political lobbying of public advocacy law groups, created in 1974 a special education revolution in our nation's schools.

PROGRAM IDEAS ALSO GROW
OUT OF OUR DREAMS AND VISIONS

Not all program ideas are fueled by outrage, anger, or despair. Some are the results of our dreams and visions of a more satisfying and richer life. Pick up a copy of your local newspaper and almost any day you can find an example of someone's dream becoming a social program. In Harwich, Massachusetts, for example, an 11-year-old girl, hospitalized for lupus and cerebral palsy, began writing letters to children she had met in the hospital. With time on her hands and a vivid imagination, she created puzzles and jokes, sending them out on a computer bulletin board. Many hospitalized children in distant cities responded. Eventually, her letters and puzzles turned into a newsletter titled "The Bearable Times." It now has a hefty mailing list. Other hospital recreation departments are using this new technology to help sick children share their unique experiences with each other. The accounts written by these children are also used in training workshops to help sensitize hospital personnel to the inner life of their small patients.

Vacation guidebooks for mobility impaired people, special sign language performances of Broadway plays, and a regular delivery of chicken soup dinners and flowers to shut-ins all improve the quality of people's lives. All these programs were organized by dreamers.

PROGRAM IDEAS OFTEN HAVE
TO FIGHT INERTIA AND FEAR

Program-generating sentences that begin with

- There ought to be a law that . . .
- It's not fair that . . .
- If only we could . . .

- It's a disgrace that . . .
- Wouldn't it be wonderful if we could . . .
- I've always wanted to . . .

are often followed by program-inhibiting sentences that begin with

- You can't fight city hall!
- What do you know, you're only a . . .
- It probably wouldn't work anyway.
- But we have always done it this way.

Planners need to create their personal mantra to silence these crushing phrases. In reality, all great ideas started as fleeting thoughts and most seemed overwhelming at first. We all possess more creativity and power than we realize we have or have ever used. To fight the internal and external naysayers, we can collaborate with other positive voices and other sources of energy.

PROGRAMS ARE ALMOST ALWAYS
COLLABORATIVE ENDEAVORS

Rarely, if ever, is a creative idea and a successful program the result of one person's work, although it might appear to be. That creative little girl who started her newspaper responded to a nurse's suggestion that her first poem was so good it should be shared. Others followed the nurse's lead by adding their support:

- Her teacher suggested she use her computer to reproduce the copy and send off the first issue.
- Her parents turned their playroom into a newspaper production room.
- A local plumber heard about the project when he came to repair a pipe and he offered to pay for the postage to send out the first hard copy issue.
- A newspaper reporter heard about "The Bearable Times" and wrote the article that I read. This project has been included in a forthcoming book about ways to harness volunteer energy.

PROGRAM IDEAS SPREAD AROUND LIKE
SEEDS IN A FIELD ON A WINDY DAY

Programs in social service agencies carry a label that says "Steal this idea, please!" Rarely, if ever, does anyone start an entirely new program that no one else has ever thought of. When starting to plan a new program, we inevitably discover that we are piggybacking on a program concept we have read about in a newspaper or professional journal, seen on TV, or visited in the past.

PROGRAM IDEAS USUALLY ARE HYBRIDS, SIMILAR TO BUT SLIGHTLY UNIQUELY DIFFERENT FROM THOSE THAT HAVE COME BEFORE

Sometimes our best ideas come to us during the sessions of conferences when speakers are presenting their program model for the homeless or addicted or physically disabled people. While listening to the speaker or watching the accompanying video, we start to think about how that particular program could be adapted to fit our own town or agency.

We read about a new program in a magazine or newspaper, clip out the article, store it away, and then one day reach into the file. Perhaps the time is ripe for that idea, but first we have to answer some tough questions: "How do I know that we really need a program like that?" "Is there any agency in town that is already conducting a similar one?" "Would a program like that be supported by my agency, church, or town?" "Could I overcome resistance to it?" and "If we started a program like that one, what modifications would we have to make to fit our specific age group or ethnic or socioeconomic group?"

One day I read in the newspaper that two men who had survived wrenching divorces decided to help others in the same boat avoid their experiences. Their divorces were conflict filled and expensive, and the couples ended up much angrier at each other at the end than they had been at the start. They decided to offer consultation to people starting down the divorce trail. First, they wrote a jargon-free manual on the ins and outs of separation and divorce agreements, arrangements for child custody, and so on. They decided that the process of mediation they had experienced when negotiating with union representatives could be equally useful for divorcing couples. Both had been impressed with the power of support groups such as Alcoholic Anonymous which break through the isolation of those experiencing a painful experience. Putting all the pieces together—manual, mediation, and support groups—they incorporated as the Divorce Resource and Mediation Center. This was the only program of its kind in the city.

A few months later, I read about a new program for blended families called Stepparent Associates. It offers a similar mix of information, mediation, and therapeutic support groups. Within a year, the local newspaper listed a program called Elderly Resources and another called The

Adoption Connection. These programs were not simply clones of the divorce program, but their originators might well have had their creative juices fueled by reading about that first pioneer program.

An interesting example of the spreading of a program seed is Elder Hostel (EH), which sponsors educational travel programs for older adults. EH began as a fortuitous juncture of two sets of needs. A few colleges seeking a source of revenue to keep staff employed over the summer break began to offer vacation courses to alumni. They were well received, but the pool of potential attendees was obviously limited. Then, someone came up with the idea that a much larger pool of summer attendees was the community of energetic, middle-class, retired adults looking for stimulating vacations on their limited budgets. They began with an initial offering of a handful of summer courses on a few college campuses. Now, their catalog lists several hundred year-round opportunities to learn and travel all over the world, on and off campuses. By linking up with Habitat for Humanity and Global Volunteers, they have added several service projects in Third World countries. So it goes—one program idea stimulates and builds on another but always with variations.

PROGRAMS ARE BUILT AROUND A LIMITED
NUMBER OF SERVICE DELIVERY MODELS

Although there are an infinite number of ideas for new programs, there are a small number of basic program formats. These can be combined in an infinite number of ways to fit the needs of different populations and problems. A large agency is likely to incorporate several or all of the following formats. A small-scale program might utilize only one format or might start out in that modest fashion. The basic program formats are the following:

Public Education, Outreach, and Fund-Raising
Resource and Referral
Direct Care or Individual Counseling
Time-Limited or Open-Ended Groups

Public Education, Outreach, and Fund-Raising Programs

Public education and outreach are the ultimate goals of all social service programs. Behind their specific services lies the unstated hope that they can someday prevent the emergence of problems. In the social services, we are all trying to work ourselves out of our jobs.

For example, a program committed to ameliorating child abuse might create the following education and outreach programs:

- Training teachers and medical personnel to recognize the warning signs of child abuse
- Teaching high school students and parents alternative techniques of discipline
- Consulting with a filmmaker who is creating videos on using techniques of conflict resolution aimed at primary-grade children
- Raising funds for recreation and respite care services to relieve the stress in overwhelmed families
- Recruiting and training Big Brothers and Big Sisters to befriend children in one-parent families

Education and outreach programs often use the same types of techniques that commercial advertisers use to get their message across. Instead of selling toothpaste, however, they are trying to convince the public to stop drinking and driving or reassure employers that hiring handicapped workers is not only the law but also good for their business.

Using these program formats, the planner might

- Conduct a workshop introducing the service to other professionals
- Write articles about abuse for the popular press or professional journals
- Compose and circulate a newsletter
- Raise funds to make a public service video or convince the media to devote time to showing documentaries on social issues
- Educate legislators and voters about an issue
- Lobby to create or change legislative mandates
- Write a proposal to receive funds from a government bureau or private foundations

Resource, Referral, and Advocacy Programs

Resource, referral, and advocacy program formats do not offer a new or expanded service; rather, they help staff and clients to locate and use existing resources. A planner using these formats might be

- Publishing a directory of social services
- Operating an information telephone or computer hotline
- Creating and disseminating a database of resources

- Providing written or visual resources for in-service training workshops and conferences
- Sending out public service advertisements of resources
- Producing a manual or video on how to file an appeal when an entitlement or other resource is denied

Some programs simply disseminate information. Others actively link clients to a resource, cutting through the red tape that confuses them. Others prod and monitor public-sector bureaucracies or file complaints for poorly delivered services.

Direct Caregiving or Counseling

Delivering services directly to people is the program format with which social service workers are most familiar. These programs are typically housed in community mental and physical health agencies, hospitals, community residences, public schools, and, to a growing extent, in the homes of clients, especially the elderly. We deliver services directly to individuals by

- Caregiving
- Case managing and coordinating
- Counseling
- Training, modeling, mediating, and coaching
- Intervening in crises

These services are generally offered one-on-one (or to a family group). They might be given face-to-face or offered via telephone or computer on a hotline. Both volunteers and trained workers with a wide array of credentials staff these programs.

Time-Limited or Open-Ended Groups

There are a variety of group formats. They can be classified according to their central purpose, which then helps one to decide on the optimum size, leadership style, meeting frequency, duration, and the flexibility of their agendas. The following are some of the most common categories of groups.

Therapy or Counseling Groups. All groups can be therapeutic in the largest meaning of the word, but some are narrowly focused on helping members resolve or cope with emotional problems or crises. These groups are likely to be led by workers experienced and trained in a method or theory of counseling or therapy. They are small and selective because the material they work on is emotionally charged. Sharing some common characteristics, members usually have a similar level of functioning.

Support or Self-Help Groups. Support group formats are more wide ranging than counseling group formats. They aim at providing emotional support and sharing of information and resources primarily by the members to each other. The support group leader is a facilitator who might be a social service worker or volunteer. In the specifically self-help model, the same goals prevail, but the leader generally currently has or has had a life situation much like that of each of the members. Both support and self-help formats often use some variant of the 12-step model pioneered by Alcoholics Anonymous.

Enrollment is often open-ended, frequently the programs are free of charge or very low cost, and groups vary in size, intensity, and duration. Sometimes, program planners are asked to help clients organize a group around their special problem and then they leave the group to its own resources once launched.

There are literally hundreds of different subjects around which support groups are organized. This format is probably the largest source of social service delivery in the country. Because of the fiscal limitations on mental health services under managed care, self-help groups will undoubtedly continue to proliferate (Wuthnow, 1994). The following is a small sampling of some of the support groups listed in *The Human Services Yellow Pages* (1996):

Food addictions
Sex addictions
Psychiatric illnesses
Physical illnesses
Learning disabilities
Victims of violent crime
Children of survivors of the Holocaust
Survivors of the Vietnam War
Gay and lesbian parents
Children and parents of gays and lesbians
Interracial families
Family members of incarcerated people
Women who have been battered and men who batter them

Training and Orientation Groups. These groups usually have an articulated purpose, content, and time frame. Their goal is to educate and influence the attitudes and behaviors of participants. They generally use experiential learning techniques with a great deal of participant interaction. Many are organized so that members can practice the tasks of daily living, parenting, and other interpersonal skills.

Task-Focused or Problem-Solving Groups. These groups begin with a clearly specified goal and usually are small and time limited. Their tasks are often preset by a board of directors or administrator trying to fill a need or resolve a pressing problem. They have an anticipated end product that might be put to immediate use. Committees, task forces, study groups, and interdisciplinary teams in agencies use this format.

Social or Recreational Groups. The goals of these groups are more diffuse and multidimensional than those of the preceding ones. A children's after-school program, YMCA, or town recreation center might have as their primary purpose one of the following broadly stated goals:

"to have fun";
"expand one's horizons";
"get to know others"; and
"encourage moral development or self-esteem."

Sports teams, a drama club, 4-H, scouts, or a fraternity, for example, have more specified agendas in addition to all the above. Often, subgroups develop within them that use other group formats. The drama club might appoint a task-focused committee to plan a fund-raiser, whereas, for example, some members of a sports team might decide to meet one night a week to give support to each other regarding the special problems common to women athletes in a male-dominated sport.

ATTITUDES AND VALUES
OF THE CREATIVE PLANNER

Collecting data to assess problems and designing and implementing action plans are necessary acts in the planning process that need to be done within a context of appropriate attitudes and values. The following are a few of the attitudes and values that are bedrock for the planner (Clifton & Dahms, 1993; Drucker, 1985; Schram & Mandell, 1997):

- *Open-mindedness:* To keep oneself open to receive new insights requires that the program planner strike a balance between automatic rejection of the traditional and facile acceptance of the trendy. Open-minedness helps us to eliminate our prejudices and biases about what we know will work. We should be willing to scrutinize an idea or an offer of assistance from any source. It also calls for a healthy dose of skepticism toward absolutes and a conviction that there is always more to learn about every problem. To keep a creatively open mind, planners provoke themselves and others to produce a great amount of associative content. Many free-wheeling ideas constitute the raw material of program planning.

- *Adaptability:* This quality is closely related to openness. We need to accept the inevitability that stumbling blocks will be strewn in our pathway. There will never be enough resources, time, energy, funding, or people to help, so the planner learns how to convert adversity into opportunity. Planners assess what they can realistically obtain, then they find ways to maximize scarce resources. Surprisingly, some of our best moments in the planning process come from the satisfaction of finding a way around a stumbling block. Throughout the book, I will suggest techniques to do this.

- *Innovation:* This characteristic involves the calculated development of new ideas built on solid data collection, experience, and the wisdom of others who have struggled with the problem. Innovation uses both the left and the right sides of the brain to analyze a situation and find the opportunities within it. This quality involves the ability to act bravely after a thorough analysis of the balance of risk to opportunity. It implies accepting occasional failures as part of the creative quest and learning from them.

- *Capacity to ask for help and offer feedback:* When we are open-minded, adaptable, and innovative, we are traversing uncharted waters. The only way to keep adjusting our course is to constantly ask, "How are we doing?" and "What could we do differently?" We constantly analyze our progress and problems and then feed the data back into our system to trim the sails. Conversely, we have to believe that others also need our honest, focused criticism, even when they may not accept it. Thoughtful feedback is a gift we give to ourselves and to others.

- *Perspective:* This is an angle of vision that sees the glass as half full rather than as half empty. It acknowledges that change, even when it will undoubt-edly be helpful, is still a fearful prospect. Uncertainty creates tension. Taking leadership in a planning task exposes one to a larger audience than most of us are accustomed to. Caseworkers can close their office doors! The program planner's work is exposed to public view. If one self-consciously views taking risks from the vantage point of potential failure, however, then no new programs that change painful situations will ever be tried.

- *Faith:* Although faith is not usually thought of as part of the arsenal of a social service worker, it is intrinsic to the program planning process. Plan-ners have to believe in the capacity of people, agencies, and communities to change. They also need to have faith in the power of ideas and in the limitless possibilities when people work together. The challenge is to keep believing this when faced with setbacks. Faith cannot be blind, but it also cannot be conditional. Strangely enough, when we place trust in people and in the process, we often create a self-fulfilling prophecy.

- *Resilience, humor, and a light touch:* Despite the fact that program planning can be tense and frustrating, and the agencies we work in must cope with painful problems with limited resources, planners have to develop a capacity to laugh at themselves. They also need to be able to shrug off their irritations with their colleagues and see humor in the inscrutable nature of people and the human condition. When program planning with clients in group and community settings, we often socialize. At impromptu dinners, over late-night snacks, and during bus rides and celebrations, we are treading the fragile boundary line between worker and client, worker and supervisor, and clients and the public. When we make the occasional misstep, a good belly laugh is as useful a tension reducer as a scream or a cry.

TRANSLATING ATTITUDES INTO BEHAVIORS

Of course, the qualities described in the previous section are easier to describe than to develop. Most of us have been schooled in convergent thinking. Too frequently we were expected to memorize or repeat. Rarely have we been encouraged to let our minds range freely, taking risks and learning from mistakes. We need to be patient with ourselves as we try on new attitudes and skills. They are not intended to be end products. Rather, they are goals to which we aspire. We need to relax and revel in the joy of being proactive.

We should take a few moments to relish a beautifully conceived and executed program, both for its humanistic and for its aesthetic qualities.

THE 5-MINUTE RECAP

- Because the future never just happens, we need to use planning skills to create a reality out of our dreams, desires, and crises, using—as much as possible—rational means to bring about improvements in the human conditions.
- Social planning aims at reducing the impact of social problems and remove barriers that impinge on the well-being of a targeted population.

- Social planning is often done by workers in administrative roles or coordinating agencies, but small-scale programs are created by a wide range of staff and volunteers.
- Rational plans inevitably are constrained by institutional and political pressures. Planners are forced to make difficult choices and trade-offs and juggle the demands of efficiency and creativity.
- Social planning builds on many of the planning techniques we use in private life.
- Small-scale planning relies on the same techniques and is as critically important as the larger-scale, strategic planning. It is usually done by frontline workers whose daily activities implement the overall goals set by the directors of their organization.
- Many agency workers, regardless of job title, are propelled into the planning of small-scale social programs by the following recent changes in the field:

    There are an increasing number of small community-based agencies.

    There is a growing focus on public education and outreach.

    There is a recognition that varying a staff member's tasks can lessen burnout and prepare him or her to move up the administrative ladder.

- When planning any small-scale program (such as an agency retreat, support group, or volunteer recruitment campaign), staff follow the same pattern of activities they would use if they were doing counseling or case management. They begin by collecting all the relevant data and then proceed to

    store and share information;

    negotiate contracts;

    build relationships;

    design action plans;

    implement action plans; and

    monitor and evaluate work.

- Once the decision is made to create a new or expanded program, planners continually fight against the inertia and lack of confidence that often stifles innovative efforts.
- Most social programs utilize a limited number of formats that are combined in a variety of ways to fit the unique needs of a particular problem and population and the skills and priorities of the planners. The most commonly used program formats include

    public education and fund-raising programs;

    resource, referral, and advocacy programs;

    direct caregiving and individual counseling; and

    time-limited or open-ended groups for therapy or counseling, support, training, the accomplishment of specific tasks, social interaction, or recreation.

- The successful completion of planning tasks depends on the planner's ability to develop the following positive attitudes and values:

    open-mindedness coupled with skepticism;

    adaptability to find ways around barriers;

    innovation that creates new ideas built on a foundation of data;

    capacity to ask for help and offer feedback;

    perspective that sees the glass as half full rather than half empty;

    faith in the power of ideas and in the limitless possibilities of change; and

    resilience, humor, and a light touch.

- Appropriate attitudes and values are not prescriptions that can be mandated. All of us work to achieve them, with varying success, throughout our planning careers.

PUTTING THEORY INTO PRACTICE

EXERCISE 1: IMAGINING POSSIBLE PROGRAM IDEAS

Collect five help-wanted advertisements for social service positions from the local newspapers. Suggest five small-scale programs that might conceivably be carried out in each of the agencies mentioned in those ads.

Advertisement:

Day Care Assistant for preschool program needed.

The following are possible small-scale programs that a day care center might plan:

- A Thanksgiving luncheon for the children and their parents
- A series of activities to prepare the children for transition to the local public school
- A fund-raiser to purchase new playground equipment
- A campaign to overcome the resistance of the neighborhood association that opposes the center expanding into the house next door
- An intergenerational program with residents of a nearby senior citizen residence
- A conference at the center on the mainstreaming of handicapped youngsters into the program
- A recruitment effort to attract volunteers after a major budget cut

- A book, toy, and clothing exchange for the parents
- A series of staff orientations before the imminent enrollment of a child who has AIDS

EXERCISE 2: ASSESSING PREVIOUS PLANNING ENDEAVORS

Choose an event in which you have been involved as either a planner or a participant. It should be one that you are familiar with, perhaps a high school dance, a celebration for parents' anniversary, a surprise party for a friend, a wedding shower, a pep rally, a walk or run for a charity, and so on.
Try to reconstruct what the planners did to complete each task.

Questions you should try to answer about the event:

How did the planners collect data before they began? What did they need to know before they could start?

How did they store and share information. How effective was the system they used?

What were some of the items in the contract negotiated with the members of the committee? What did each get out of the activity and what was each expected to give? To what extent was the contract made clear? What were some of the rules of the road of the event?

How did the planners try to build positive relationships among the planners and between the planners and the participants? How did it work out? What kind of feeling tone was generated? What happened when conflicts occurred?

What was the action plan for the event. Was it written out? How clear was it, how realistic was it, and how much input did the planners or participants have in shaping and modifying the plan?

How was the plan actually implemented? How close to the real event was the program concept or design? What needed to be changed? How was it done if things had to be changed in process?

How would you evaluate the event? What do you think went well during the event and what could have improved? What do you think others felt about it? To what extent were they encouraged to express their feelings about changes they wanted? If you were in charge of that program the next time, how would you do it differently?

CITATIONS AND SUGGESTIONS
FOR FURTHER READING

Aldridge, T., Macy, H., & Walz, T. (1982). *Beyond management: Humanizing the administrative process.* Iowa City: University of Iowa Press.

Dyckman, J. W. (1983). Social planning, social planners and planned societies. In R. Kramer & H. Specht (Eds.), *Readings in community organization practice* (3rd ed.). Englewood Cliffs, NJ: Prentice Hall.

Ecklein, J. L., & Lauffer, A. (1972). *Community organizers and social planners. A volume of case and illustrative materials.* New York: John Wiley/CSWE.

Journal of Non-Profit Management and Leadership. See for a variety of useful articles and to keep current.

Pincus, A. H., & Minahan, A. (1983). *Social work practice: Model and method.* Itasca, IL: F. S. Peacock.

Schumacher, E. F. (1975). *Small is beautiful: Economics as if people mattered* (p. 217). New York: Harper/Calaphone.

FOR FURTHER INSIGHT INTO THE
IMPACT OF POLITICS ON PLANNING

Cloward, R. A., & Piven, F. F. (1971). *Regulating the poor.* New York: Random House.

Forester, J. (1989). *Planning in the face of power.* Berkeley: University of California Press.

Gummer, B. (1990). *The politics of social administration: Managing organization politics in social agencies.* Englewood Cliffs, NJ: Prentice Hall.

Jansson, B. S., & Taylor, S. H. (1978, Summer). The planning contradiction in social agencies: Great expectations versus satisfaction with limited performance. *Administration in Social Work, 2,* 176.

Patti, R. J. (1983). *Social welfare administration: Managing social programs in a developmental context.* Englewood Cliffs, NJ: Prentice Hall.

Weinbach, R. (1994). *The social worker as manager, theory and practice* (2nd ed.). Needham, MA: Allyn & Bacon. In a relaxed style with little jargon, the author gives practical insights into the role of the human service manager as planner.

FOR EXAMPLES OF
PROGRAM DEVELOPMENT

Christian, W. P., Hannah, G. T., & Glahn, T. J. (Eds.). (1984). *Programming effective human services: Strategies for institutional change and client transition.* New York: Plenum. Authors provide very good case studies of workers making revisions, program additions, and modifications in social programs.

Fram, E. H. (with Brown, V.). (1994). *Policy vs. paper clips: Selling the corporate model to your non-profit board* (2nd ed.). WI: Families International.

Rothman, J., Erlich, J. L., & Teresa, J. G. (1976). *Promoting innovation and change in organizations: A planning manual.* New York: John Wiley.

Rothman, J., Erlich, J. L., & Teresa, J. G. (1981). *Changing organizations and community programs* (Rev. ed.). New York: John Wiley.

Shore, W. H. (1995). *Revolution of the heart: A new strategy for creating wealth and meaningful change.* New York: Riverhead Books. This book provides an entrepreneurial approach to program development that offers excellent insights into the use of resources as well as an inspiration to think big and take risks.

Wuthnow, R. (1994). *Sharing the journey: Support groups and America's new quest for community.* New York: Free Press.

2

PLANNING TO PLAN
Assembling the Tools

He has half the deed done, who has made a beginning.
　　　　　　　—Horace, Roman poet and satirist

TOOLS OF THE PLANNER

THE BIG QUESTION MARK

A spirit of adventure and the courage to take risks
The ability to motivate others to believe in the ultimate success of the plan
A clearly articulated set of goals
The skill of breaking large goals into tasks with small steps
A strictly maintained recording and monitoring system
The skill of finding resources and using aids for planning

THE BIG QUESTION MARK

The only stupid question is the one that never gets asked. (Anonymous)

Only foolish people sit alone in their offices trying to figure out how to solve a complex problem or recoup a failed effort. The creative planner understands that to tackle a perplexing problem he or she begins by asking searching questions, often a loud and to everyone in shouting distance. Asking questions is the sign of a creative intelligence. It begins to shine a light in an overcrowded and disorganized cellar loaded with random facts, emotions, and endless possibilities. The set of questions planners ask are the same ones that a seasoned editor suggests to novice reporters writing a news story: *why? who? what? what if? where? when? how? how else?*

Imagine the meeting of a task group convened to explore the escalating number of young adults thrust out into the community with inadequate preparation to find and hold a job. The members might ask the following:

Why are so many youngsters dropping out of school before they graduate?

Why is the number of dropouts so much higher than it was 5 years ago?

Why has this problem been allowed to grow for so long?

Who are the youngsters who are dropping out. From what socioeconomic or ethnic group do they come? What is the gender distribution? What are their achievement test scores?

Who are the people in this town who work with teenagers and might have some ideas?

Who, besides me, has an interest in this problem and might join with me in proposing some solutions? Shall I look to members of the school board, local business leaders, politicians, mental health workers, the police department, professors at the college, or the leadership of the church, synagogue, or mosque?

What do the parents, teachers, and students think the reasons are that so many youngster have dropped out of high school?

What strategies to prevent dropouts have already been tried?

What program strategies seemed to work well and which ones proved to be inadequate?

Where can I find other programs that are dealing with the problem of reducing the rate of school dropouts?

Where can I apply for funding for programs to prevent the problem or assist those who have already dropped out?

Where shall I locate my program for school dropouts? Is it better to be outside the school building, perhaps in a storefront center, or should the program be integrated into the regular school building?

When should dropout prevention programs start? Is freshman year too early? Is junior year too late?

When can I realistically aim at beginning this program? Should it begin with a summer session or when school begins in the fall?

When should sessions be held: during the day, in the evenings, or over weekends?

How can we convince the school board that our proposed programs are worth the investment of their limited time and resources?

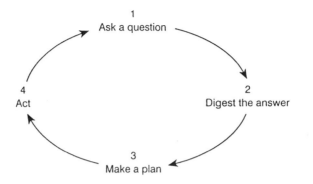

Figure 2.1. The Information Loop (From Schram & Mandell, 1993, p. 357)

How will we evaluate our work to judge how successful we have been and decide what changes need to be made once we have started?

How will we engage the interest of the youngsters who have already turned off to school?

Michael Quinn Patton, in his very useful book, *Practical Evaluation* (1982), stresses that the quality of the initial questions determines the quality of the data collected and, just as important, it sets the conceptual framework for the eventual measurement of program outcomes. He offers a simple guide to help us remember the questions to ask. He borrowed the following poem from Rudyard Kipling, and I borrow it from him:

I keep six honest serving men
They taught me all I knew
Their names are What and Why and When
And How and Where and Who

THE INFORMATION LOOP

In program planning, the process of generating questions and seeking answers will probably never end. Each question gives rise to the next one, like peeling an infinitely large onion. We digest the answers, choose the ones that seem most useful, and then use that information to create an action plan. We implement the plan and then ask a whole new set of questions about how it worked out or might have been better. The answers lead us back around the circle again in what we call the information loop (Figure 2.1).

A SPIRIT OF ADVENTURE AND THE COURAGE TO TAKE RISKS

After we have practiced the art and skill of asking questions, we sort through the mound of answers our questions stimulated. Many answers will be vague. Other answers may be clear, but one person's analysis will often contradict another: The teenagers we interviewed analyzed the problem one way, the parents saw it differently, the professionals propounded their reasons for the problem, and, of course, there were differences of opinion within each of these groups. Some parents thought that the drop out rate would diminish if schools were allowed to be tougher on the kids, and some thought that it would help if parents were given more training in discipline. Some of the respondents agreed that many teens suffered from a lack of exposure to the world of work in high school. To some extent, they were all correct. What do we do when "doctors disagree on the diagnosis"?

Planners who listen carefully can then distill the nuggets of wisdom in all the opinions they have collected. Ultimately, however, they will create their own list of priorities. Therefore, for example, that planner might choose to design internship activities for the high school. Workshops for parents and teachers might be organized to review school standards and expectations and propose changes to the school board.

The process of selection of ideas would continue as the planner helped members of each of the constituencies clarify their goals and visualize activities that would address pieces of the larger problem. Each program idea will necessitate trade-offs and compromises.

Even though the planner believes that the internship program should be made available to every student, this might not be feasible. Perhaps there is government funding available to work with "youths at risk"; therefore, realistically, the world of work program might have to concentrate on serving that subgroup within the high school population. If a local church offers financial support and the use of their basement for a teen service program but is adamant about excluding youngsters with drinking or drug problems, however, the planners might concentrate on serving a low-risk population that would be a broadly based preventative program. No one will ever be completely satisfied with the plan. It will inevitably ignore some significant aspects of the problem and exclude some subgroup that needs service. The planner has to live with ambivalence and ambiguity.

Finally, after the program has been in operation for a while, we will be expected to document its impact on the drop-out rate. Although there might be evidence of short-term satisfaction with the program—the young adults attend regularly and their mentors are enthusiastic about them—it may not be possible to show a decrease in the drop-out rate after only a year of program operation. Maybe it takes longer than that to stop the slide. Perhaps the economy is in the doldrums and more high schoolers quit school to help out their families, the church pulls back its funding, and the government grant is wholly inadequate and full of distracting red tape.

Program planning in a social agency involves, similar to counseling, a large amount of rolling up one's sleeves and starting to work on a problem despite ambiguity. We often lack accurate information, have limited control over all the forces at work, and have inadequate research tools to measure the long-term impact of our work

Having a spirit of adventure about the planning endeavor helps us keep perspective. Each new plan blazes its own trail through uncharted wilderness. Having patience with our clients, coworkers, and especially ourselves fortifies us as we set out on this perilous journey.

We gain firsthand insight into that animating spirit of adventure when we read the words of a program planner who obviously revels in the thrill of the process, much as a mountain climber exults in his conquest of a peak. In *Revolution of the Heart,* Robert Shore (1995) breathlessly relates his triumphs in creating a nationwide alliance of groups that help relieve hunger. As one reads of his wheeling and dealing, one cannot help but be swept up in the spirit that fueled his program development process and drew others into sharing his vision.

Despite its inherent ambiguity, small-scale planning is still more of a technology than are the other social service interventions.

Although nothing involving human beings is ever 100% predictable, if goals are realistically focused, and carefully implemented a sound planning model, a competent planner raises the possibilities of mounting a credible piece of program. As an experienced planner, for example, I can confidently assure my agency director that if assigned to design an orientation program for new volunteers I am likely to achieve the following objectives:

- The volunteers will perceive the warmth of their welcome to the agency.
- The volunteers will increase their knowledge of the goals and tasks of the agency.
- The volunteers will learn about the tasks the agency expects them to perform. Then they can decide if they want to do that job.
- The volunteers will have the chance to get to know each other and the staff on a first-name basis.

- The agency staff will gain information about the qualifications of the volunteers so that they can be placed appropriately.

Contrast this high probability of outcome with that of the following casework encounter. A counselor begins working with a young pregnant teenager with the goal of helping her (and her mate, if possible) choose the option that best fits her life situation and then set a plan in motion. No matter how skillfully the caseworker does the job, however, a number of internal and external variables over which he or she has no control can impinge on that rational process. The young woman might be under so much emotional pressure from her parents, her mate, or peers that she may end up choosing an option that is thrust upon her.

Also, the pregnant teenager may equivocate so long that the inexorable passage of time renders termination of the pregnancy, for example, a mute choice. Opting to raise the child, after waiting too long to make any other decision, she might find herself ejected from her home by her reluctant mate or angry parents. The slashing of welfare funding in her state might result in there being no money to support the baby, perhaps she suffers an emotional breakdown before or after the delivery and loses custody of the baby to the Department of Social Services or to the parents of the father, and so on.

This infinite number of interactions of social and personal forces, luck and chance, leaves the outcome far more open to chance than is likely when planning and conducting the small-scale program. As I assert this, I remind the reader that the outcome of any program will depend on the care with which a realistic goal and a set of implementing activities have been chosen. Experience helps sharpen our capacity to do this.

THE ABILITY TO MOTIVATE OTHERS TO BELIEVE
IN THE ULTIMATE SUCCESS OF THE PLAN

Workers who are more accustomed to counseling and casework roles may find significant differences in their posture and level of involvement when they undertake a planning assignment. In the casework or counseling encounter, the trained worker reflects and restates the client's thoughts and wishes and is careful not to assume too direct a role in advocating for one course of action over another. When program planning, this nondirective stance could be counterproductive. The planner often works for two masters—his or her committee members and that other group out there that is the proposed recipient of the plan. When the problems of the planners conflict with the needs of those who need the program, the planner might act as cheering squad or Greek chorus, providing motivation and courage.

Many planners try to exert a great deal of positive, upbeat control over the elements in the intervention. Assuming that the groundwork has been well laid, the planner shares his or her conviction that the plan is worth doing and the outcome is possible. The planner might suggest the utility of one technique or resource over another. He or she might urge the members to establish and adhere to a sensible time sequence and suggest alternative solutions if they become immobilized or travel too far down an unproductive pathway. If, despite advice and encouragement, the chestnuts look as if they might burn, the worker might have to pull them out of the fire.

For example, the director of student activities at an urban college related the following cautionary tale:

I had written a small grant to fund a program we called, Beyond Your Major. It was a very modest attempt to cross over rigid academic discipline lines to encourage math and science majors (who are traditionally very narrowly focused at our school) to become involved in one-shot community service projects. By even this brief exposure to the neighbors who lived in the inner-city area surrounding the campus, we hoped they would think about ways that social problems could be worked on through their own disciplines. Math majors might tutor in a GED program or engineering majors might help design a playground, for example.

I hired a very bright human service intern to coordinate the program, and we set up a schedule of meetings so I could help him to plan the nuts and bolts of mounting it. Twice he asked if we could set a date to meet with the funding committee to decide what to do if he couldn't get enough students to participate. Each time he proposed the "bail-out" meeting I reminded him that the number of students we needed to fill the service projects was so modest, that if we networked through the fraternities and sororities and put notices on enough bulletin boards we could surely fill all the slots.

He was doing a great job of contacting agencies, finding projects, locating transportation, sending out flyers, etc. But he just wasn't reaching out. I'd talk with one of the campus club presidents and get her all excited about participating, then I'd pass the name along to the intern to follow up, but nothing seemed to jell. When I called the prospective participants to find out what had dampened their interest, I'd find out that the intern had such uninspired conversations with them that the listeners lost interest.

Several times I role-played phone calls with him, trying to pump up his courage and enthusiasm. I encouraged him to phone the students early in the morning or late at night to avoid playing phone tag. But, bright and efficient as he was, he couldn't reach out with any self confidence.

I felt obligated to the shelters with whom we had made commitments to provide dinners for three evenings. I also had a commitment to the alumni group that had given us the grant and to the many students who could benefit from participating in the service projects.

Finally, I just sat down and made a bunch of phone calls. By gently twisting a few arms and with a lot of good-natured banter, I signed up enough students for each evening. Once they started serving the food and interacting with the guests at the shelters, their enthusiasm grew. I think several will return to the agencies on their own. And my intern basked in the success of the project. But I'm still not sure whether he got the message!

It sounds almost simplistic to say this, but if you do not believe a program is going to work, or you cannot inspire others to believe in it, it probably will not!

A CLEARLY ARTICULATED SET OF GOALS

A clearly articulated set of goals creates the skeleton, or infrastructure, around which every plan is built. Without clear goals, the whole planning process sags and falls apart in randomness and frustration. You may not know which road will take you to your destination when you start a planning process, but you absolutely have to know why you are setting out on the journey. Planning is a process that moves a set of goals into action in the most rational way. Without clearly articulated goals, we cannot evaluate how well we have done after a plan has been acted on.

Simply having a set of agreed on goals, however, is not enough. The goals need to be stated in specific or operational terms and they should be feasible and constantly reviewed and revised. Biting off more than they can chew has led to the death of many otherwise excellent programs.

For example, we set ourselves up for guaranteed failure if we plan a program around the stated goal of "Stopping the abuse of alcohol in our town" or "Stopping teenagers from driving when drinking."

Those goals are certainly too grandiose to be accomplished with one single program, if at all. Alcohol abuse is a complicated multifaceted problem. It has been with us since the first cave dweller discovered the immediate rush he got when he drank a gourd full of fermented grape juice. Our country once outlawed the manufacture and sale of alcohol, but prohibition was a disastrous failure that created more problems than it solved. Self-help groups such as Alcoholics Anonymous (AA) seem to be successful for many people who abuse alcohol, for at least some amount of time, but there is no formula to get people who abuse alcohol into AA or keep them coming back. Raising the legal drinking age, restricting the sale of alcohol on certain days and places, and increasing the liability risk to those who serve it all seem to help to some extent. The designated driver advertising campaigns about the effects of drinking and driving and tougher sentences for driving drunk seem to also help slightly. We need each of these program approaches and many others yet untried.

All we should set our sights on with an alcohol abuse program is to chip away one small piece from this gigantic mountain of a problem. We can only work on

- One aspect of alcoholism
- Among one specific group
- In one town
- At one particular time

For example, many chapters of Mothers Against Drunk Driving have chosen the narrowly focused but important goal of reducing the number of drunk driving incidents at prom time. Some groups sponsor lavish, all-night alcohol-free postprom parties. Other chapters acknowledge that the seniors are probably going to drink, so they try to cut down on automobile accidents by underwriting the costs of rented limousines for prom night.

Notice how clearly articulated the goals of these programs are. They aim at cutting down, rather than totally cutting out, the amount of liquor consumed or the potential deadliness of its effect on one particular high-risk occasion.

The politicians may trumpet their singular solutions with rhetorical flourishes that make good headlines and sound bytes, but social planners know they cannot possibly intervene in major social problems with overgeneralized solutions.

THE PLANNER NEEDS TO PAY ATTENTION
TO SECONDARY GOALS

Although every set of plans needs a clearly articulated, agreed on, and feasible central goal, there are also likely to be secondary goals that might be unarticulated but should be attended to. For example,

- A young man attends the meetings of his block association because he is genuinely concerned about a proposed shopping complex that will destroy the last lovely piece of parkland in his neighborhood. He is also newly single, however, and wants to meet some eligible women.

- A parent enrolls her toddler in a play group so that her child can interact with other youngsters. She also desperately needs a few hours to herself so she can read a book or work out at her health club.

These are legitimate goals and should be acknowledged by the planners. If socializing makes the meetings of a social action group more appealing, then a period of time can be established at the beginning or end of the meeting for coffee and conversation. If free time for parents is an ancillary hoped-for outcome of a toddler play group, then the leader should make sure its scheduling works for both the children and the parents.

THE SKILL OF BREAKING LARGE GOALS INTO TASKS WITH SMALL STEPS

After we have translated our goals into operational statements, we can specify the logical activities that can turn them into reality. Next, we try to describe in detail the many small tasks needed to mount the activities. We sequence these tasks and delegate them to committees or individuals.

This is the same process we used when we moved into a new office or apartment. We tried to figure out when to paint the walls, scrape the floor, and have the couch delivered. Of course, we were often forced off schedule. Perhaps we had been unrealistic or had not foreseen one aspect or consequence of our plan. That is to be expected, however; we learned to do it better next time from those glitches.

Barriers, mistakes, and unanticipated consequences of actions are opportunities to exercise our creativity, flexibility, and resilience. After we have survived them, we have an obligation to warn those who might replicate our plans about the potential pitfalls.

Some potential disasters can be anticipated. Every parade we plan faces the possibility of being snowed out or rained out. Therefore, the following is a rule of thumb: *For every plan there needs to be a clearly articulated backup plan with delineated step-by-step procedures for a reasonable list of "what ifs."* When anticipating the likelihood of inclement weather, a backup indoor location or a cancellation and postponement drill are the program's "umbrella"! For every person assigned to complete a task, there should be someone else waiting in the wings to jump in if it does not get done.

A STRICTLY MAINTAINED RECORDING
AND MONITORING SYSTEM

At a cocktail party, it may sound winsome to say *"I just can't remember names,"* but in human service practice, it is professionally unacceptable. By missing or being late for a meeting or omitting a name from an important mailing list, we negate our professed "caring" for others. Nothing dooms a planning project more profoundly than habits of disorganization and procrastination.

When urged to think back on a major planning endeavor in our lives, most of us would confess we have specialized in both disorganization and procrastination. I offer the following impressive illustrative example:

> I can remember when I was leading a student work project to Haiti. I had spent weeks arguing with my reluctant dean, assuring him that I could be trusted with the smooth operation of the service project in this admittedly tense country. I took care in orienting the students to the culture, making sure they had the proper inoculations, passports, duplicate drug prescriptions, parent's permissions, sturdy shoes, and so on. As we were finally settling down on the plane going to Detroit where we would pick up the flight to Haiti, I leaned over to my seatmate and pointed out in my most "I told you so voice" that it was dangerous to carry his passport so carelessly in his shirt pocket. As I said the word *passport*, I did a double take, realizing in a flash that I had left mine in the backpack that I had decided at the last moment not to take. A very red face, a dash off the plane, and a cab ride to home and back assured that my students would never let me forget that.

Important phone numbers or to-do lists scribbled on the margins of newspapers are guaranteed to be thrown out in the next orgy of housecleaning. Every lost bit of information takes us hours of work and frustration to reconstruct. Every deadline that is missed, because we thought the grant had to be turned in on the 21st of February and it was really due the 12th, is a lost opportunity for us and a crushing blow to those who depend on us.

Just as we expect human service workers to practice and increase their empathy and nonjudgmental attitudes, so do we expect them to master techniques for the efficient storing and retrieval of information. Both the popular literature and the professional texts on time and information management can improve skills in this area (e.g., Frame, 1995; Lakien, 1974; Wilson, 1978).

A seminar in gaining control of one's time and life often can be found in a continuing education catalog. Organizational skills require muscles that need to be constantly exercised to grow strong.

THE SKILL OF FINDING RESOURCES
AND USING AIDS FOR PLANNING

There are several aides to the planning process. Prominent among them are the following:

Pencil and paper, computer, calendars, and memo books
Chalkboards and erasable poster board
The planners' personal and professional network

PENCIL AND PAPER, COMPUTER HARD DRIVE
AND DISC, CALENDARS, AND MEMO BOOKS

Proposing that writing instruments and calendar books are basic tools of the planning process seems like a very simplistic statement. Surprisingly, however, many people do not approach planning tasks with them in hand. Lakien (1974), an organizational development expert, asserts that systematic planning is an act of writing and not simply one of thinking. Many English teachers assert that writing is, in fact, an act of thinking.

When involved in a planning project, most of us think about it almost constantly. Before falling asleep at night or waiting for the traffic light to change, the mind buzzes with details and wonderful ideas. Although profound, insights can be easily forgotten when we wake up, the traffic light changes, or the TV attracts our attention to the description of some cataclysmic event. Finding the correct piece of equipment to record those random ideas is a personal quest. Some of us carry a small notepad that is our security blanket, whereas others use a pocket tape recorder or computing devices.

Every planner needs a home base where the great ideas, newspaper clippings, names of agencies and experts, price lists of equipment, and so on can be warehoused. The project also needs an archivist, secretary, or report assembler who is the ultimate repository of everyone's bits of paper.

The written materials and database connected with a project need to be constantly updated. A computer file with appropriate subsections named for each of the component parts of the project works well, as do sections delineated in a loose-leaf notebook with many pockets. File folders in a special drawer or cabinet or a box in the corner of the office are logical resting places for later retrieval.

Shopping for and assembling the right folders, software, and calendar books to suit one's personal organizational style is a serious beginning act in the planning process. Each time we write down an important name and address, a price quote, or a task that needs to be done and who volunteered to do it under the appropriate heading, we are cutting through the turmoil and panic that can accompany the starting of a project.

Information committed to black and white and easily shared provides the basis for collaboration. Minutes of meetings are critical to the planning process, alerting each person to the jobs they volunteered to do and keeping absent group members inside the loop.

CHALKBOARDS AND ERASABLE POSTER BOARD

Take a moment to think about the way in which you take in and hold information. I am a visual person. I need to see little boxes and circles, words, numbers, and dates spread out before me. When I start a new project, I immediately hang up an erasable blowup of a calendar page on the wall above my desk. Then I start filling in the boxes with notes on tasks that should be done, deadlines and dates, and times of meetings. A large chalkboard, sheets of newsprint, erasable boards, and other devices help concretize vague notions of time and space. The more erasable the surface, the more the planners can shift around the assignment of tasks, time frames, and so on. These very visible charts are especially critical when planning with others. They help members review the progress of the plan and remind them of commitments.

Newsprint sheets with lists of goals, activities, and deadlines, generated early in the planning process and reviewed regularly, provide the group with a history of its progress that can be used later as part of its evaluation. When filed with other project notes, these sheets can be retrieved a few years later when a similar project is beginning. They are catalysts, providing stimulation and realistic time frames for a new project. Sometimes they are quaint reminders of how naive we were and how much wiser we have become.

DIRECTORIES, SCHEDULES, STATEMENTS OF POLICY AND PROCEDURES, AND OTHER RESOURCE MATERIALS

In this information age, there is a plethora of material. If you need to find out how many homeless teenagers there are in your state or how many women were widowed last year and their average salary, there are many sources of data. When writing an analysis of the dimensions of a problem and the justification for a program, it is imperative to include the most updated and carefully cited background statistics.

Although we are sure the data is out there somewhere, we often do not know how to access it. A reference librarian—especially in a college—can be a valuable resource for resources, demonstrating the creative skills needed to search a computerized data bank. The librarian points you in the direction of the major index or guide that leads to the publications with the information sought. A librarian led me to *A Guide to Information Sources for Social Work and the Human Services* (Mendelsohn, 1987), which has saved me many hours.

The telephone company's advertising slogan, "Let your fingers do the walking" is sound advice. At some point in the planning process, you will need to walk your fingers through resources such as the following:

Telephone directories
Directories of local or national social services for a specific population
Books listing private foundations and corporations that fund nonprofit programs
Price lists and the rules for the use of facilities such as public parks
Eligibility requirements for different types of agencies or services
Schedules of civic and recreational events in a town
Catalogs of specialized supplies and equipment

These are grist for the planner's mill. Before a group gets too deeply wedded to a plan, members need accurate information about how they can use a particular resource they need. It might be necessary to know, for example,

- If they can meet the eligibility criteria for a donation from a supermarket or food pantry
- What the deposit is to rent a van or bus and if it is refundable
- What the rules are that govern the issuing of permits to use a public park
- What other major events are going on in town the week they hope to hold the open house for a new community residence
- Which days are the religious observances of the main group they hope to involve in their event

Accurate data helps planners make difficult choices. For example, no matter what weekend in June a parents' group chooses for their conference on the special needs child, there is bound to be scheduling conflicts. A high school graduation, a major sports event, or a church bazaar will inevitably compete with it. If June is the only time they can book the local college campus and the local college campus is the only place with the facilities they require, however, there is not much choice. Therefore, they set the date for the conference, understanding that those competing events are likely to lower attendance. Perhaps they can design strategies to minimize the negative influence of the conflicting events. At the very least, they can make sure the conference sessions are recorded and the videos or reports are made available to those who could not attend. Every program decision is an equation, "If I do X, then I lose Y, but gain A and B."

THE PLANNERS' PERSONAL
AND PROFESSIONAL NETWORK

Of all the tools of the planner, the ability to creatively use his or her own network is probably the most useful. The directories, resources guides, schedules, and telephone books provide the raw data of people and places to use in planning. It is through our ability to go beyond the basic data, however, that we fine-tune our information. By asking the people we trust about how those resources have worked out when they or a client used them, we learn about inconsistencies between the services as they are described and the services as they have actually been delivered. For example, an agency might state in its brochure that it welcomes a diverse population. If it can only be reached by climbing a steep flight of stairs, however, then wheelchair-bound program participants are de facto excluded. If, despite the statement that they are an "equal opportunity employer," the staff is homogeneous, your clients who are gay or from a minority ethnic group might not feel welcome. Agencies have endless waiting lists, eligibility criteria, and "modes of operation" that they do not commit to print. This information can only be accessed through a phone conversation with a client or colleague who has had firsthand experience.

Our network of contacts smoothes the pathway to a resource. For example, perhaps after months of searching, we have found the appropriate empty storefront for our inner-city drop-in day care center. Then, we collected information from the building, health, fire, and police departments on licensing requirements. After months of bureaucratic foot dragging at the real estate agency, bank, or public bureaucracy, however, we might need to seek help from a city counselor (whom we play bridge with) or the police chief (who is a friend of a friend of one of our board members). Perhaps we met a legislator at a conference and she said, "call on me if you ever need help." Her name occupied a place of honor in our database, awaiting this day.

When you ask for a city official by proper title and name and begin the conversation by saying, "Reverend Jones, the director of United South End Housing, suggested I call you," you might speed up the wheels of progress or find out why they are turning so slowly.

Donations of funds, services, or equipment are most likely to come from people in the extended network of contacts. A friend who has a brother in the plumbing business might be the source of a donation of a free or reduced-cost watering system for our community garden. If you have a part-time job as a waitperson at a restaurant, perhaps your manager might contribute food or paper goods to the fund-raising dinner at the recreation program where you work the rest of the week.

Cynics often say, "It isn't what you know, it's who you know that helps you to get ahead in life." In program planning we say, "It is what you know and who you know that unlocks doors."

When our personal network cannot help us, we summon up the courage to go beyond it. We pick up the phone and call the author of an article we read to ask if he or she will speak at our conference, or we call every supermarket in the phone book, tell the manager about our food pantry, and request a contribution. The worst that can happen is the person may say "no." Surprisingly, most people want to help a social service agency. Many merchants, public officials, and even our own friends have simply been waiting to be asked.

The more specific and time limited the request, the better the chance of getting to "yes." The person who declined when asked to join your board of directors is likely to accept if asked to do one task that he or she enjoys. He or she might willingly paint the signs or design the poster for your event. Someone else might agree to invite his or her artist friends to donate work for a silent auction, play an instrument for a senior citizen dance, or drive a van to pick up chairs for an event (see Howe, 1991, and Shore, 1995, for excellent ideas on networking).

When word gets around that you have developed a support group for people living with a family member with Alzheimer's disease or that you have a good track record getting students who are brain injured into college, you become an important part of someone else's network.

If your reputation for mounting successful small-scale programs grows, you might be asked to chair a committee at the social service coalition.

UNDERSTANDING THE PHASES OF THE PLANNING PROCESS: TROUBLESHOOTING, MAGNIFYING MICROSCOPING, THE PROGRAM IN ACTION, WRAPPING UP, AND DISSEMINATING

Planners wear many different hats when following the planning model from the first tentative idea to action to evaluation. Each phase calls for an essentially different set of attributes or special kinds of intelligence.

In the first stage, the planner is a gadfly or troubleshooter. He or she listens sensitively to people's complaints, collects problems and inadequacies, and encourages them to join together to work on changing their situation. The planner is a skeptic, asking hard questions about the validity of those complaints, knowing that eventually he or she will have to back up his or her assertions with hard data. The planner is a passionate believer in the possibilities of social change, but does not go out on a limb without doing the necessary "homework."

In the second phase, having explored the dimensions of the problem, the planner dons a different kind of hat. Now the planner thinks big and creatively. The planner holds a magnifying glass to the problem. The planner steps back and views it in its fullest context. He or she visits other programs, gathering ideas and brainstorming alternative ways of tackling the problem. Visualizing many possible arrangements of appropriate activities, the planner assesses each for its strengths and weaknesses. Finally, he or she energizes others to join in grappling with the problem (to learn more about these skills, see Bobo, Kendall & Max, 1991; Kreztmann & McKnight, 1993).

In the next phase, having chosen a set of goals and activities and put them together into a proposal, the planner is ready to act. Now the planner adopts a much narrower and intensive focus. Placing each part of the proposed program under a microscope, the planner enumerates all the minute details that can turn a creative idea into a program that has a high probability of achieving its goals. Now there is much counting, sorting, list making, and deciding which activities will be done by whom and when. The planner solicits feedback as he or she proceeds, always ready to learn from miscalculations and recalibrate the plan (to learn more about microscoping skills, see Covey, 1990; Frame, 1995; Winston, 1978). In the next phase, the creative idea generating and list making are put to the test as the program unfolds. In-process corrections are made and the program is brought to its ending. Then, immediate follow-ups close this phase.

Of course, the program is far from over even though the chairs are now empty or the children have gone home. In the final phase, the housekeeping details are carefully completed. Those who could not come have some type of follow-up, and the evaluation documents are analyzed. Then the report is written and disseminated and these planners or others start the program loop all over again.

HOW CAN A PLANNER ADOPT EACH OF THESE PERSONAE?

Occasionally, I encounter a planner who appears to shift smoothly from troubleshooting to magnifying to microscoping and then can orchestrate the events and evaluate systematically. Years later, he or she continues to lead the program in the nitty-gritty tasks of its day-to-day work. Those people surely exist in the social services, but they are rare and uniquely talented individuals.

It is far more typical, however, for planners to feel more competent in one phase of planning than in the others. We have all encountered a colleague who can generate a host of creative ideas and inspire others with his or her passion and charisma but frustrates everyone he or she works with by coming late or unprepared to meetings. During the early phases, he or she is indispensable, but in the later ones this colleague is a roadblock. We have also probably worked with his or her colleague, who freezes up during a brainstorming session and can find a hundred reasons why your idea will not work. He or she loves, however, to compile lists of tasks and he or she can make a computer sing.

The psychologist, Howard Gardner (1983), has written extensively about the need to recognize, nurture, and credit different but equally important types of intelligence. Although we might excel at one aspect—and should acknowledge where our skills will be the most useful—we can still become more comfortable in the creative phase and more proficient at keeping track of details.

This recognition of different but necessary styles of intelligence adds strength to the dictum that the best planning efforts are collaborations in which workers complement and support each other's strengths and compensate for weaker areas.

In the chapters that follow, we will look in detail at each of these phases, detailing the several steps we climb to achieve each.

THE 5-MINUTE RECAP

- The primary tool of the planner is the energy and courage to tenaciously seek answers to questions such as why? who? what? what if? where? when? how? and how else?

- Asking probing questions to a variety of people, in appropriate places, is the sign of a creative intelligence at work.

- The process of generating questions, getting information, and then asking more questions creates an information loop.

- Answers often elicit an overload of vague and contradictory opinions, but from this raw data, the planner distills nuggets of useful wisdom, rolls up his or her sleeves, and creates his or her own understanding of the problem at hand.

- All social service interventions are inherently ambiguous, but small-scale planning is more of a technology than are the other strategies.

- The ability to motivate others to believe in the ultimate success of the planning endeavor and the ability to estimate when worker action is needed to salvage a faltering plan are invaluable skills, although they might not be as appropriate to use when doing counseling or casework.

- A clearly articulated, achievable set of primary and secondary goals create the skeleton around which the final plan can be built.

- Once articulated and accepted, goals are translated into operational statements and then broken down into a series of tasks to be sequenced and delegated.

- A carefully constructed and maintained recording and monitoring system assures that the plan can be readjusted and implemented in the most caring and efficient manner.

- Competent planners use writing tools, resource materials, and their network of personal and professional contacts to implement a plan and prepare for contingencies.

- The planning process is an organic whole that incorporates several phases of activity, beginning with problem identification (troubleshooting) and proceeding onto

  program design (magnifying);

  program specification (microscoping, program implementation; and

  program evaluation and follow-ups.

- Although planners need to be able to function well in each of these phases, most will discover that they have stronger skills in one phase than in the others. Thus, planning endeavors work best when they are collaborations in which members complement and support each other's strengths.

PUTTING THEORY INTO PRACTICE

EXERCISE 1: GETTING STARTED

Reread the quotation at the beginning of this chapter:

"He has half the deed done who has made a beginning!" This statement can be interpreted in several ways. What do you think the Roman writer meant by it? What does it mean to you? Before reading the following example, list at least five ways that this quotation could be interpreted.

Example of one worker's answer:

I think that the author meant several things, first is that we often keep ourselves from starting on a venture by obsessing about "what will happen, if." But once we allow ourselves to start asking serious questions about the problem, we find that there are many resources available to us that we didn't realize existed. Often others join us in the venture and a dynamic begins that can feed on itself.

I often think back to when I was a recreation worker running teenage dances. Sometimes for the first hour, most of the teens stayed outside the center, waiting for it to get going. A few would wander in, see the floor was almost empty, and then they would leave. Finally I would go out on the street and strong arm 10 kids into coming inside. As soon as they entered, the dance began to take on a life of its own and the others would be drawn in. But no one wanted to be the first one inside. It takes courage and a lack of self-consciousness.

I think the other interpretation is that if you really think through a project in advance of starting and line up everything you will need, you are halfway to completing it. I think about when you have a term paper assigned. No matter how overwhelmingly difficult it seems, if you just go to the library and get out a book on the topic and start jotting down random thoughts, instead of fretting about it, you find that an outline begins to emerge and that outline points you to the next step.

To what extent are the experiences of this writer similar to yours?

EXERCISE 2: RESOURCES SCAVENGER HUNT

You work as a counselor at a nonprofit residence that provides low-cost lodging to out-of-town families who are visiting their children while they undergo cancer treatment at a nearby major medical center.[1] You have been assigned to coordinate a block party to introduce your agency to the neighbors and thank the volunteers for the work they have done in fixing up the house.

Task 1

Generate at least five questions you should ask about the safety issues and legal problems that might be involved in having a large outdoor event on a pubic street. After you list the questions, suggest people or places in your town that might be knowledgeable resources for answering each question. For example:

Question	Resource
Is it legal to block off a street to traffic?	Ask at police headquarters
If it is, what do I have to do?	

Task 2

Your director has warned you that with all the expenses of opening a new program there is virtually no money left in the program budget. She expects you to put on a festive event with entertainment and refreshments, however. List at least 10 resources you could turn to for help with the party. Remember to begin your list by tapping your own personal and professional network. After you list each resource, find out what you have to do to obtain help. Does it require some type of special request letter? If so, what is the time frame, and so on.

**Examples of resources in
one worker's personal network**

- My mother works in a bank and the employees there have a fund that charitable groups can apply to for small grants. I need to write the manager.

- My boyfriend plays in a rock band, perhaps they would perform. Ask after we know the date for certain.

- I have a friend who used to work for a YMCA and I know she put on a lot of events. She could give me ideas.

Task 3

You have decided that it would be very festive to have shirts and balloons printed with the agency name. They could be sold at a nominal cost. Using your phone directory and any other resources you have, locate places where these might be obtained. Find out what the cost would be and how far in advance they have to be ordered.

Task 4

List and describe at least two kinds of record keeping you think would be appropriate for a block party.

CITATIONS AND SUGGESTIONS
FOR FURTHER READING

Gardner, H. (1995). *Frames of mind: The theory of multiple intelligences.* New York: Basic Books.
Patton, M. Q. (1982). *Practical evaluations.* Beverly Hills, CA: Sage.
Schram, B., & Mandell, B. R. (1993). *Introduction to human services policy and practice* (2nd ed.). New York: Macmillan. (See especially Chapter 11, pp. 425-464).

AIDS FOR PLANNING: TWO USEFUL BOOKS

Leibert, E. R., & Sheldon, B. E. (1974). *Handbook of special events for non-profit organizations.* New York: Association Press.
Mendelsohn, H. N. (1987). *A guide to information sources for social work and the human services.* Phoenix, AZ: Oryx Press.

FOR FURTHER INSIGHTS INTO
THE MICROSCOPING STAGE

Covey, S. R. (1990). *The 7 habits of highly effective people: Restoring the character ethic.* New York: Simon & Schuster.
Frame, D. J. (1995). *Managing projects in organizations: How to make the best use of time, technique, and people.* San Francisco: Jossey-Bass.
Lakien, A. (1974). *How to get control of your time and your life.* New York: New American Library.
Winston, S. (1978). *Getting organized.* New York: Warner.

FOR FURTHER INSIGHTS INTO
THE MAGNIFYING STAGE

Two well-written compilations of the wisdom of community organizers with very concrete suggestions for building vision and commitment for civic projects, especially in the face of declining governmental resources, include the following:

Bobo, K., Kendall, J., & Max, S. (1991). *Organize! A manual for activists in the 1990's* (2nd ed.). Santa Ana, CA: Seven Locks Press.
Kretzmann, J. P., & McKnight, J. (1993). *Building community from the inside out, a path towards finding and mobilizing a community's assets.* Evanston, IL: Northwestern University, Neighborhood Innovation Network. (Distributed by ACTA Publications, 4848 N. Clark St., Chicago, IL 60640)

A recent book full of the excitement and creativity of program planning and the think-big stance of the early stages of program development is the following:

Shore, W. H. (1995). *Revolution of the heart: A new strategy for creating wealth and meaningful change.* New York: Riverhead Books.

NOTE

1. The agency described in this exercise is patterned after the nonprofit Ronald MacDonald Houses sponsored by the fast-food corporation in many cities in the country.

3

MEET THE PLANNERS FROM LIFT HOUSE (LET INFANTS AND FAMILIES THRIVE)

Only unreasonable people will not accept the world as it is. Therefore all change depends on unreasonable people.

—George Bernard Shaw

PLANNING IS NOT AN ABSTRACT EXERCISE

While learning how to plan and while actually doing it, the skillful planner needs to visualize the event at the end of the road he or she is traveling. This process of visualization is like the role playing we have done during in-service workshops or during a counseling session when preparing a client for an important job interview or an emotion-laden encounter.

Like the director of a theatrical performance, the planner closes his or her eyes and visualizes a well-lit stage filled with actors, scenery, and props, facing a live audience. The planner conjures up the conference room, sports field, or lodge of the camp where he or she is contemplating mounting a program. In the planner's mind's eye, he or she positions the crafts or refreshment table, arranges the chairs in a pattern that facilitates the agenda, and decides where posters, the microphone, and spectators should be strategically placed. In the planner's mind's eye, he or she "sees" the participants—their ages, genders, ethnicity, physical disabilities, and so on. The planner's first visualizations will probably paint the ideal or best program imaginable.

By the time the event occurs, the visualizations, now transferred onto many sheets of paper, are closer to the way the event is actually likely to unfold. At each stage, the planner has been forced to make several less than perfect choices of place, schedule, staff, budget, speakers, refreshments, and so on. Each time a barrier presented itself—perhaps the space the planner requested was not available, the speaker had to cancel, or the mail room buried the planner's notices so that they did not get sent out in a timely fashion—the planner readjusted the program elements. He or she tried to turn each barrier into an opportunity and to find a creative alternative. Sometimes, that actually happened. Some unexpected pieces of luck and chance also set the stage for the final scene; perhaps a reporter from the local newspaper was intrigued by the project so he or she wrote a full-page story about it, or perhaps the last-minute fill-in speaker turned out to be much more engaging than the one who had canceled.

VISUALIZING THE STEPS IN THE
PROGRAM DEVELOPMENT PROCESS

So that the reader can visualize the steps in the planning process that I will describe in the following chapters, I have "created" a small social service agency that I have named LIFT House (Let Infants and Families Thrive). It is a private, nonprofit, residential program for young mothers who are homeless.

I have also created a staff coordinator, board member, volunteers, and residents who fill the house with their laughter, arguments, and newsprint planning charts. As I describe each of the steps in the planning process, I will use the people of LIFT House to illustrate the techniques of creating the small-scale program.

I could have chosen any one of an almost limitless number of actual or hypothetical programs to use as an illustration. The content of various programs and the populations they serve vary, but the steps necessary to create a sound program are the same. The model I will be describing could be used just as effectively to plan any one of the following:

- A suicide prevention hotline
- A support group for couples who struggle with infertility
- An apprenticeship or outward-bound program for students who are learning disabled
- A gleaning program that collects surplus food from restaurants and transports it safely to shelters for homeless adults

- A drop-a-dime program that identifies crack houses and pressures the police to shut them down
- A program that sends books to men and women who are incarcerated
- A citizen's action group that is mobilizing the community to prevent the closing of their only super market
- An intergenerational program that links up college students and the elderly residents of an assisted-living home to exchange oral histories
- A midnight basketball program that offers teenagers an alternative to the violence that often plagues their community and their lives

Therefore, although I care profoundly about creating useful programs for young mothers and their children, this topic is incidental to the central mission of this book, which is to present a model useful in developing all small-scale social program.

VISUALIZING LIFT HOUSE

Close your eyes and create a mental picture of LIFT House. It is a large four-story Victorian-era house with gabled roofs and a wraparound porch. It is a faded "painted lady"—timeworn but solid. It sits on a narrow side street among a row of wooden double- and triple-deckers of smaller size and newer vintage.

The house has been in the neighborhood since the early 1900s. When the board members of LIFT purchased it, it was a boarded-up eyesore. Three years ago, the board members renovated it, creating a transitional home for eight young women and their infant babies. It is located in an outlying section of a small industrial town. A bus on a nearby street runs into the center of town and out to the suburban shopping malls.

Along the front of the house, there is a cross-hatched fence and a row of newly planted evergreen bushes. In the back of the house, there is a low, wooden play structure with two small caged swings and a tiny seesaw. There are also two picnic tables and a small vegetable garden in the back-yard. Several folded baby strollers sit on the back porch. A sloping ramp leads from the back porch to the street.

LIFT is a private nonprofit corporation run by a nine-person board of directors. The women who live at LIFT House were referred by social workers at the Department of Social Services or the local family service agency, by staff at the local hospital or homeless or battered women's shelter, by a doctor, or by a person from the clergy. In a few instances, the women heard about it by word of mouth and referred themselves. Each young woman can live at LIFT House for 1 year. After that, she can choose to move into a small apartment within a three-block radius of the main house for another 2 years. To be admitted to the house, the women must meet the following eligibility criteria:

Unable to live with family members or a mate

Under 21 years of age

Have an infant under the age of 1 year

Be reasonably mentally and physically healthy

Be drug and alcohol free at the current time

Commit herself to trying to live at the house for 1 year

Commit herself to finishing school with a diploma or general equivalency diploma (GED), working, or entering a training program or college

The house employs one full-time program coordinator, a child care teacher, a few part-time house counselors, and has many volunteers. There is a day care program at the house and parenting classes and support groups that are open to both residents and other young parents from the community. The women attend programs at many community agencies. Those who have jobs pay a portion of their salary to the house, some receive financial assistance from the fathers or their families, and the shortfall is made up by funding or in-kind assistance from the Department of Social Services and private foundations.

LIFT's board of directors is composed of professionals and community activists and two elected residents. In day-to-day routines, the house is self-governing. The current residents meet regularly to discuss and make decisions about the many details of shared living.

The primary goal of the program is to act as a bridge to independent living for each of the parents and as a solid launching pad for the infants. It provides a special kind of "extended family network" for the mothers and their babies, helping them to negotiate their critical first years. Although they can only live at LIFT for a maximum of 3 years, the resources of the house are committed to helping the alumni make the transition to their next living and working situation. Some of the mothers pool resources and share an apartment, whereas others may live with family members or a mate. It is hoped that when they leave, each will have a realistic plan for the future and some solid parenting skills. Perhaps they will also be able to contribute their experience and knowledge to the agency to help other young parents.

MEET THE PROGRAM PLANNERS
WHO WORK AT LIFT HOUSE

Now that the reader has "seen" the house, I introduce you to five of the volunteers and workers at LIFT. You will come to know them as I describe their planning tasks as they create their own small-scale programs.

Ana Lee Chu

Ms. Chu is a 48-year-old woman who seems to comfortably juggle many roles in life, doing each with a surprising amount of ease and a quick smile. She works full-time as a dental assistant in a large group practice. She is also the mother of five children, who range in age from 7 to 22. She and her husband, who is an architect, are active in many groups within their town. Of all their volunteer roles, LIFT House has been the most important.

Several years ago, Ms. Chu was doing volunteer dental care at a shelter for men and women who were homeless. The program was begun by the minister and supported by the members of her church. Once each week, while her husband and children served food and distributed blankets and towels, she examined and cleaned the teeth of as many as 20 men and women. When she found serious cases of decay, she would arrange to have the person treated by one of the volunteer dentists she had recruited.

Through her sensitive work at the shelter, she began to be known and respected by many of the "street people" in her town. On several occasions, a woman would tell her about her own impending pregnancy or a pregnant friend who was on the streets with no place to live. Several times, she had let a young woman and her baby stay on the couch in her living room because she could not imagine them spending the night on the streets or in an overcrowded shelter. It was a kind act, but it was stop-gap measure that made scant difference in the future of the young family. It also raised some thorny personal problems about her own boundaries because she had her own children to care for.

Several times she called the local welfare office in a desperate search for financial or medical assistance for a young woman. The more she searched for services, the more frustrated she became. Phones were often busy, and the workers were out in the field. Usually, the women did not have any of the documentation required to file for pubic assistance.

At the same time, the state legislature was busy cutting the welfare department's budget. Sometimes the women found a place to stay but it lacked the child care that would enable the women to look for work or finish their education. Occasionally, one lucky woman would find an apartment but could not raise the "up-front" money for the first month's rent and security deposit.

Inevitably, these young mothers would be forced to give up their children to the foster care system. Ms. Chu would watch helplessly as they drifted into drugs, prostitution, or the abusive relationships that had propelled them out onto the streets in the first place. She also watched the babies start a downhill slide. With poor nutrition, little health care, and a mother who was loving but unable to nurture them, they had little ballast with which to face the world.

Through her many phone calls and visits to the Department of Social Services (DSS), she became friendly with Kristen Connelly, a social worker at DSS. Kristen was sympathetic but often came up empty-handed. She agreed with Ms. Chu that if these women could find reliable child care, a decent place to live, a job, and help in learning how to parent, they might be able to "make it" on their own some day. A small investment now could break the cycle of dependency and depression in the future.

Eventually, they came to the conclusion that if they wanted a well-thought-out program for these young mothers they would have to create it themselves. They gathered some of their friends together in Kristen's living room and, after much discussion and reality testing, decided to start off with a small child care program designed for mothers living in shelters. That program evolved, with many interim steps, into the multiservice residence that is LIFT House today.

Now, there is talk of expanding the agency to include a second LIFT House designed especially for mothers who have AIDS. Ms. Chu, however, is not sure if she can handle another major project and keep juggling her own balls. Currently, she serves as chair of the LIFT board. She is also the "house mother" and a general inspiration to everyone.

When asked what it was that made her take on so much leadership, Ms. Chu said,

I've been an active volunteer for as many years as I can remember. My mom used to take me with her to visit her dad when he was in a nursing home. After he died, we continued going back once a week to visit his friends. I joined the Girl Scouts and worked on neighborhood clean-ups, then I became a "candy striper" at the local hospital. When I was in high school and all through dental hygiene school, I tutored kids who had recently come from Haiti and Central America. That's how I met my husband. He and I ran a three-legged relay race together in a fund-raiser that I helped organize for that program. We've been tied up ever since.

My husband came to the first meeting when we dreamed up LIFT. Since he is an architect he located the house we purchased and he has been in charge of renovations and maintenance. My two kids, who are in college now, come to LIFT House to play with the babies or take them out when their moms are at work or in class.

Ms. Chu has been planning small-scale projects for all her adult life. Now, however, as board chair she does much more strategic or long-range planning than actual small-scale program development and implementation. As the reader will see, there are both differences and similarities between these two types of planning.

Kristen Connelly

Kristen Connelly is 31 years old and a graduate of the local college and graduate school of social work. She is engaged to be married and currently lives with two roommates. She is the full-time program coordinator at LIFT. During her rare time off, she plays the conga drums in a band. Kristen and Ms. Chu have been personal friends and professional colleagues for the past 6 years.

When she graduated from social work school with a master's of social work, she swore that she was not going to end up in a fancy office doing therapy or being a supervisor. She said,

I wanted to be "on the front line," working with people. So I went to work for the Department of Social Services where I had done one of my internships. The minute I got there, they wanted to make me a supervisor because I had an advanced degree, but I insisted on remaining a social service worker.

For 2 years, I was between a rock and a hard place. I treated the clients with respect and tried to help them work toward their goals, but too often I couldn't get them the resources they needed to become self-supporting. There aren't enough decent vacant apartments for a low-income person. There are never enough slots in job training programs. My clients were often being discouraged from going back to school to improve their prospects.

I'd finally locate an apartment with reasonable rent, but then I couldn't get the money to pay the first and last month's rent. Worse still, many landlords refused to rent to a mother on welfare. I'd see blatant discrimination, but the agency wouldn't allow me to file complaints of discrimination.

Mostly, there were just too many people assigned to my caseload and too much red tape. In the name of accountability to the public I spent valuable time filling out forms proving that the client's weren't cheating. I was drowning in a sea of paperwork and had a supervisor who never had enough time to help me help the clients. I knew my job was vital, but I was ready to branch out and try new ways of fighting poverty.

When the LIFT planning committee asked Kristen to become the first paid coordinator of the house, she felt honored but conflicted. She still had to pay back school and car loans, and her parents were on her case to buy some new clothes and "get a life." The committee had obtained a 4-month seed grant for planning, but it could not guarantee salary beyond that time and could not offer the health care benefits that she received as a municipal employee. She was excited, however, at the prospect of so much responsibility and of being in on the ground floor of starting an agency. Working with a small number of clients meant she could facilitate genuine change in a young person's future.

She accepted the challenge and took the lead through months of hearings at the town planning and zoning boards, through all the tearing down and rebuilding of the house, and through the recruiting of the first residents and volunteers.

She sees herself as a conductor of an orchestra, trying to get the best out of everyone. She supports and encourages the staff and residents while being sensitive to the needs of the board members, the foundations that give financial support, and the neighbors, who are LIFT's best friends and severest critics. She states,

No two days are alike in this job. I arrive at LIFT House at about eight o'clock just as the overnight counselor is leaving and the day staff are arriving. I find out what problems have occurred and those set the agenda for my day. A stuffed up sink and blown away down spout can be my central problems. Or maybe a sick baby needs to get to the hospital and our van is broken, or an argument broke out among the residents the night before that is still simmering. Perhaps one of the residents came home stoned or let her boyfriend into the house after curfew. I hate to be strict, but these rules have been created in response to past disasters. We began with very few rules and let them evolve. They all make a good deal of sense and I can defend them with conviction.

Often, I have to go to court or a lawyer's office with one of the residents. I might be accompanying a young woman to DSS for an appeal hearing because she was refused a service we believe she is entitled to. Or I might be training a volunteer to do all of the above. I have had to learn the fine art of delegating work.

She also does some crisis counseling and emergency child care and is the group leader of the house council. She organized and offers resources to a chapter of Coping With the Overall Pregnancy Experience (COPE), which is a chapter of a nationwide support group for parents.

At the end of each day, she is exhausted and perhaps frustrated, but there are many immediate rewards. When her spirits are low, she revives them by watching one of the babies break into a great big smile or by remembering how depressed and angry one of the residents was when she arrived at LIFT and how she had grown 10 feet tall by the time she left. The board and staff are like a family. They disagree but always resolve their differences—"kiss and make up."

She is getting married next year, so she hopes to reduce her hours at the house and resign from one of the citywide committees she chairs. Her fiancé is an airline pilot who works odd hours. She would like to spend blocks of time with him and take advantage of his free airline trips. For now, however, she cannot imagine quitting her job at LIFT.

Earlier this year, Kristen organized and co-led an 8-week series of parenting seminars at the local hospital. This was her major small-scale planning work for the year.

Raymond Bucoli

Raymond is in his early thirties and is employed by a computer corporation. He has been a volunteer at LIFT for 2 years. He became involved when Kristen convinced his company to donate a computer and printer to the house. He was assigned to set up the system and train Kristen and the part-time secretary-bookkeeper on how to use it.

Later, Kristen asked him to show several of the residents how to use it. He taught them basic word processing and then donated some educational games that would help improve their skills for the GED, for training programs, and for college. He fell into the pattern of coming once a week to troubleshoot the machines and teach the residents to use them.

Recently, Raymond took a leave of absence from his job to spend more time with his long-time companion whose health was deteriorating. Since his companion's death from AIDS, Raymond has thrown himself into volunteering at the house. He says it takes him outside of himself and helps him deal with his terrible loss. Because one of the residents and her baby are HIV positive, this is his way to memorialize his lost lover.

He has become the chairperson of the newly formed mentoring committee. Many of his coworkers have heard about LIFT and he is convinced that they can be persuaded to tutor and befriend the residents. He also is confident that between himself, his employers, and his friends, he can raise the money for the project. This will be his first major planning task at LIFT.

Gardenia Dennis

Gardenia has been an important part of the LIFT House family since the building was first renovated. She lives on the same street in a small house that she came to as a bride. She raised her own family there as well as a long list of foster children.

When the board was first negotiating to purchase the house and many neighbors were organizing to oppose the sale, Ms. Dennis was one of the few who spoke up loudly in support of the project. After the sale went through and the carpenters were working, she stopped by to say "hello." Ms. Chu was looking harried, so Gardenia invited her to take a coffee break. Around her kitchen table, Ms. Chu and Ms. Dennis discovered how much they both loved children and they started what has become a great partnership.

Soon after her first visit, Ms. Dennis became "Grandma" to Kristen, Ms. Chu's children, and the parade of carpenters and plumbers. She not only kept them supplied with hot coffee but also continued to speak eloquently in their behalf at community meetings. Even after the town issued a permit, many neighbors worried that a social service agency such as LIFT would lower their property values, which were already in a steep decline. They worried about the extra cars the house would bring into the already narrow street and about the kind of people the house would attract. Many neighbors had negative views of what they called "unwed mothers" and "loose teenagers." Despite the fact that some of them had unplanned births in their own families, they still worried about the influence that these young women might exert on the neighborhood children.

Grandma understood their fears, but because she was a respected woman who had befriended many of their children—of diverse races and social classes—her positive vision prevailed. The block association placed some limitations on the amount of expansion the house could do, but it agreed to withdraw the petitions opposing the house that it had sent to the zoning board.

Gardenia was already enrolled in the Foster Grandparent Program, which paid her a small stipend to assist in nonprofit agencies. The extra money she earned made a big difference to her because her social security check never covered her expenses. She arranged to be placed with LIFT and now works there for 3 hours every day unless she is seriously ill.

Most of her work is in the child care program, in which she models for the parents those nurturing skills she developed during many years of raising her family and foster children. She looks after both the staff and the parents—baking cakes on their birthdays, knitting scarves for everyone who looks chilly, and stenciling lovely ornaments as housewarming presents for new apartment dwellers.

She is also in charge of the LIFT garden. She spent many of her happiest times in the rural South and is eager to share with the young residents her love of nature. She finally convinced them to go on a camping trip with her.

Although she is 81 years old and is beginning to be bothered by arthritis, she is fiercely independent, refusing to slow down. She responded to the problem of aching joints by registering at a health club and learning weight training.

This program season, her small-scale planning project is a single-event weekend camping trip, a first for the LIFT mothers.

Paulo Mejia

Paulo, a 19-year-old college student, has been working part-time at LIFT since the beginning of the school year. He was born in the Dominican Republic and has been in the United States for 6 years. He is majoring in recreational therapy at the local community college. As part of his financial aid package, Paulo was awarded a work-study grant. He chose to perform his 20 hours a week of work at LIFT House after hearing about it in a sociology class.

When Paulo started at LIFT, he was an accounting major. He was assigned work in the LIFT office helping with bookkeeping and other clerical tasks. As soon as the staff and residents got to know him, however, they quickly found many other things for him to do.

Working at LIFT House has given him two gifts for which he will always be grateful. First, he found that being bilingual, Spanish and English, is a plus rather than the hindrance he had thought it to be. He has been able to translate for the family members of some of the residents who are not comfortable speaking English. On several occasions, he has translated during a grandparent support group. He has also gone to court with a resident who was seeking a restraining order against her former boyfriend. She feared that she would miss something that the judge or a lawyer said. He understands that when a person is emotionally stressed, he or she often reverts to his or her first language, which makes the person feel more secure. He has also translated the LIFT House manual into Spanish. He recently convinced a friend at school to translate it into Korean. Now he is looking for a student who speaks the dialect of Russian spoken in Belarusse because one of the residents at LIFT is from there.

The second gift that working at LIFT has given him is the courage to change his major. He had initially chosen business because that would please his family. Therapeutic recreation, however, even if he will earn less money, is what he found he really wanted to do. He has a natural flair for teaching and motivating others that he discovered when he worked with some of the residents to prepare for the GED. Because he had to take it himself to qualify for college, he is unusually sensitive to the styles and feelings of adult learners.

Through his work at LIFT, he is also less self-conscious about that short period in his life when he too was without a place to live. When he first came to the United States, his father could not find a job. His mother cleaned houses, and he worked "off the books" stocking the shelves in a convenience store. When his mother became ill and his father went into a depression, Paulo had to stay home and take care of both parents. There was no money coming in for rent. He tried to get welfare assistance, but his family did not qualify for it, or at least that is what the worker said.

Ashamed of being turned down and not knowing that he had rights to appeal that decision, he had no option but to tell the landlord that he simply could not pay the rent. His family was evicted from their apartment. His mother and father stayed with two different relatives. Neither one had any space for him, and he did not have any close friends he could turn to for help. He spent each day taking care of his mother and father, and each night he slept at a shelter, rotating among the three in his town. For 5 months, he joined the ranks of the homeless. Eventually, he got a night job, rented a room, and passed his GED. Now he attends college and lives at LIFT, doing maintenance work in exchange for room and board.

This semester, he is doing an independent study on the problem of homeless families and the strategies used to deal with the problem. Paulo wants to share what he has learned with the other students at the community college. He thinks that many of them are insensitive to the problems that can propel hard-working people onto the streets.

With two of his college friends, he has begun planning a homelessness awareness week. In addition to raising consciousness about homelessness, he also hopes to raise money for the LIFT House program fund. This is his small-scale planning project this year.

WHAT DO THE LIFT WORKERS HAVE IN COMMON?

LIFT House's mixture of professionally trained staff, highly skilled volunteer board members, neighborhood, business world and college volunteers, and part-time workers is a staffing pattern that one is likely to find in a small-scale social program. In fact, it is not at all unusual to find a social program in which the lay staff far outnumber those who are professionally trained and credentialed.

This is certainly very different from the staffing patterns of other helping professions. Whereas volunteers perform many valuable tasks in hospitals, schools, and court clinics, for example, the main work of these agencies is performed by highly trained and licensed professionals. Obviously, one would not feel very safe having his or her tonsils taken out by a well-intentioned garage mechanic who practices a little medicine in his or her spare time.

Although it is not at all accurate to assert that "anyone can perform human service work," it is true that the ability to constructively intervene in a personal or social problem is widely spread within the general population. Some of the most sensitive group leadership one can find might be going on right now as a layperson conducts a self-help support group for infertile couples or for the mates of people who have eating disorders. Brilliantly sensitive casework is often done by a layperson covering the phones for a suicide prevention or AIDS information hotline.

What is it then that binds all these workers, lay and professionally trained, into a field called social services? I think that it is a common core of attributes that determines which people are skillful workers, regardless of their superficial differences. Although formal training in college (and beyond) is likely to increase the competence of a human service worker, creativity, compassion, and warmth, for example, are attributes that a person is likely to have before entering a training program. Through careful screening, orientation, in-service workshops, and much action followed by reflection, an understanding of the structure and content of the professional helping relationship can be nurtured in a wide variety of people who are open-minded and willing to grow.

THE STRUCTURE AND CONTENT OF THE
PROFESSIONAL HELPING RELATIONSHIP

The structure of the professional helping relationship, as opposed to the purely social relationship, has the following five qualities that distinguish it from a purely social relationship:

It is time limited.
It has a clear, agreed-on focus.

Table 3.1   The Content of the Helping Relationship

Attitudes/Values	Skills	Knowledge
Patience	Gathering data	Human growth and develop-ment
Empathy	Interviewing—active	
Self-awareness	looking, listening,	Abnormal growth and devel-opment
Capacity to deal with ambi-guity and take risks	and question asking	
	Reviewing referral data	The impact of society and culture on behavior
Capacity to ask for help and offer feedback	Researching	
	Visiting	The dynamic of groups and organizations
	Observing	
Belief in people's and sys-tems' capacity to change	Storing and sharing infor-mation	The social and political forces that affect helping
Open-mindedness, skepti-cism, and rejection of stereotypes	Keeping records	Social problems, special populations, and resources
	Writing reports	
	Building relationships	Issues of research and evaluation
Humor and a light touch	Negotiating contracts	
	Forming action plans	
	Implementing action plans	
	Intervening	
	Referring	
	Monitoring and evaluating	
	Giving and receiving feedback	
	Constructing evaluations	

SOURCE: Schram and Mandell (1994, p. 129).

It has an articulated division of labor.

It is disciplined.

It is built on acceptance rather than simply on attraction.

The content of the helping relationship has three component parts: attitudes and values, skills, and knowledge. The following chart lists many of them. Of course, no one worker ever embodies the components in the same way or to the same extent. They form a model against which one can measure one's strengths and weaknesses and chart a course for further growth as a volunteer or paid worker (Table 3.1).

THE 5-MINUTE RECAP

- As planners move through the phases of the planning process, they sketch a progressively more detailed portrait of the program they are creating.

- On paper and in their mind's eye, planners visualize alternative arrangements for the audience, the speaker's platform, refreshments literature tables, and so on.

- In the beginning phases, planners visualize the best-case scenario, but by the time the program opens its doors that first vision has undergone adjustments and compromises until it approximates how the actual event might look.

- To help the reader visualize each phase of the processes described in this book, I have "created" a private nonprofit residence for young, previously homeless women and their children. It is named LIFT House.

- LIFT is home to nine young women and their babies. Each of the women is enrolled in a school or work training program.

- By following the program planning activities of the staff, board, and volunteers at LIFT, the reader can see the program planning process unfold as it might in the real world of small social agencies.

- The first person the reader meets is Ana Lee Chu, a passionate visionary, cofounder of LIFT, and chair of its board of directors. She organized the first LIFT program after being a volunteer for many years at a shelter for homeless women. In Chapter 4, the reader follows her struggles to establish the part-time day care program that was the precursor of the current LIFT House.

- Next, the reader is introduced to Kristen Connelly, the other founder of LIFT, who is a trained social worker and LIFT's salaried program coordinator. The reader learns about her planning efforts both in Chapter 4 and in Chapter 8 as she finishes up working with a parenting group that she has facilitated and is now evaluating.

- Raymond Bucoli is the third member of the LIFT staff. He is a dedicated volunteer who works at LIFT two evenings a week and is a computer professional during the day. In Chapter 5, the reader will follow his planning work as chair of the newly established LIFT mentoring program.

- Gardenia Dennis (Grandma) works as a "foster grandparent" at LIFT. She is a neighbor who, after raising her own and several foster children, has taken the women of LIFT under her wing. In Chapter 7, the reader learns how she prepares for and triumphantly returns from the first LIFT camping weekend.

- Paulo Mejia is the youngest worker at LIFT. He is an immigrant from the Dominican Republic who was once homeless but is now attending college and working at LIFT through a work-study financial aid grant. He also works as the night custodian in exchange for room and board. In Chapter 6, he plans a series of activities for a campuswide homelessness awareness week that aims to raise funds for LIFT while raising the consciousness of the students.

- LIFT House's mixture of professionally trained staff, part-time workers, and volunteers from various fields is a staffing pattern typically found in small-scale social programs.
- Although their educational backgrounds, experience, and skills may vary, all competent human service workers share a common core of attributes.
- Through careful selection and training of staff, and by constantly reflecting on what they have done, the helping relationship can be nurtured in a wide variety of people who are open-minded, warm, and willing to grow.
- The structure of the helping relationship is different from that of the purely social relationship in that it

  is time limited;

  has a clear focus;

  has a division of labor;

  is disciplined; and

  is built on acceptance rather than simply on attraction.
- The content of the helping relationship is composed of three components: attitudes and values, skills, and knowledge.
- A chart was presented that lists the attributes of workers in each of the three components discussed previously. It is not likely that any worker embodies all of them. Models are useful, however, as a ruler against which workers can measure their progress toward an ideal type and set goals for future development.

PUTTING THEORY INTO PRACTICE

EXERCISE 1: STRUCTURE AND CONTENT
OF THE HELPING RELATIONSHIP

All of us have had periods in our lives when we have wanted to yell, "Stop the world, I want to get off." Try to recall and describe an episode in your own life when you grappled with a vexing personal problem. It could have been something as seemingly trivial as needing help in changing your major or being homesick at camp, or it may have been a major crisis. What is important is that the situation was troubling you.

Reflect on those friends, family members, or professionals who tried to help you resolve your problem. Choose two of these people. To what extent did these "helpers" embody each of the attitudes and values listed as being important in the helping person? (For example, to what extent were they nonjudgmental or open-minded or empathetic? How did they express—or neglect to express—those characteristics?)

EXERCISE 2: EXAMINING YOUR ATTITUDES
AND VALUES, SKILLS, AND KNOWLEDGE

1. Choose three concepts from each category in the attitudes and values, skills, and knowledge chart.
2. Describe how each is integrated into your own character, personality, and work style. Tap into all your past helping experiences as friend, family member, volunteer, and worker to examine the attitudes and values, skills, and knowledge you chose.
3. Suggest ways in which you might strengthen or further test those areas that seem weakest. Try to be as specific as you can as you set your goals for your professional development. General statements such as "I'll get more experience in . . ." are too broad to be useful. A better approach would be "I think that I should try to get over my shyness by taking some public speaking courses or maybe joining a club and taking on a leadership role." (Note: It is easier to talk about one's negative points. Social service workers also need to be clear about their positive attributes.)

CITATIONS AND SUGGESTIONS
FOR FURTHER READING

ATTRACTING, TRAINING, AND RETAINING
VOLUNTEERS IN A NONPROFIT AGENCY

Ilsley, P., Jr. (1990). *Enhancing the volunteer experience: New insights on strengthening volunteer participation, learning & commitment.* San Francisco: Jossey-Bass. See several other suggested readings on this topic in Chapter 6.

FOR UNDERSTANDING THE COMPLEXITIES OF POVERTY
AND HOMELESSNESS FOR PARENTS AND CHILDREN

Berrick, J. D. (1995). *Faces of poverty, portraits of women and children on welfare.* New York: Oxford University Press. Although the whole book offers dramatic insight into the potential futures of the women of LIFT House, Chapter 3, "Sandy, Working but Poor," is especially useful. It describes the life of a 24-year-old working woman who began her struggle with poverty as a teenage mother.
Families in Society. The Journal of Contemporary Human Services. See issue on fathers (January 1993) and issue on teen pregnancy (June 1993)
Horowtiz, R. (1995). *Teen mothers: Citizens or dependents.* Chicago: University of Chicago Press.
Lee, J. A. B. (1994). No place to go: Homeless women. In A. Gitterman & L. Shulman (Eds.), *Mutual aid groups, vulnerable populations and the life cycle* (2nd ed.). New York: Columbia University Press.
Walsh, M. E. (1992). *Moving to nowhere, children's stories of homelessness.* New York: Auburn House. This is a series of eloquent stories composed by children whom the author

encountered in shelters for families who are homeless. Through reading these stories, one can achieve a new understanding of the human cost of moving to nowhere—and an appreciation of the resilience of the youngsters, their parents, and the human service professionals who, despite these difficult and often cynical times, have not given up on the value of helping those in need.

EXAMPLES OF PROGRAM MODELS
FOR HOMELESS MOTHERS

Brown, J. (1994). Agents of change: A group of women in a shelter. In A. Gitterman & L. Schulman (Eds.), *Mutual aid groups, vulnerable populations and the life cycle* (2nd ed., p. 273). New York: Columbia University Press.
Ovrebo, B., Ryan, M., Jackson, K., & Hutchinson, K. (1994, Summer). The homeless prenatal program: A model for empowering homeless pregnant women. *Health Education Quarterly, 21*(2), 187-198.
Wayne, J. (1995). Group work model to reach isolated mothers: Preventing child abuse. In L. Schulman (Ed.) (with Group Work Faculty, Boston University School of Social Work), *Readings in differential social work practice with groups.* New York: American Heritage.
Siefert, M. B., & Strauch, K.-S. (1991, April). Skill building for effective intervention with homeless families. *Families in Society, 72*(4), 212-219.

4

TROUBLESHOOTING
Describing the Full Dimensions of a Problem

In a far-off land a long time ago, a vain emperor spent all his kingdom's money on clothing himself in the most expensive fabrics in the world. One day a shrewd tailor came to him and told him that he could spin a garment so fine that only the pure in heart could see it. The emperor bade him to begin and in a short time he produced what he said were the rarest of garments. He helped the emperor discard the clothes he was wearing and put on his fine new clothes.

Proud of his new possessions, the emperor led a triumphant parade through the town. None of the onlookers could see the emperor's new clothes. But they oohed and aahed anyway, assuming that they were the only ones who couldn't see them. They were certainly not going to publicly admit that they were not pure of heart. After many minutes of adulation a little boy in the crowd looked up at his mother and said, "Gosh, the emperor is naked!" Emboldened by the innocent little boy's blunt statement, the spectators began to shout, "Hey, the emperor has no clothes on at all."

Based on *The Emperor's New Clothes* by Hans Christian Andersen

When the little boy announced to the assembled throng that the emperor was naked—and he really was—he was taking the first step of the troubleshooter.

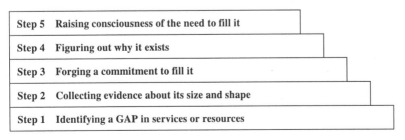

Step 5	Raising consciousness of the need to fill it
Step 4	Figuring out why it exists
Step 3	Forging a commitment to fill it
Step 2	Collecting evidence about its size and shape
Step 1	Identifying a GAP in services or resources

WHAT IS A TROUBLESHOOTER?

When a planner takes the role of a troubleshooter, he or she identifies a serious problem in the delivery of services or a lack in the quality of life of a group of people. Once the planner has stated that a problem exists, he or she begins a process that may eventuate in a program being created to remediate the deficits. To be a competent troubleshooter, we need the following two capacities which can be mutually exclusive and which can pull us in opposite directions:

- We need the sensitivity to observe that a GAP exists and the compassion and dedication to insist that it be filled.
- We need to restrain our impulse to jump in and try to "fix it" before we have carefully analyzed the problem.

The impulse to act decisively when we see that people are in pain is understandable. We chose social service work because we believe in the possibilities of change, that people's lives can be made more productive. Adding to this inner drive to action, our clients, who live on the front lines of that pain, urge us to act. Also, an impatient public demands that we show results for their tax dollars. We dance to the tunes of many drummers.

An increasingly wide array of people from different venues also express their concern about the massive social problems in our communities. The politician, the minister, the talk show host, or the president of a civic group or taxpayer's association all voice their opinions on who has caused the problems and how they can be fixed. There are great differences of opinion about both causes and cures.

Headlines in newspapers and sound bytes on TV quote their pronouncements:

Rising delinquency rates are due to mothers who are out working instead of staying home to supervise their children!

The rise in crime is a result of the decline in church attendance!

Welfare payments create dependency, encouraging the large numbers of unwed mothers!

After these pronouncements, the "experts" often propose "a one-size-fits-all program strategy":

Throw those "unwed" mothers off the welfare rolls and make them go to work!

Teach sex education!

Teach abstinence!

Outlaw abortion!

Put those disruptive teenagers in jail and throw away the key!

Hold the parents responsible if the kids get into trouble!

Responding to these problem definitions and program strategies, social service workers repeat an axiom attributed to H. L. Mencken, a cynical social critic, who said, "For every complex problem there is one elegantly simple—but usually wrong—solution!"

Troubleshooters have to resist jumping on the bandwagon of the oversimplified solution. They plan and implement a program only after fully describing the problem and exploring each of the alternative strategies in all their complexity. Of course, they must be careful not to postpone action indefinitely by endless perseveration.

After acknowledging the inevitable tension between reflection and action, we begin the program development process by climbing up the first step.

STEP 1: IDENTIFYING A GAP

A GAP is defined as the chasm that lies between

What exists now

G   A   P

What ought to be happening

The planner's goal is to close that GAP by designing a "what-ought-to-be" program. Although it is unlikely that any single program will eliminate the whole GAP, each one can protect some people from the GAP's worst effects. Let Infants and Families Thrive (LIFT) House, for example, is a small but significant part of a safety net. It does not eliminate the problem of homelessness, which forces so many young mothers to fall into the chasm. It fills a small section of the GAP by offering a handful of mothers a path toward independent living. Its founders hope that there will be many other programs like LIFT to care for young mothers while the community continues to design other strategies that close the overarching GAPs in affordable housing, family life, education, child care, and so on.

A GAP EXISTS IN THE EYES OF THE BEHOLDERS AND
THEIR VIEWPOINTS OFTEN CHANGE OVER TIME

From the brief review of sound bytes and headlines, it is clear that there is widespread disagreement on what constitutes a significant GAP and who has the responsibility to fill one. Also, definitions keep changing. For example, from the colonial era until the Great Depression of the 1930s, personal and social GAPs were assumed to be primarily the responsibility of families and, to a lesser extent, the church and local municipality. During the Great Depression, however, that perspective radically altered. Responding to the massive economic dislocations, the federal government began to take the lead in closing the GAP created by the widespread unemployment. The strategy of using government-sponsored entitlement programs, such as social security and unemployment insurance, to fill the GAPs created by loss of jobs through the vagaries of the economic system or through aging and disability has expanded enormously since then (Axinn & Levin, 1997).

Recently, however, assumptions about the role of federally sponsored social programs in filling social GAPs have been questioned. Since the congressional election of 1994, many of the program strategies we have come to view as the "rights" of citizens and the "obligations" of the federal government have been sharply cut back or passed on to the states to do what they will. As in an earlier era, I suspect that the family, the church, the local municipality, and, now, the private sector and volunteerism will be expected to fill the GAPs.

The downsizing of entitlement programs and the shifting of auspices from the federal to the state level create an increasing demand for planners who can cope with budget cuts with creative solutions, stringing together resources from different sectors of the society. If the states do indeed use the promised block grant funds to replace the large-scale federal mandates with many small programs tailored to local needs, this might be a period of great program experimentation. It remains to be seen, however, how much of the demand for local control is a ploy to simply cut taxes and divert tax money from solving social problems to other, less controversial municipal projects.

GAPS ARE OFTEN IDENTIFIED BY PEOPLE
AT THE GRASS ROOTS OF A COMMUNITY

It often appears as if the directors of the major health and social service agencies or government officials are the ones who alert us about the necessity and strategies for filling GAPs. If you trace the history of most social programs, however, you will discover that people on the grassroots level had been grappling with those problems long before the bureaucrats noticed and were motivated to design an official program for it. Listen in on conversations at the local bar, hairdressing salon, and on the benches where parents wait to pick up their children after school. It is there that you will hear GAPs being identified and alternative strategies debated. Like the boy who cried out that the emperor had no clothes on, it takes a while for little voices to be heard, but they are often highly articulate and insightful.

EXAMPLES OF GAPS AND PROPOSED STRATEGIES IN CONVERSATIONS ON THE GRASS ROOTS

The following are some of the GAPs that a few laypeople and professionals identified at a meeting of their neighborhood association. Although the members might not agree on the relative importance of each GAP, each is critical to those people tottering on the edge of the chasm.

Example 1

What is happening now

My son has Down's syndrome and he is being mainstreamed in the local public school. When he was in the early grades, he was invited to parties and sports events. Now that he is a teenager the kids don't want him around. He is getting so lonely and depressed.

G A P

What ought to be happening

There ought to be a social club where my son could go for activities with other teenagers who have problems of mental retardation. I bet their parents are having the same worries I have about what the kids will do after high school. There ought to be a support group for the parents so we could exchange ideas and gather courage from others who share our disappointments and hopes.

Example 2

```
                     What is happening now
```

In our neighborhood, there is so much tension between the college and the local children. The kids have no place to play, so they wander onto the campus and are chased away by the campus police who automatically assume they will cause trouble. The community has so little and the college kids have so much.

G A P

```
                   What ought to be happening
```

There ought to be a way for the neighborhood kids to use the sports facilities on the campus. Maybe the college students would volunteer to play sports with the local youngsters. Everyone would learn from each other.

Example 3

```
                     What is happening now
```

There are so many people in prisons who don't have high school diplomas and they get out and can't find a job. So they turn back to crime. They've cut out most of the classes in the jails and they say they don't have money to keep the libraries open.

G A P

```
                   What ought to be happening
```

There ought to be a way to get books—even secondhand ones—to prisoners who can't afford to buy them. Then they could study for the general equivalence diploma (GED). There are retired teachers and other professionals who could hold classes in prisons. I bet they'd do it if they were given transportation and some training.

Example 4

What is happening now

Women who are date raped almost never report it or follow through on the legal process of apprehending the criminals. They feel too scared or ashamed to cope with the police or face their friends.

G A P

What ought to be happening

There ought to be a way to support the women if they decide to press charges. The police officers ought to be trained to understand the pain of the victims and be more proactive in stopping the sexual abuse of women and children before it escalates.

GAPS ARE IDENTIFIED
WHEN A WISH LIST IS CREATED

GAPs do not arise only from crisis situations. They can also be identified when a group of people, such as the staff of a social program such as LIFT, creates a wish list. This list is composed of resources that the agency lacks, preventing staff from delivering needed services. Some items on the list could be used to expand services or create new ones. Table 4.1 presents a list that was created at the LIFT annual retreat.

After creating the list in Table 4.1, LIFT staff tried to reach consensus on which resource GAPs were priorities and which could be put on the back burner. They were planning several fund-raising programs for the coming year. Now they were ready with their list of priorities. If donations exceeded the amount they needed to just survive, they would refer back to the list to allocate the surplus funds to fill some of the GAPs.

The wish list is also useful if a foundation or individual donor is willing to give LIFT a special onetime donation. Sometimes, donors want a few alternative choices about how their donation will be used.

Of course, the best laid plans of mice and men oft go astray. By the time a small sum of extra funding does materialize, the hot water heater or the roof might have sprung a leak. Those are GAPs that always take priority!

Table 4.1   LIFT House Wish List

If we had a laser printer, we could produce better newsletters and fund-raising appeals.

If we had a camcorder, we could make videos to use for staff and parent training.

If we had a lending library of children's books and toys, the parents could return to the house after they left to keep their babies stimulated.

If we could hire a part-time assistant director, Kristen and Ms. Chu would not have to work so hard and burnout and maybe leave.

If we could buy the house next door, we could cut down on our waiting list or permit some of the mothers to live here longer.

STEP 2: COLLECTING EVIDENCE ABOUT THE SIZE AND SHAPE OF THE GAP

Although each of the members at the civic association meeting described the GAP that he or she perceived with great conviction, the members will need much more than passion to mobilize others to fill it. They must support their assertion with statistical and theoretical evidence that indicates at least some of the following about the GAP:

- The moral, ethical, or legal principle that impels people to fill it
- The specific harm that has already been done by it
- The number of people who are currently adversely affected by it
- A projection of the numbers of people who will be affected in the future if no remedial action is taken
- The harm in other spheres that will occur if it continues to be ignored
- Evidence that there are no other programs designed to eliminate the GAP or that those that exist are not accessible to a specific group

When turning to the public sector, those who state that there is a GAP must be prepared to document, to the best of their ability to predict the future, the absolute bottom line, which is stated, for example, as follows:

If we don't spend X amount of dollars now, we will spend XXX more later on!

To conduct a GAP analysis (also called a needs assessment), planners must be genuinely open to the possibility that the GAP they perceive as so critical, when looked at more closely, is not as significant as they thought it was at the beginning of their exploration. Perhaps they can find ways to fill the GAP without the expenditure of scarce funds. For example, maybe LIFT House does not need to own their own laser printer but rather could arrange to use one at the local high school or bank. Also, perhaps the day care program at the YMCA would be willing to expand its toy and book-lending library to include the LIFT mothers.

THE FOUNDERS OF LIFT RESEARCH THE GAP IN SERVICES FOR YOUNG MOTHERS*

For 3 years before LIFT House opened its doors, Kristen and Ms. Chu spent endless hours finding data to support their assertion that a new program was needed for young homeless mothers. Their anecdotal evidence was important but not sufficient. Of course, they had been warned that no assessment can completely boil down the urgent needs for service of a population into a row of hard numbers. The following several problems occur as we try to collect evidence of need:

- Agency personnel may have difficulty admitting limitations in the services they are now providing.
- Prospective clients may fear revealing their personal concerns, weaknesses, or shortcomings.
- Often, there is a lack of access to respondents.
- How questions are phrased and how answers are interpreted can bias the data in unknown ways.

Rather than being conclusive, therefore, needs assessments suggest the probable need for services or programs (Soriano, 1995, p. 3).

ESTABLISHING THE SERIOUS CONSEQUENCES
OF AN UNFILLED GAP

Kristen and Ms. Chu began the search for corroborating data by accumulating research reports that demonstrated the disastrous long-term effects on the educational achievement and health of malnourished and under-stimulated babies. Articles, books, and interviews with professionals also supplied information about the potential for physical abuse and sexual exploitation in families headed by young, homeless, isolated mothers.

AUTHOR'S NOTE: For materials on conducting a needs assessment, see Epstein and Tripodi (1977), Moroney (1977), Powers, Meenaghen, and Toomey (1985), Kettner, Moroney, and Martin (1990), and Soriano (1995).

They also found data that supported their own conviction that young parents who lacked adequate housing during their first year of parenting were likely to lose their babies to the foster care system. The bottom line was that the costs of maintaining these mothers in a supportive environment such as LIFT were far less than the costs to provide foster care for their children. Providing services to keep a family together is easier and more humane than terminating parental rights and searching for adoptive families for the children of homeless young mothers.

ESTABLISHING THAT THE GAP EXISTS IN A SPECIFIC COMMUNITY OR POPULATION

Once Kristen and Ms. Chu had created a stack of papers supporting the gravity of the problem, they had to demonstrate that it existed in this particular town, right now. Therefore, they searched for statistics on the size of the homeless young mother population. This was a tall order because it is frequently very difficult to find statistics about the victims of social problems, especially those that carry stigma and the potential of punishment or harassment.

Much of the homeless problem is hidden. For example, the young women might be living in dangerously overcrowded homes, bunking with abusive mates or stressed family members. Many of them keep moving from one temporary shelter or a friend's couch to the next. Young mothers often do not admit that they are without a permanent home, because they fear that they will lose their children to the welfare establishment they are so dependent on but afraid of.

Because no source of credible statistics existed for their town, Kristen and Ms. Chu had to do the collecting of data themselves. They arranged to do an inventory of four family shelters on five evenings and discussed their quest for data at a welfare rights group meeting. In this way, they hoped to estimate the size of the target population. They also wrote an article for *Spare Change,* a newspaper published by a homeless advocacy group.

ESTABLISHING EVIDENCE OF THE INADEQUACY OF EXISTING SERVICES

Kristen and Ms. Chu also had to find out about the services and GAPs of all the other facilities in town that worked with young mothers. The techniques they used for their GAP analysis are very much like the market research surveys routinely conducted by commercial companies. Before expanding into a new town or adding a new product line, the wise

Table 4.2   Sources of Information About the Need for a Program for Young
Mothers Who Are Homeless

Staff at the obstetric and emergency clinic at the hospital

Department of social services staff

Staff and clients at the battered women and homeless women's shelter

Staff of adoption and foster care agencies

Guidance staff and nurse at the high school

Staff at the mental health clinic

Local clergy

Staff at the town hall who deal with public housing

Real estate agents

Members of the board of selectmen

Chairs of neighborhood associations

Faculty in the human services, psychology, and sociology departments at the community
   college

Staff at the Boys and Girls Club and YMCA

The reference librarian

A group of teen mothers

---

businessperson makes sure there is indeed a cohort of consumers available
and interested.

FINDING ADDITIONAL SOURCES OF INFORMATION

When Kristen and Ms. Chu first began exploring the GAP, it seemed
like a complex task for novices. As with every other part of the planning
process, however, they knew they must break down the job into small steps
and recruit others to take a few of the tasks. Each member of the planning
committee agreed to take on at least one data-gathering task. Their
interviewing tasks were facilitated by the fact that every person on their
list had already shown a commitment to serving the homeless population
or young mothers in general.

Kristin also recruited a sociology professor at the local college and an
investigative newspaper reporter. They gave her their expert advice and
assigned their students to do some of the legwork. Most important, they
gave the project the imprimatur of two respected community institutions.

Table 4.2 shows the list that they composed of the people to interview
in person or by phone. Obviously, the decision of who to interview and
the questions to ask must be tailor-made for the specific GAP being
researched.

Table 4.3   Sample of GAP Analysis Interview Questions for Agency Staff

In what specific ways does your agency serve young, homeless, or inadequately housed young mothers?

What number of persons do you reach and are there waiting lists for the services to young mothers?

How do you interact with other agencies around this population?

What other services do you hope to offer in the future?

What services do you wish some other agency would offer?

What trends do you see in this population? Is it growing, shrinking, or maintaining?

What trends do you see in the housing situation?

How do you think we could best use our time and energy?

Who else should we speak with who is involved in delivering services to young homeless mothers or has valuable resources?

At each interview, they asked similar questions so they could combine the results into one comprehensive report. Realizing that words can be imprecise and a question can be interpreted differently than was intended, they decided to conduct a small pretest. By asking their questions in a few "sample" interviews and reviewing them with each respondent, they spent more time but created a more useful instrument. Table 4.3 shows a few of the questions asked.

Although the list of questions to ask and people to interview might seem daunting, often others have already done most of the data gathering. Using the phone book and local directories of services in your area, seek out the headquarters of umbrella organizations such as the following:

The Coalition for the Homeless

The National Association of Social Workers

The Cancer Institute

The American Association of Retired Persons

The Council on Aging

The Welfare Rights Organization

Legal Services for the Poor

The Disability Law Center

If the umbrella groups do not have the data already collected, it might be possible to conduct interviews with the participants who attend their meetings. If the specialized groups cannot be located, most cities have some type of social agency consortium variously called the community council, Red Feather Agency, or a similar title. With many social service workers in one place, at one time, your survey could be filled in, and a discussion about the data you seek could add anecdotal richness to the facts collected.

Research and statistical data can also be found in articles in professional journals. They can provide much of the background to the problem one is working on and point the way to other sources. Because so many of us need to obtain this type of information with the smallest investment of time and energy, Mendelsohn (1987) has prepared a book, titled *A Guide to Information Sources for Social Work and the Human Services,* that assists information gathering.

STEP 3: FORGING A COMMITMENT
TO FILL THE GAP

Social service workers cannot read a newspaper, visit an agency, walk through a downtown area, or take a friend to an emergency room in a hospital without noticing some glaring GAPs in service. Most of the time, we notice, comment on it, and get on with our lives. Making a commitment to fill a GAP is undoubtedly the step at which many of us opt out of the program development process. We have busy lives and roles that are already set for us. Also, as previously discussed, many of us have a feeling of powerlessness when faced with an unfamiliar task.

It must be stressed that when people doubt their capacity to create a program to fill a GAP, it will persist. Yet most innovations have grown out of the commitment to follow up on a GAP made by people with little formal training in program planning.

Examples of laypeople creating small programs that blossomed into large, innovative agencies abound. The widely sold and much translated women's health book, first written in the 1970s and revised many times, *The New Our Bodies Ourselves* (Boston Women's Health Book Collective, 1992), grew out a women's consciousness-raising group. The group members had been surprised to discover how little each of them knew about their own bodies. Most of the books in the library discussed women's health and sexuality from the male author's perspective. Therefore, the women began reading all the articles they could locate that were emerging from the women's movement. Then they visited other women's groups, asking many questions and recording the responses. They went on to interview those health care providers whom they trusted.

From this mass of data grew a well-written, inexpensively printed book distributed through women's centers. When the demand for it surpassed the capabilities of the small printing company they had used, it was republished by a major distributor. It has since been regularly updated, expanded, and translated into 10 languages. Today, it can be found in local bookstores, libraries, hospitals, and schools throughout the country. The same authors incorporated as a nonprofit group called the Boston Women's Health Book Collective and went on to write books about parenting, teenage women's concerns, and women at mid-life (*Our Bodies Ourselves,* 1976, 1992; *Ourselves and Our Children, 1978; Ourselves Growing Older,* 1984). By donating a portion of their royalties, they created a foundation that funds other nontraditional women's health projects.

Staying on the pathway to their goal was not the hard part of their work because the excitement of shared discovery and the urgency of the need for information propelled them forward. The hard part was taking the first step.

STARTING SMALL HELPS TO BUILD
EXPERTISE AND COMMITMENT

People concerned about GAPs and who have ideas on how to fill them need reassurance that creating a program does not necessarily take a vast sum of money or specialized expertise. For example, the lending library of books and toys that was on the LIFT wish list would not need much to get started. It requires some storage space with shelves (and perhaps a lock) and the time and energy of two or three volunteers who could do the following:

- Devise a set of rules and a system for borrowing items
- Purchase used books and toys at yard sales and public library sales
- Write a letter soliciting donations to the local churches and civic groups
- Contact the owners of the local toy shop to find out who their wholesale suppliers are
- Call a few publishers of children's books for remainders

If they still have some energy, during the Christmas-Chanukah-Kwanza season, they might set up a display in a large bookstore and ask customers to purchase a book for a child in need when they buy one for their own child.

GAPs get filled because a few people keep plugging away, learning as they go. In fact, all human progress probably depends on a few unreasonable people who refuse to take "no" for an answer and have a seemingly ridiculous confidence in themselves and their project.

STEP 4: FIGURING OUT
THE REASONS FOR THE GAP

Once the GAP has been described and we are committed to filling it, we need to figure out what causes lie behind the GAP. Then the programs we design to close the GAP should flow logically from this analysis. This linear approach appears to be a good approach—describe the problem, find the causes, and prescribe the remedy—but unfortunately it works better for the computer engineer or dentist, who are trying to figure out the source of a computer glitch or a pain in your mouth, than it does for the social service planner. When dealing with a troubled human being or a vexing social problem, we have few dependable diagnostic tools. Still, we must try to understand as much as possible about causality in all its complexity.

We explore the reasons behind a GAP by once again seeking out answers to hard questions from every available source.

Why do american adolescents commit suicide at such an alarming rate?

Why do inner-city adolescents have such an alarming rate of high school dropouts?

We listen to the social scientists, solicit the views of our clients, and then use our own inductive reasoning. The answers or hypotheses we come up with, however, will always remain speculative. Thus, when we mount a suicide prevention or drop-out prevention program we can rarely build it on a sure understanding of the causality behind those problems. Every strategy derived from an analysis of causality begins and usually remains an experiment.

In addition, even when we have a fairly good grasp of the many causes of a social problem, we can never be certain which particular reason accounts for the behavior of any one individual who falls within that category. For example, although all the member at an Alcoholics Anonymous meeting probably drink to excess, the reasons that any one person in that group abuses alcohol are complex and ultimately unknowable.

Given a similar set of life circumstances—for example, growing up with an alcoholic parent—each sibling in a family responds differently. One child might follow the parental pattern of abuse, another totally abstains, whereas a third child can drink socially with few ill effects.

Even after we have chosen a program strategy consistent with our analysis of causality, we still cannot assume that any changes in the behavior or life chances of a participant are a direct result of our program intervention. Our program, no matter how carefully chosen and well conducted, is only one of a multitude of forces influencing our client's life. Positive changes or negative setbacks might be attributed to those intervening variables.

Finally, the analysis of causality is not a neutral activity. Planners bring to it their own proclivities and ideological biases.

THEORIES OF CAUSALITY RISE AND FALL AS
SOCIAL ATTITUDES AND CIRCUMSTANCES SHIFT

The understanding of the causes of social GAPs is particularly suscep-tible to shifts in the prevailing ideology. Thus, for example, at one point in our history lax punishment for criminal acts was thought to be a major reason behind the escalation of the crime rate. Imposition of the death penalty was used as a program strategy. Decades later, in the 1960s, an era more sensitized to the social factors that lie behind crime and the biased administration of justice, the Supreme Court limited its use. The Committee to End the Death Penalty disbanded and an energetic set of programs called the War on Poverty promised to reduce criminal behavior by providing an array of opportunities for the economic advancement of the poor.

The "lack-of-opportunity" analysis of crime and the strategies that flowed from it, however, are now being successfully challenged in many states. In the 1990s, frustration with the inability to eliminate violence has brought back the death penalty, tough mandatory sentencing, boot camps, and even the chain gang. Researchers continue to produce contradictory sets of data supporting or refuting the efficacy of using harsh programs for crime prevention. We accept or reject their findings equally because of our ideology and because of careful analysis.

At times, our understanding of causal factors and program strategies that flow from them are recycled after years of disuse. The police officer walking his beat and interacting with neighborhood residents was long viewed as a strategy for crime prevention. That strategy was gradually replaced by the more technologically advanced use of squad cars and portable phones. Recently, criminal justice planners, analyzing the causes of crime, have proposed programs of "community policing" to reduce the social distance between the community residents and those who protect them. Long-time police officers must be shaking their heads in disbelief as they are once again "walking their beat" and hearing it hailed as an innovative strategy.

In Chicago, the large, publicly supported housing projects once hailed as major program innovations to eradicate the problem of poverty are now being bulldozed. Rent-control strategies put in place to protect the stock of affordable housing have virtually disappeared all over the country, propelled by a widespread belief that they caused more harm than good. Program planners now propose small, mixed-income housing developments, vouchers that subsidize low-income people in private-sector housing, or simply leaving the market to its own devices.

THEORIES OF CAUSALITY ALSO RISE AND FALL
AS KNOWLEDGE AND SKILLS EXPAND

Although many causality analyses rise or fall due to shifts in social attitudes and political power, some are the result of advances in diagnostic tools and strategies of remediation. The area of mental health programming yields some striking examples. For many years, mental health practitioners believed that schizophrenia was primarily caused by emotional traumas and failures in parent-child bonding. Intensive psychotherapy was the program strategy for those who could afford it. Long hospital confinements were routine. Now, advances in brain research have shown that imbalances in the chemistry of the brain are also major causal factors. Brief hospitalizations, time-limited therapy, often including the family, and trials of medication are now the most typical program strategies.

PERFORMING A CAUSALITY ANALYSIS
PRIOR TO CHOOSING PROGRAM STRATEGIES

After accepting all the inherent limitations of establishing solid causality, Kristen and Ms. Chu knew they must still try to perform a causality analysis before choosing the program strategies. They began their analysis by drawing a circle to represent the whole set of reasons behind the problem of homeless young mothers (Figure 4.1).

Next, they cut several pie-shaped wedges, each one representing one possible reason (or hypothesis) for the problem. They left one wedge blank to remind them that there were causes they had not yet discovered.

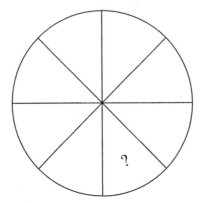

Figure 4.1. The Whole Problem Is Composed of Many Possible Causes

Although there are as many individual stories as there are young homeless women, the reasons for homelessness of young mothers fall into several categories. The following is the list that Ms. Chu and Kristen came up with after reviewing all the data they had gathered:

- Health issues
  - Problems of alcohol and drug abuse
  - Physical or mental or learning disability
  - Child with special health problems
- Lack of family and social support
  - Rejected by family because of the stigma of the birth or because of their own personal problems
  - Lack of peer group support—friends are still in school or in same circumstance
  - Lack of financial support from the fathers
- Lack of information about their rights and resources
  - Lack of knowledge of how to obtain the resources for income maintenance
  - Lack of knowledge of legal rights (or weak enforcement) to obtain support from fathers
  - Lack of confidence in foster care system and fear of losing child permanently
  - Lack of knowledge of alternative forms of adoption
  - Lack of understanding of complexity of single parenting

- Difficulty in getting and holding a job

  Has job but cannot save enough money for first and last month rent and furniture

  No high school diploma limits job options

  Lack of marketable skills

  Learning disabilities limit job options

  Lack of job-seeking skills

  Lack of transportation makes commuting from suburban areas impossible

  Job discrimination due to race, age, gender, or marital situation

- Lack of affordable child care

  No relative or friend to care for child while going to school, training, or work

  Child care too costly or not accessible

  Fear of low quality of child care

- Lack of affordable housing

  Low vacancy rate of low-cost and subsidized housing

  Few small apartments in town

  Landlords will not rent to single women with babies (problems of lead paint and fear of rowdy or promiscuous behavior)

- Emotional problems

  Low self-esteem and self-confidence

  Had to flee an abusive mate or family situation

  Need for someone to love—baby seems only alternative

  Wanted to have child because it gives a role and purpose to life

- Problems with sexuality or male-female relationships

  Pressures toward early sexuality by peer group and media

  Social attitudes that equate masculinity or femininity with fertility

  Blocks to male-female communication

  Lack of emphasis on parenting skills and responsibilities for males

  Lack of knowledge or access to birth control methods

  Lack of safe birth control methods

LOOKING CLOSELY AT EACH REASON LEADS TO DESIGNING A DIFFERENT TARGETED PROGRAM

After they finished drawing up the previously discussed list, Kristen and Ms. Chu could see how each of the categories of reasons they listed could lead them to design a different set of program strategies. For example,

- If they chose "nonsupport from the fathers" as the reason they would focus on, they might lobby at the state legislature for more creative ways to locate the fathers and extract payment. They might also design a high school-based fathering education and support program. This would aim at turning "men who impregnate women" into "fathers."
- If they chose to concentrate on lack of a high school diploma and lack of job-seeking skills, they might design a variety of catch-up, back to school, and stay in school programs. These might include workshops, mentoring, and internships. Perhaps they could do outreach to employers for job placement.

Homelessness requires so many different program strategies that Kristen and Ms. Chu knew they could not deal with all of the strategies.

RARELY CAN ONE SOCIAL PROGRAM INCORPORATE ALL THE PROGRAM STRATEGIES NECESSARY TO DEAL WITH ALL THE CAUSES OF A GAP

A new program should concentrate its creative energies on targeting a few of the causes. A narrowly focused program can add other components after its expertise and base have grown.

Kristen felt frustrated by this incremental approach. She wanted to jump right in and create a residential program that targeted the wedges of affordable housing, education, job training, and a healthy support network. She had the vision of LIFT House in her mind's eye. Ms. Chu, however, was not ready to make such a gigantic commitment of time and energy.

After much debate, Ms. Chu's more cautious approach prevailed. They decided to begin by targeting the wedge "lack of affordable child care." Even a small part-time child care program would give the mothers time to look for apartments and jobs or attend classes. The babies could also benefit from attention and consistency of a few experienced caregivers. It was not the "whole pie," but it was a start.

MS. CHU AND KRISTEN PLANT THE SEEDS OF LIFT WITH A PART-TIME CHILD CARE PROGRAM

The plan they proposed was to create a program of supervised child care for young parents who were homeless or inadequately housed. It would meet three afternoons a week for 3 hours. The planning committee assured Kristen and Ms. Chu that there was a good pool of volunteers. Before they could go much further, however, they had to find out how feasible it was to find an appropriate and safe facility that was rent free or very low cost and accessible to the shelters and bus line.

Utilizing their network of friends and family, they located a neighborhood church with a well-maintained Sunday school classroom. Elated, they assumed they could now shift into high gear. A barrier lay ahead, however!

STEP 5: RAISING CONSCIOUSNESS ABOUT THE NEED TO FILL THE GAP

Good intentions, carefully researched data, and creative program strategies should be sufficient to commit others to join us in creating a program. Unfortunately, however, often good intentions, data, and ideas are not enough.

It will probably be necessary to convince those who are the gatekeepers to our resources not only that we are correct but also that our request cannot be ignored. Decisions about who will obtain support and critical resources are often idiosyncratic—or conspiratorial, according to the planner's perspective. Often, resources are allocated on the basis of who is doing the asking, on the popularity or safety of the issue, or on whether it is believed by those in charge that the program has widespread support. Social service programs have always had an image problem. We work with clients whom others might not want to deal with. Until people need our services, they rarely will take to the barricades to make sure our programs receive support. Funding decisions tend to be inherently political and funding relationships between requestor and donor are inherently unequal (Gummer, 1990).

We need to prepare ourselves to search beyond the one agency we are negotiating with and market our vision to a wider constituency. Marketing, a concept more often associated with the business world, is equally necessary in the nonprofit sector. *Social marketing* is defined as the design, implementation, and control of programs seeking to increase the acceptability of a social idea, cause, or practice in a target group. It is simply a planned system of achieving organizational objectives—a program intended to sell a program!

There are some dramatic differences between social marketing and the marketing done in the business world, however. The social program planner does not try to convince the public that it needs a novel program that he or she has created. Rather, the planner first assesses the pressing needs of a community and then proposes ways to satisfy them (Kotler, 1982; Lauffer, 1984; Rothman et al., 1981; Rubright & MacDonald, 1981).

WHEN THE DEMAND THAT THE GAP
MUST BE FILLED FALLS ON DEAF EARS!

When Kristen and Ms. Chu requested permission to use the Sunday school classroom for the child care program, they naively assumed the answer would be a resounding "yes!"

At their first meeting with the church council, they distributed a well-researched report documenting the urgent need for their proposed child care program. They distributed letters of support from local merchants promising to donate equipment and from volunteers committing their time. Both Ms.Chu and Kristen had solid reputations in the volunteer and professional service community.

The next day, however, they received an apologetic "no" from the embarrassed minister. Although their presentation was deemed excellent and everyone agreed it was a worthy project, the problem of young homeless mothers was near the bottom of the church council's agenda. They raised concerns about insurance liability and the dependability of volunteer caregivers. Several council members had raised the money to equip the Sunday school classroom and they were very protective of it. Although no one actually said it out loud, the minister thought that at least one member worried that this kind of program would be "condoning promiscuity."

DEALING WITH RESISTANCE TO FILLING A GAP

When program planners encounter resistance to their requests, it is likely to be the result of one or more of the following factors:

- They are competing for scarce resources with other social programs that also make a strong case.
- The strategies proposed are controversial or not fully understood.
- People who exert influence or power have, for their own personal reasons, chosen to oppose it.

In addition to these factors, many social planners encounter the not-in-my-backyard syndrome. Community members might worry that the negative stigma or consequences of a social service program located close-by will rub off on their homes, diminishing their sense of security and their property values.

When we encounter resistance, it might be a sign that we have not planned adequately or carefully prepared our case. Therefore, we step back, rework our design, and then organize a campaign to push our program higher up on the agenda of the group we are trying to convince. That process is called *consciousness raising,* a term popularized by the women's liberation movement. It is a process that provokes people to look at an old issue in new and more encompassing ways.

Consciousness-raising activities take many forms. In the 1970s, as a part of the feminist revival, small informal discussion groups sprang up throughout the country. Women of all ages came together to create a new understanding of their roles in society. They read, talked, listened to each other, and often held each other's hands as they tried new ways of thinking and acting (much as did the Boston Women's Health Book Collective).

Other forms of consciousness raising are more short term. They are intended to emotionally "hit you over the head or in the heart." The AIDS Quilt, composed of thousands of decorated squares of fabric, each one constructed to represent a person killed by the virus, is one powerful example. The quilt (now too gigantic to spread out in one continuous piece) travels in segments around the country. It is displayed on college campuses, in shopping malls, and in churches, usually sponsored by the local AIDS support group. Its main goal is to provoke the realization in viewers of just how much like their own loved ones—and themselves—the victims of this disease are. This empathic recognition might move the viewers to act less judgmentally toward people with AIDS. It might also encourage the viewers to support the funding of AIDS research, social services, and education programs.

Observing this powerful consciousness-raising technique, a women's crisis center created The Clothesline Project. On a line strung across a public space, they hang shirts that are filled with the words and pictures of women who have been sexually harassed, raped, or stalked. Onlookers are encouraged to decorate a blank shirt to add to the line if they too have painful memories of a similar assault. Watching the discomfort and pain of the spectators, one realizes the power of this kind of message presentation. It forcefully communicates the gravity of the problem while giving succor to the victims and pause to potential perpetrators or apologists. The following are some other ways that program planners have tried to raise the consciousness of the public:

- An alcohol awareness program on a college campus displays a wrecked automobile on the front quad accompanied by a video of the crash that killed the young driver and her friends. In the student center, a state trooper demonstrates how one can monitor a blood alcohol level.

- A Holocaust commemoration committee of an interfaith council displays horrific photographs of emaciated survivors of concentration camps in the lobby of a federal office building, and for 2 days, the names of victims of the camps are solemnly read aloud.
- A delegation of Irish Americans who are also homosexuals march in a St. Patrick's Day parade despite the objection of the organizers, and then press a very public lawsuit when they are ejected.
- A group of advocates for the mentally ill erects crosses on the town green to dramatize the number of deaths that have occurred among the mentally ill because of the lack of outpatient services for them in the community.

THE MASS MEDIA PLAY A MAJOR ROLE
IN CONSCIOUSNESS RAISING

Making effective use of the mass media is one course of action that may significantly influence public sentiment and the decisions of policy-makers. It might build the groundswell of support that carries the program up and over the objections or timidity of those who are withholding the resources. Planners need to learn how to create a news release, hold a press conference, develop relationships with local reporters (especially investigative reporters), call into talk shows, write letters to the editor, and use the communication power afforded by the Internet (for other helpful media techniques, see Brawley, 1983).

Consciousness-raising materials can also be disseminated at conferences, forums, seminars, teach-ins, and rallies and through the showing of documentary films. The information, especially any statistics presented, should be as accurate as possible. Libraries and government reports can provide access to data (Mendelsohn, 1987). Written materials add depth to the public's understanding of an issue that has not been widely understood. They also create a sense of credibility and urgency.

Sometimes, consciousness-raising techniques feature charismatic personalities. They can spread a message about the need for resources in a very engaging and dramatic way. Everyone has probably seen or heard on a talk show one of the following:

- An actress or high-ranking official who grew up in an alcoholic family and has written a book about the experience
- The heir to a tobacco fortune who leads an antismoking campaign
- A political figure who has survived breast cancer and talks about it at rallies
- A famous scientist or athlete who is severely physically handicapped but whose achievements contradict stereotypes about the limitations imposed by disability

KRISTEN AND MS. CHU RAISE THE
CONSCIOUSNESS OF THE BOARD MEMBERS

Kristen and Ms. Chu realized that they had to intensify their consciousness-raising activities. They had to spread their message about the tragic consequences of the lack of child care for homeless young mothers to a circle outside the church. In the congregation and in the broader community, they might find sources of clout that had the influence or power to reverse the board's refusal.

Being the sole proponents of the LIFT program put them in a weak position, and they could easily be ignored. They needed to draw strength from being a part of a coalition of individuals or groups. A *coalition* is defined as a time-limited organization (or cluster of individuals and groups) in which there is a convergence of interest on the part of a number of actors and an interaction around furthering these common interests (Dluhy, 1990). Although coalitions serve other more benign purposes, such as disseminating information and networking, in this instance the need for a coalition was political in the most basic sense. The board had resources to allocate, and the LIFT committee had a program that made sense but was being blocked.

Expanding the scope of their consciousness-raising activities to a wider audience had a secondary goal. If their campaign to change the board's vote did not succeed, by stirring up the waters and informing many others about the issue, another facility might be offered to them.

The following are the consciousness-raising activities the LIFT committee members performed:

- Wrote an article about the job search struggles of young mothers for the local newspaper
- Convinced the local public access TV channel to film a panel discussion on the LIFT project with Kristen, a minister from a church that sponsors a similar program, and two previously homeless mothers who are now employed after graduating from nursing school
- Convinced a sociology professor to write an article for the newspaper stressing the diverse backgrounds of young mothers who become homeless
- Obtained a social work intern and a communications major from the local college to work on a brochure and fact sheet about the child care program
- Arranged to speak at a chamber of commerce luncheon about the need to support the efforts of young mothers to find work and complete school to avoid continued dependence on the public sector
- Enlisted the Key Club at the high school to do a toy drive for the program

- Convinced the high school principal to speak with the church council about the difficulty of young women obtaining a GED diploma if they have no child care
- Created an advisory committee of a pediatrician, the minister from the church, the high school principal, an officer of the chamber of commerce, two young mothers who had been homeless, and two retirees from the parish

Through these consciousness-raising activities, the message reached many local residents, some of whom were members of the church. Kristen and Ms. Chu received donations of materials and offers of volunteer help. One of the people who contacted them was a parishioner who had been a young single mother for 3 years and had been close to being homeless several times. She volunteered to speak in support of the child care program at the next open meeting of the church community.

The chair of the Ministry Beyond the Walls Committee of the church promised to speak with each of the board members about his group's enthusiasm about the LIFT proposal. Kristen and Ms. Chu were no longer alone, and they were no longer outsiders asking for a favor!

At the open meeting of the church community, Kristen and Ms. Chu came prepared with the following:

- Copies of the articles about their proposed program which had appeared in the local newspaper
- A copy of the video made by the public access TV channel
- A list of the names and positions of the people who had agreed to serve on their advisory committee
- A paper on teenage parenting and the need for a child care program written by a sociology professor
- An eloquent spokesperson who was well-known as a member of a family long affiliated with the church

At the meeting, a motion was made to allow the space to be used and to join in sponsorship of the program. The motion passed—although not without a heated debate. Finally, the first program of LIFT had found a home in a supportive environment!

WHEN EDUCATIONAL CONSCIOUSNESS-RAISING STRATEGIES ARE NOT SUFFICIENT, PLANNERS CAN BIDE THEIR TIME

Despite planners' best efforts at consciousness raising, often a desperately needed program still cannot garner support. When that happens, the planners might decide to accept the reality that at this time and in this place, the soil still is not fertile enough for their program to take root and grow. Perhaps they can continue educating the public and the power brokers who control the resources. The program, however, might need to be put on hold until the message finally gets through or until the field of forces and the cast of actors have changed. For example, a turnover in membership or an election might bring in a new, more supportive set of church council members. Perhaps a new Sunday school director will be hired who is more supportive of the LIFT program.

The time spent in educational consciousness-raising activities is rarely wasted. It can produce valuable serendipitous results. For example, had the church board not reversed its decision, the dean at the local college might have been moved to offer space, or he might have organized a coalition of agencies to pool their resources for LIFT. His activism would demonstrate the college's sensitivity to the needs of its neighbors while providing internships for its early childhood and human service majors.

The recent upsurge in attention paid to volunteer service initiatives might make the time for such a move propitious. On a more practical level, the LIFT board would be likely to support the college's attempt to purchase a new property in the face of resistance from the local block association. The strongest coalitions are symbiotic ones in which everyone gains something they need.

WHEN EDUCATIONAL CONSCIOUSNESS-RAISING STRATEGIES ALONE ARE NOT SUFFICIENT, PLANNERS MIGHT USE PRESSURE TACTICS TO PRY OPEN THE GATE TO THE RESOURCES

If their creative outreach techniques were exhausted and patience worn thin, the LIFT planners might have eventually abandoned their hope of raising consciousness through education and influence. Then they might have chosen to employ pressure tactics. They would be stating,

We have tried every way we can to help you understand that this is a serious GAP that needs attention. We have pointed out to you the advantages that such a program would bring to fulfilling your mission in the community. Now we are going to use all our skills to force you to change your refusal.

The LIFT committee could have joined forces with sympathetic members of the congregation to organize a petition or a letter-writing campaign protesting the board's refusal. Also, they might have mounted a campaign to convince congregants to withhold their contributions to the church building fund until the church agreed to meet its civic responsibility by hosting the child care program.

Community groups that believe their demands are not being taken seriously often take this route, although it is obviously a last resort. The union movement that improved the oppressive conditions of workers in the early 1900s was built through the use of these strategies of protesting and boycotting.

In the 1960s, the civil rights movement utilized pressure tactics after years of using education and exerting influence to achieve racial desegregation in the southern states. The 11-month boycott of the buses in Montgomery, Alabama, by the black community provides an excellent example of a pressure campaign. After months of walking to work, thereby withholding their bus fares, it became clear that the bus system and the town's merchants could not survive without the business of the black citizens of the town.

Entering white-only waiting rooms in train stations and sitting in and demanding service at segregated lunch counters kept the momentum for change building throughout the South. These activities eventually forced many discriminatory laws and behaviors to change. They also changed the consciousness of many of the black protesters who had for years accepted their lack of resources and privileges.

A close scrutiny of the history of most social programs, whether they be a schoolwide sex education campaign or a bill mandating the rights to a mainstream education for students who are disabled, reveals that ultimately the decision to proceed to fill a GAP is reached after there has been a mixture of education, influence, and pressure (Schram & Mandell, 1997).

THE 5-MINUTE RECAP

- Troubleshooting is the act of identifying a serious problem in the delivery of social services or a lack in the quality of life of a group of people. These problems are called GAPs.

- A GAP is the space that lies between what now exists and what ought to be happening.

- A GAP is a subjective estimate of a problem, likely to vary according to when it is described and by whom.

- GAP statements often begin as complaints, as statements of alarm, or as hopes and dreams.

- The troubleshooter needs the sensitivity to identify a GAP in services coupled with the restraint needed to carefully analyze the problem before prematurely jumping in to "fix it."

- Those who would define a GAP as needing to be filled should support their assertion with the following:

  Statistical data demonstrating its extent

  Evidence of its serious consequences

  A projection of what will happen if it continues

  Evidence that no other program can close it

- The research conducted regarding the size and shape of a GAP is often referred to as "conducting a need's assessment."

- The founders of LIFT had to turn to many sources—people as well as written materials—when they explored the need for a child care program for young mothers who are homeless.

- To make sure they obtained a full picture of the situation from each person they interviewed, Kristen and Ms. Chu constructed and then "pretested" a set of probing questions.

- Once the data have been collected, the troubleshooters need to summon up the courage and commitment to work to fill the GAP.

- Although it can seem overwhelming to design a program to fill a GAP, many innovative approaches have been created by laypeople who had little money or formal training but kept plugging away, never taking "no" for an answer to their legitimate requests.

- After the GAP is described and the commitment to fill it made, troubleshooters speculate about the possible reasons for the GAP. This is vital because each reason will point the way to a possible program strategy.

- Theories of causality are hypotheses that are likely to change to fit the prevailing social attitudes and the current state of knowledge and skills.

- There are multiple causes for social problems. Some might not be amenable to change with the tools available, and some causes will inevitably remain unknown.

- Rarely can one social program deal with all the possible causes of a problem. Planners usually choose to focus their program strategies on one or two causes of the overall problem. Perhaps later on they can add programs to deal with others, or perhaps another agency will take on that task.

- Despite being well documented and analyzed, a GAP might still continue to be ignored by those who control the necessary resources.

- When that happens, planners employ the community organization techniques for social change. They educate, persuade, and might finally turn to direct pressure to overcome inertia or resistance to change.

- Most planners employ a subtle mix of all three sets of organizing techniques as they try to restructure or expand on a current program or innovate a new one.

PUTTING THEORY INTO PRACTICE

EXERCISE 1: COLLECTING EVIDENCE ABOUT A GAP

The Situation

In the past few years, there seems to have been an alarming increase in teenage vandalism, auto accidents, and cases of attempted suicide among the teenage population of a small, affluent suburb. A task force composed of two town councilors, two high school peer leaders, and the director of the regional mental health association has met several times to discuss this problem or GAP.

At their meetings, they have shared stories about episodes they are aware of and agree that this appears to be a serious problem that is growing worse. They are convinced that too many parents in the town are busy ignoring the signs of this alarming GAP in services for this vulnerable population.

Task

1. Acting as a member of the task force, list at least four places (and/or people) you would visit in your town to collect data about the extent of teenage adjustment problems and the resources that already exist to deal with them.
2. List at least five questions you would ask the people you interview to gather data about the problems and services for teenagers in this town.
3. List any publications or any other sources you could use to learn more about the problems of teenagers in suburbia in general and this town in particular.
4. How might you best solicit the opinions of a cross section of the teenagers in this town about the extent of teenage problems and the strategies they think would help to deal with them?

EXERCISE 2: FIGURING OUT CAUSALITY

The committee that has been researching the problem of teenage destructive behavior has now collected a large amount of material from interviews, surveys, and reading. The committee is ready to try to define the reasons for the alarming increase in teenage vandalism, auto accidents, and attempted suicide. From this analysis, the committee will propose its program design.

Using your own knowledge of the subject, create a list of at least eight possible factors that might account for a growth in destructive teenage behavior. After you have listed all the causes you can think of, divide them into the following general categories:

Family issues

Developmental pressures (e.g., search for identity, etc.)

Environmental pressures (issues in the town)

Community or societal pressures (e.g., mass media, etc.)

What other categories arose as you sought to categorize the reasons you came up with?

Understanding that a single program cannot possibly tackle all the causes of a problem, choose those three causes that seem to be the ones most amenable to small-scale program interventions (e.g., the escalating divorce rate might be a major source of stress for teens, but the lack of recreational outlets, one of the other proposed causes of stress, is a problem that could be dealt with more directly and realistically in a small-scale program).

EXERCISE 3: RAISING CONSCIOUSNESS
ABOUT THE NEED TO FILL A GAP

Although the task force has compiled an impressive report and proposed some feasible programs, the town council members vote to table the report and spend their remaining discretionary funds on physical improvements to the downtown shopping area. What six arguments would you use to try to convince them to reorder their priorities and fund a program that aims to lessen teenage violence.

Describe five strategies the task force might employ to raise the issue of the lack of social services for teenagers to the top of their agenda. Remember to begin with education and then move to persuasion and pressure.

CITATIONS AND SUGGESTIONS
FOR FURTHER READING

Boston Women's Health Book Collective. (1976). *Our bodies ourselves: A book by and for women.* New York: Simon & Schuster.

Boston Women's Health Book Collective. (1978). *Ourselves and our children: A book by and for parents.* New York: Random House.

Boston Women's Health Book Collective. (1992). *The new our bodies ourselves: A book by and for women.* New York: Simon & Schuster.

Doress, P. B., & Siegel, D. L. (in cooperation with Boston Women's Health Book Collective). (1994). *The new ourselves growing older: Women aging with knowledge and power.* New York: Simon & Schuster.

NEEDS ASSESSMENTS

Epstein, I., & Tripodi, T. (1977). *Research techniques for program planning, monitoring and evaluation*. New York: Columbia University Press. See especially Chapters 2 and 3 on conducting a needs analysis survey and Chapter 4 on being an alert consumer of research studies in the problem area you are exploring.

Kettner, P. M., Moroney, R. M., & Martin, L. L. (1990). *Designing and managing programs: An effectiveness based approach*. Newbury Park, CA: Sage. This very well-written book devotes Chapters 2, 3, and 4 to an in-depth look at the criteria, techniques, and some of the inherent dilemmas of exploring a GAP—which they refer to as a problem analysis or needs assessment.

Moroney, R. M. (1977). Needs assessment for human services. In B. J. Friedan & M. J. Murphy (Eds.), *Managing human services*. Washington, DC: International City Management Association.

Powers, G. T., Meenaghan, T. M., & Toomey, B. G. (1985). *Practice focused research, integrating human service practice and research*. Englewood Cliffs, NJ: Prentice Hall. See especially Chapters 5 and 6 for suggestions for using the library and accessing other special sources of information when documenting a GAP. Chapter 7 provides a useful discussion of needs assessment strategies.

Soriano, F. I. (1995). *Conducting needs assessments, a multidisciplinary approach*. Thousand Oaks, CA: Sage. This book provides a useful step-by-step approach to needs assessment. Chapter 7 focuses on reporting your findings. Chapter 8 offers suggestions to increase social and cultural sensitivity in creating a needs assessment instrument and in approaching community members.

RESOURCES FOR MARKETING AND CREATING SUPPORT FOR PROGRAMS

Brawley, E. A. (1983). *Mass media and human services: Getting the message across*. Beverly Hills, CA: Sage. This book provides good nuts and bolts examples of using the more conventional print media to raise consciousness about a problem and program.

Kotler, P. (1982). *Marketing for non-profit organizations* (2nd ed.). Englewood Cliffs, NJ: Prentice Hall.

Lauffer, A. (1984). *Strategic planning for not-for-profit organizations & resource development*. New York: Free Press.

Mendelsohn, H. N. (1987). *A guide to information sources for social work and the human services*. Phoenix, AZ: Oryx Press. This book is an invaluable time-saver that leads to finding statistics and other information that can be used for needs assessment and program proposals.

Rothman, J., Erlich, J. L., & Teresa, J. G. (1976). *Promoting innovation and change in organizations: A planning manual*. New York: John Wiley.

Rothman, J., Erlich, J. L., & Teresa, J. G. (1981). *Changing organizations and community programs* (Rev. ed.). New York: John Wiley.

Rubright, R., & MacDonald, D. (1981). *Marketing health and human services*. Rockville, MD: Aspen Systems.

COALITION BUILDING

Dluhy, M. J. (with Kravitz, S. L.). (1990). *Building coalitions in the human services*. Newbury Park, CA: Sage. This book provides a useful set of strategies for planner consciousness-raising efforts. It also provides ideas on how to achieve acceptance for a program by mustering support from agencies to influence and exert pressure on reluctant sponsors or funders.

FURTHER INSIGHTS INTO CONSCIOUSNESS-RAISING TECHNIQUES

Gummer, B. (1990). *The politics of social administration: Managing organization politics in social agencies.* Englewood Cliffs, NJ: Prentice Hall. This book provides an insightful analysis of the politics of social service programming which divest us of illusions that simply documenting a need is sufficient to garner support. The book also prepares a planner to meet the barriers that might be thrown up in the planner's path as he or she seeks approval for innovations.

Schram, B., & Mandell, B. R. (1997). *Introduction to human services policy and practice* (3rd ed.). New York: Macmillan. See Chapter 11, pp. 425-464.

5

MAGNIFYING THE GAP
The Program Design Process

Unless we foster versatile, innovative and self renewing men and women, all the ingenious social arrangements in the world will not help us.

—John W. Gardner (1964)

Step 5	**Spelling out program details, presenting a program proposal**
Step 4	**Weighing the trade-offs and prospects of program ideas**
Step 3	**Sorting, ranking, and selecting appropriate ideas**
Step 2	**Generating program ideas through specific techniques**
Step 1	**Taking an inventory of similar programs**

A caveman watching his neighbor chipping away at a large, flat piece of stone said, "Hey Torvor, what are you doing?" Torvor replied, "I am trying to invent the wheel." His neighbor looked surprised and said, "Don't waste your time, that guy in the next cave has already invented one." So Torvor put down his ax and went to see his neighbor's wheel. He liked it, so he went home and copied the design and the method. But a few months later, he was back at it again, looking perplexed as he chiseled away at a large stone. His neighbor, looking surprised, asked, "Torvor, now that you have seen the other guy's wheel, why are you spending so much time trying to figure out how to make one?" "Well," Torvor replied, "His was pretty good, but I want one that is a little different. And anyway, what if I want to make a wheel and he isn't around to show me how to do it?"

This parable has two messages. First, there is no reason for any of us to think that we have to invent a program from scratch. If we look around our community, it is likely that someone else has already thought about a similar problem and invested time and energy creating a blueprint to fill the GAP. We can utilize their blueprint. In program planning, we need not worry about accusations of plagiarism.

It is also true, however, that we can rarely ever just digest whole a program that was specifically designed for another population or a slightly different problem. Other program designs are our starting point. The program design process that Kristen and Ms. Chu embarked on once their GAP had been fully explored had much in common with Torvor's work. They were certain that somewhere, in their town or perhaps in a neighboring community, there was a program similar to the one they wanted to create. Therefore, they began to seek out such a program, hoping to copy its strengths and avoid its weaknesses.

Their program would have to be tailored to reflect the special needs of the young mothers who were living in shelters and of the ideals, values, and constraints of the church that was lending them space. The program would also reflect their own special talents and the resources and limitations of their committee members.

PROGRAMS ARE ORGANIC

Each time you put together a program, it is like going through a birthing process. You cannot risk skipping a step. Program designs are never completed; they are always in a state of dynamic change. No sooner has a program been planned than the planners start redesigning it according to their most recent feedback and their developing understanding of the problem being dealt with. The creative program planner is a manipulator in the best sense of the word, always keeping an eye on the weathervane to see which way the wind is blowing.

Five months after Kristen and Ms. Chu started the Let Infants and Families Thrive (LIFT) child care program, Ms. Chu lay awake at night trying to figure out how to expand the program from 1 day to 3 days and eventually from 3 days to 5 days. Out of that child care program grew the general equivalency diploma (GED) tutoring program for the mothers, then a course in becoming a child care assistant, and so on. Finally, it became clear that all this activity needed a home of its own; thus, LIFT House, a full-service residence for young women and their infant children, opened its doors.

LIFT has continued to grow. Each time the program has expanded or a new activity has been added, the workers have climbed each of the steps shown in the beginning of the chapter. On their first ventures into program generation, they began with a mixture of excitement and apprehension. As they have grown in skill and self-confidence, however, they have been able to walk the steps more quickly with far fewer false starts and stumbles. Program planning is a muscle that grows stronger the more it is used.

RAYMOND PLANS A MENTORING PROGRAM

After LIFT evolved into a residential program, Kristen and Ms. Chu had their hands full supervising the daily activities of the house. Planning new programs was a time-consuming luxury they could no longer afford. Innovations now depended on the enthusiasm and energy generated by the residents and volunteers. Kristen and Ms. Chu, however, were always available to give consultation to fledging planners who had a vision but lacked the experience to know how to fit together all the puzzle pieces that create a new whole.

Raymond, the computer programmer who volunteers his services in the LIFT office, is one of the people who Kristen is currently guiding through the design process. He has been assisting in the education and career training program for the residents. He thinks it is woefully inadequate, however. Many of the young women remain in the GED tutoring classes long after they should be advancing to take the test. He thinks they lack the self-confidence to even try. Others have some job training but hesitate to go to interviews. He has analyzed the causality of this apparent immobility and has decided that the major reasons for the GAP in follow-through are lack of concrete search skills and lack of self-confidence.

To support this assertion, he interviewed some former residents about their current school and work roles. He asked them what more they think LIFT could have done to help them make the transition to the world of school and work. He also spoke to each of the current residents about their goals, and through role-play he developed a sense of the skills they had in finding resources.

During this same period of exploration, he asked the personnel director of his company what she thought could be done to give the young women at LIFT more support and self-confidence. She suggested that they would benefit from a one-on-one mentoring relationship. She told him that mentoring programs are being established in many inner-city high schools. Therefore, Raymond's project idea has taken shape. He wants to link up each LIFT resident to a person in the community who has already been successful in school or in a career. These volunteer mentors would spend a considerable amount of time coaching the mentees in ways to meet their school or work goals. The mentors could informally teach the skills of locating educational and training resources, filling in applications, and practicing for interviews. He does not want this to be like a counselor to client relationship. He visualizes it as more like the relationship with an older sibling or a friend who just happens to have more experience in certain areas. He wants his mentors to be the kind of people who can empower, believe in, and cheer for their mentees. They will also need to do some hand-holding and, perhaps through their networks of contacts, they can open some doors for the residents.

The board members of LIFT have long wanted to fill that GAP, so they are excited that Raymond is taking the leadership in creating the LIFT mentor's program. They delegated two board members and a resident to work with him on a planning committee. Now, as Kristen and Ms. Chu have done many times, Raymond starts to climb the steps of the second phase of the planning model.

STEP 1: TAKING AN INVENTORY
OF SIMILAR PROGRAMS

As Raymond started the planning process, Ms. Chu reminded him that no matter how creative his idea, other equally committed people had probably been thinking along similar paths. Therefore, his first job was to link up with those programs and pick the brains of their staff and clients. At first, he thought this would be an impossible assignment. He was used to working at a computer firm that goes to great lengths to guard its company secrets. He was also self-conscious about intruding on a busy person's time. Ms. Chu, however, reassured him that "informational interviews" are like casting bread on the waters. Today, a person would give him an hour of his or her time, and in the future, when the LIFT mentoring program was well launched, someone else would approach him for a few hours worth of brain picking.

Raymond began by composing a list of questions to use in the agency interviews. Before he visited an agency, he asked the agency to send him their brochures, fact sheets, or any forms they used. Reviewing these

Table 5.1   Sample Questions to Ask When Inventorying Programs

---

What exactly is the job description of your mentors (or tutors)?

What are the basic qualifications you look for?

What kind of commitments do you ask of the mentors?

What kind of contract do you use for mentors and mentees?

How did you initially recruit your mentors? How effective were these methods?

How do you screen your mentors?

What kind of training do you provide for them?

What criteria do you use to match the mentor and mentee?

What kinds of incentives do you provide for mentors and mentees? Any financial reimbursement to the mentors, or special events?

What kind of evaluation process do you have for the teams?

What would you say have been the strengths and weaknesses of your program so far?

What are your future goals for the program?

If you were starting from scratch, what would you do differently?

---

materials gave him some basic data about the program and helped him learn its basic vocabulary. With this preparation, he could use his limited time at the interview to obtain more in-depth evaluative information.

Obviously, the questions a planner asks are tailored to the specific kind of program being researched, but Table 5.1 shows the type of open-ended questions that can elicit thoughtful responses.

Once Raymond had his survey questions organized, he set out to locate parallel programs by exploring his own network. When one is on the trail of information, it is a good strategy to let everyone know what one is looking for. It is remarkable how many bits and pieces of information friends and colleagues have filed away in their brains or file drawers. Many planners develop the habit of having a shoe box into which they put articles they have clipped out of newspapers, agency brochures, conference programs, and notices they have salvaged from bulletin boards they have encountered in their travels.

Raymond was building a network of experts to tap for ongoing advice. He was also creating a resource inventory, a mapping strategy that attempts to amass enough information to identify the resources of a total delivery system. Through the inventory, a planner can evaluate whether the existing service system is functioning to capacity, whether specific agencies in the system are capable of serving more people, and whether there is an overlap of services. This assessment may result in the conclusion that there is a need for a new program (in this case, a mentoring program), or perhaps better coordination or use of existing resources could meet this demand for service (Kettner, Moroney, & Martin, 1990, p. 63).

The director of the personnel department at the company where Raymond worked was the first resource person on his list. After he queried his own network for leads, he cast his net more widely, examining the following:

1. The phone book and a directory of area social services (Gardner, 1964)
2. The Information hotline run by the United Way, a human service consortium
3. The school department, especially the directors of special education, student support services, and vocational education
4. The local chapter of the Big Sisters and Big Brothers Association
5. The state Vocational Rehabilitation Department
6. The chairperson of the local college's department of education
7. The local library

After searching the list discussed previously, Raymond found the following:

- A nearby city had a chapter of the "I Have a Dream Foundation." This national program, founded by Jamie Bush, the former president's son, conducts extensive training of young professional volunteers who act as mentors to low-income high school youth. They promised to send him their annual report, training materials, and copies of the contracts they used for mentors and mentees. They set up a time for him to interview the coordinator as well as a mentor-mentee team.

- The school department told him that the college volunteer service ran a mentoring program with one of the public schools in the low-income community. The college president had created a program called "Ticket to Success." It guaranteed that any low-income youngster from the program who successfully completed high school would be given a scholarship to the college. A faculty member invited Raymond to their mentor retreat. This was held at the end of each program year so participants could evaluate the program and set future goals.

- The Department of Vocational Rehabilitation had a fledgling program called People Allied in Learning (PAL) that matched up adults who were learning disabled with children who had similar problems. They were in the early stages of their program, but the counselor who was running it was eager to talk with someone else who was just beginning.

- While surfing the shelves at his public library, Raymond came across a book titled *Handbook of Special Events for Non-Profit Organizations* (Liebert & Sheldon, 1974). Although it did not provide him with any immediate clues about structuring mentoring programs, he was relieved to find a book that provided specific detailed ideas on how to create a special event that promotes a cause to garner public acceptance, to raise money, to recruit volunteers, and to dramatize a program's needs and accomplishments. He took copious notes to be reviewed later, when he was further into the planning process.

A GENERAL PRINCIPLE ABOUT SEEKING OUT PROGRAMS

It is a rule of thumb in seeking resources to start with the largest umbrella agencies. Therefore, for example, if you are planning a program in the area of senior citizen programs, call town hall to find out which agency or department has oversight in this area. It is likely to be called the Council of Elders, the Senior Citizen Council, or some variation on those titles. If you are planning a program to fill a GAP in services for people who have Lou Gehrig's disease, spina bifida, obsessive compulsive disorder, or eating disorders; children with cancer; adults with developmental delays; veterans with posttraumatic stress; or gay people who are the victims of violence, it is likely that there will be a listing in the phone book of a local chapter of a national organization that has a title similar to one of these subgroups. If there is no phone listing, the social service worker at the local hospital might know the person in town who organizes those issues. Frequently, there is someone on the medical or mental health staff that specializes in a particular issue. Often, there is a volunteer working out of his or her living room. Perhaps the social service department or library will have a book that lists the headquarters of national advocacy and self-help organizations. By writing a letter or phoning the central office, you can locate their affiliates in your area.

Finding programs and knowledgeable people is like going on a scavenger hunt. Think creatively, and each time you get the wrong person on the phone, ask who she or he thinks might be the right source.

STEP 2: GENERATING PROGRAM IDEAS
THROUGH SPECIFIC TECHNIQUES

As Raymond reviewed the notes he had taken during his interviews and plowed through the stack of reports, forms, and flyers, he began to feel overwhelmed. He had almost too many ideas on recruiting, training, and maintaining mentors.

He needed to convene the planning committee to sift through the ideas and choose its own design. He found a block of time that everyone was available and convinced Ms. Chu to join in the daylong planning "retreat." She agreed on the condition that the meeting have a clear structure. During these early sessions, he must try to avoid the "groupthink phenomena," in which a few articulate people—often the more experienced ones—hold sway. Although they may not intend to dominate the discussion, their ideas and energy can overwhelm participants who are less confident or less invested. Therefore, many creative ideas never surface. Worse still, the program design may not be "owned" by all the members. Their low investment might haunt the program.

Raymond thought about the techniques used in his workplace. At critical junctures, consultants had helped the staff to focus their thinking. Using the techniques, all the staff members were able to spell out their ideas. Then, they constructively evaluated the ideas so that everyone found his or her voice and every ear heard even the quietest whisper.

In the library, he found a book titled *Assessment Tools* (Lauffer, 1982). Lauffer describes six techniques useful in focusing meetings, helping participants explore the following questions:

What is happening?
What is likely to be?
What do we want to happen?
How do we move into action?

The techniques can be used in training and staff development activities, in program planning, and in agency management. They are remarkably flexible tools, adaptable for a wide variety of situations. They all share the virtue of starting a meeting with a predetermined format. Some rely on the preparation of materials before the meeting begins. The following sections provide a brief description of a few of them, and others will be discussed elsewhere in the book.

MAPPING TECHNIQUES

Using paper and pencil or an erasable surface, the principal actors, groups, and other elements in the social environment that might be involved in the plan are graphically depicted as a series of shapes on a field. The map for the mentoring planning session could begin by drawing a big circle in the middle of the paper to represent LIFT. The chief executive officer, the training and development departments, and staff union of Raymond's firm, for example, might be triangles, the local college's education department and alumni association might be squares, and so on. Next, arrows would be drawn among and between the shapes on the map to represent the extent of their existing relationships to each other. This kind of visual analysis can be used to acknowledge linkages that already exist and can be put to good use in the plan under discussion. Just as important, however, a scan of the map can also point to spots where linkages do not already exist and might be developed. A picture is, indeed, often worth a thousand words.

TASK ANALYSIS

This is another pencil and paper technique, but in this instance we develop "mapping sentences," with action verbs to specify actual or desired behaviors and relationships that might be performed by a given group or person doing a job within the plan. A task sentence should include the answer to the following questions:

Who
performs what actions,
to whom or to what,
using what tools or methods,
to what outcome or what purpose,
using what direction or under whose supervision or instruction,
to be evaluated or monitored in what way?

NOMINAL GROUP TECHNIQUE

This is a deceptively simple technique in which participants are asked to write down their ideas, priorities, needs, or some other predetermined information about the issue being discussed or planned either in preparation for the meeting or once assembled. These lists are then sorted into categories, listed on large sheets of paper to be talked about one at a time, or any other method that seems most appropriate to the central mission of the meeting are used. Raymond planned to use a series of these types of exercises, with time limits, to move the group along in a step-by-step fashion that although recognizing the preciousness of their time and the need to accomplish much in one meeting, allowed the open flow of feelings and ideas during each exercise.

DELPHI QUESTIONNAIRES

These are questionnaires that can be administered and tabulated before the planning retreat. They are designed to tap the opinions and willingness to share resources of the experts or power brokers whose views it is necessary to know before planning because these views will probably exert a strong impact on the shape and potential success of the plan. The answers can then be dealt with constructively by the planning group. Because the cooperation of both the officers and the staff of his company was vital to the mentoring program, Raymond realized he needed to try to get an accurate estimate of his support. Because the whole topic of young, poor mothers elicits strong feelings, he made his questionnaires anonymous, protecting against false political correctness. He wanted controversies and resistances to surface early in the planning process so that they did not sabotage the program later.

GAMING AND OTHER SIMULATION TECHNIQUES

These are interactive methods used to explore the implications of employing one or another strategy to achieve given ends. By setting up a what-if scenario and playing it out with a set of constraining rules or by discussing possible outcomes, participants are forced to make decisions, establish priorities, and hone techniques of persuasion. Although the situations are created, they can provoke surprisingly "real" behavior and ideas that can then be discussed when the simulation has ended.

BRAINSTORMING

Ms. Chu suggested that after reviewing all the written material they had accumulated, they should use a technique called brainstorming (Osborn, 1957; White, 1981). This is a very simple but elegant planning device that quickly produces a great many ideas, some mundane and impractical and a few marvelously creative and usable. Brainstorming energizes the planners, freeing them of their usual reserve by sweeping them into the contagion of idea generation and shared problem solving.

The staff and residents of LIFT House have used this technique on many occasions. For example, they were once awarded a $500 grant from the chamber of commerce's Christmas holiday appeal. They had to decide how they wanted to spend it, so they had a full "town meeting" of staff residents and volunteers. Everyone had his or her say. Together, they built a "wish list" of things they would like to buy for the house. On another occasion, the weekly town meeting faced the vexing problem of what to do with a resident who kept borrowing the other women's clothes without permission. They generated a whole list of possible solutions.

To do their brainstorming, they usually split into groups of three people. Those who are hesitant to speak out in a larger assembly can be easily heard and encouraged to participate. Even the quietest of the LIFT members have, buried inside them, many ideas and solutions. Brainstorming helps them to speak up.

A brainstorming assignment has to be clearly focused. It usually starts by asking one specific question that can be answered in many different ways. The following are examples of beginning questions:

- What shall we do when X happens?
- What will we do if Y doesn't work out?
- What is our most hoped for XYZ?

A time limit of 5 or 10 minutes is set. Time pressure encourages members to keep throwing out ideas. Idea generation can also be surprisingly exhausting. Participants are given some parameters—perhaps the group is told that the ideas cannot cost more than X amount of dollars or must be completed by the end of the programs season. Generally, only the most basic constraints should be placed on the idea-generating process.

The participants should be told that there is a premium placed on thinking off the beaten track, but that no idea will be discarded and there are no right or wrong ideas. Whoever is leading the group discussion usually reviews the few simple rules of brainstorming before the session begins. The group leader can get the creative juices flowing by throwing out a few ideas, perhaps some that were gleaned from the process of inventorying programs or that have already been floated by a member of the group.

The following are a few other suggestions for using this simple but potentially highly effective process (Coover, Deacon, Esser, & Moore, 1978; Dale & Mitguy, 1978):

- Pick a diverse group to ensure a variety of ideas and approaches.
- Call the session or group by a special name to convey a sense of its importance (perhaps it might be dubbed a task force, think tank, or problem study group, assuming those titles have not already been overused in your organization).
- Set up a special meeting with a clearly defined issue to discuss and define ahead of time what will not be allowed to be part of the discussion.
- Do not censor your own ideas; let them flow. (Even if they sound foolish, impractical, or naive, they can be sorted and discarded later under closer scrutiny by the group or a higher level of authority.)
- Do censor your judgments of other's ideas. Be careful not to communicate distaste, scorn, or ridicule either verbally or by facial expression. As with one's own ideas, they can be sorted out after the initial brainstorm session.

- Give encouragement and support to others and expect it from them.
- Build on each other's ideas. Feel free to add to, expand, or change elements of ideas. No one owns an idea in brainstorming.
- Move quickly from one idea to the next with a minimum of further discussion of drawbacks or merits. Try to get out as many ideas as possible.
- List every idea so that they are not lost in the quick flow of talk and energy. Using an easily erasable surface conveys the message of fluidity and encourages members to build on each other's ideas.

STEP 3: SORTING, RANKING, AND SELECTING APPROPRIATE IDEAS

After a brainstorming idea-generating session, group members review their ideas, eliminating some and further exploring those that remain. Although there are no right or wrong ideas, there are some that are more exciting to the group of planners, easier and more doable, complex but potentially more useful, more immediate whereas others are longer range, and more or less time- and energy-consuming.

Obviously, ideas that seem to offer the largest payoff for the least amount of time and energy are always sought.

Raymond faced a blackboard brimming with ideas after he asked his committee members to map and brainstorm ways to recruit mentors.

He posed the following question to the group: "Given how overcommitted most working professionals and college students are, where can we find people who have the knowledge, time, and interest to become mentors?" Table 5.2 provides the unedited list of ideas that the committee came up with.

The places to recruit mentors fell into the following categories:

1. The general public
2. The local college campus
3. Raymond's company
4. Groups of retired seniors

They reviewed the four potential sources, discussing the trade-offs inherent in each to determine appropriate outreach strategies and to decide where to focus their efforts. After discussing category 1, they agreed that reaching out to the general public was probably the most obvious but least fruitful source. They might attract many inquires by posting signs and advertising in the local newspaper, but if they cast their net too wide they

Table 5.2   Resources for Recruiting Volunteers

Recruit at Raymond's company
Put up a big sign outside LIFT House
Advertise in the local newspaper and on the local cable station
Advertise in a computer journal
Advertise in the alumni magazine of the local college
Speak at a meeting of the alumni chapter
Speak to the honor society at the college
Speak to a faculty meeting at the college
Speak to a meeting of the faculty spouses
Contact retired faculty members and retired schoolteachers
Speak at a meeting of the Council of Elders
Contact a group called Retired Seniors in Volunteer Placements and one called Retired Executives Club
Speak at the local churches and synagogues

might attract people who were well intentioned but did not have the academic background or occupational contacts a mentor needs. Advertisements in the paper would also use up too much of their program budget.

Then they assessed the feasibility of category 2. College faculty and honors students were certainly qualified, but their daily lives were heavily committed. They also took long breaks midyear and during the summer, which limited the continuity of the mentoring relationship. The faculty spouses used to be a wonderful source of volunteers, but with more of them working, that pool has almost disappeared. Campus-based work study students such as Paulo were often dependable, but their academic readiness to mentor was in question.

When they discussed category 3, Raymond was unsure how many of his colleagues he could actually recruit. Many commuted from the suburbs and had young families. Excluding these workers, there was still a good-size pool of workers who had fewer family responsibilities and lived within the city. Raymond's personal relationships with coworkers could also be a motivating factor in overcoming any reticence. Because everyone he worked with was computer literate, that would add a special dimension to their mentoring. They also might have useful personal networks of other young professionals who knew about job opportunities. In the long run, the best recruiting is done through personal contacts.

Finally, they discussed category 4, retired professionals. Because many people take (or are pressured into) early retirement, the senior citizen groups, especially those with retired professionals, appeared to be a very rich source of mentors. Many senior citizens were well educated and looking for roles that used their skills. There was an agency in town that placed senior volunteers, so that agency was certainly a fruitful source. The following is how they eventually ranked the places they would focus their mentor recruitment efforts (from most useful to least useful):

Priority 1: Staff at Raymond's workplace

Priority 2: Retired teachers and businesspeople

Priority 3: Current faculty members and honors students

Priority 4: The general public

Ms. Chu suggested that they think about the list and return to the next meeting ready to develop a specific plan of recruitment activities. Some of the best thinking occurs in the privacy of one's home as one reflects on what has transpired at a meeting. Although it usually works best to use the idea-generating techniques with others, the experienced planner develops the ability to hold a pretty good conversation with himself or herself.

STEP 4: WEIGHING THE TRADE-OFFS
AND PROSPECTS OF PROGRAM IDEAS

Once program ideas are sorted and ranked for their attractiveness, feasibility, and power, we systematically weigh and analyze each one. Every program has inherent trade-offs. We gain one thing while we give up something else. There are no perfect program strategies, but there are better ones and worse ones. After analyzing a strategy, we can be alerted to potential problems within it and then devise activities that might overcome, minimize, or work around them.

For example, Raymond was eager to start recruiting his colleagues to volunteer as mentors. He also wanted to get them fired up about the employee's fund-raiser that would be donating its proceeds to LIFT. He wanted to set a meeting to start the ball rolling. He was convinced that if his coworkers visited LIFT House and met the mothers and babies, his coworkers would be "hooked." He had established the optimal place for the meeting and now had to decide just when it should be scheduled. To his surprise, he discovered that to make even a simple decision like setting a time and date for an event, he had to analyze the multiple trade-offs inherent in that choice. These trade-offs flowed from the lifestyles and characteristics of the people involved.

If he scheduled the first planning meeting for sometime in the middle of the winter, because he lives in a snowbelt, he had to be concerned about the possibility of a storm that might force a last-minute cancellation. He knew, however, that if he waited too long to begin, the fund-raising project would compete with graduations and the start of summer vacations. If the event was to be in early spring, then he had to begin at least 3 months before.

He had been warned to check the calendar to make sure he did not choose a date right before or after a 3-day weekend or a major holiday such as Thanksgiving or Christmas. The people he worked with often linked extra days onto holidays to visit far-flung family or go on a short vacation. He knew to avoid the dates of the Super Bowl and Academy Awards. He finally chose four possible dates from which the group members could choose at the first meeting.

Now he had to decide what day of the week and what time of the day to have the meeting. Random thoughts crowded his mind:

> If I choose a midweek evening, there are bound to be people who are wiped out by a long day of work and decide at the last minute not to come. But of course I can cajole them into coming before they slip away home. But if they are exhausted and I drag them to the meeting, they will all be in a hurry to get away early in the evening. That's no way to show off the house and have them get to know the residents.

Then, he examined another possibility—holding the meeting on a weekend afternoon. His internal conversation went as follows: "If I hold it on a Saturday afternoon, everyone will be fresher, free of work pressures, and possibly much more willing to spend a substantial amount of time." Clearly, that seemed like the most productive atmosphere for a planning meeting. Then a doubting voice inside him said, "When you commute from the suburbs, you dread one extra day of coming into the city. There is an inertia to being at home, once you get there. They will have good intentions, but I think very few people will actually show up."

Immobilized by indecision, Raymond kept putting off setting a time for the meeting. Kristen noticed this and decided to help him. She assured him that like all wise planners, it was good that he was thinking through all the potential problems inherent in each choice. She told him, however, that he needed to be more systematic in his estimating the trade-offs and then put his energy into maximizing the positive forces and minimizing

Table 5.3   Force Field Analysis: The Assets and Liabilities of Having the
Meeting on a Midweek Evening After Work

Positives	Negatives
What we have going for us:	*What we have going against us:*
Staff members are all downtown	Staff are tired after a day of work
Staff can easily be rounded up and reminded	Staff may have to work late
They can come with their colleagues	They have to drive home or catch commuter trains that will shorten the meeting
They do not have to give up precious weekend time	They may be nervous about coming into the LIFT neighborhood at night

the negative ones. Finally, he needed to set a time limit on his deliberations
and make a decision. She said,

> I am giving you 1 hour to make a thoughtful decision and design strategies
> to get the best possible turnout. I am going to show you how to do a force field
> analysis, a wonderfully simple, but effective decision-making technique.

She handed him a pad and pencil and told him to list each of the benefits
of having a midweek meeting on the left side of the page and the
drawbacks of the midweek meeting on the right side. Table 5.3 shows
Raymond's force field analysis.

After reviewing the positives and negatives of a midweek evening
meeting, Raymond decided that the midweek meeting definitely had more
going for it than did the weekend meeting. Kristen told him to move to
the second part of the force field analysis—make a chart listing all the
negatives of a midweek meeting on one side and then brainstorm strategies
that might overcome or minimize their impact. Table 5.4 shows what
Raymond wrote.

Raymond probably would not need to use all the strategies shown in
Table 5.4, but they all made a great deal of sense.

Making his decision and visualizing strategies to implement it mobilized Raymond. He thanked Kristen and went to the LIFT office to
compose a letter to his boss and an invitation to his colleagues.

As he reflected on the evening, Raymond felt he had accomplished
much. He had finally set the fund-raising event into motion, added a useful

Table 5.4   Force Field Analysis: Strategies for Overcoming the Negative
Forces in a Midweek Evening Meeting

Negative Force	Possible Strategies to Overcome it
Staff are tired	Monday or Tuesday nights are early in week; folks are less tired then
	Have coffee and cake at work before we leave for LIFT
May have to work late	Meet with boss and try to get his or her commitment to support this event by not assigning overtime to those who volunteer
	Promise to use company name prominently in advertising the final event to the public
	Have one car wait for those who have to work a little later
Have to drive home or catch commuter trains	Promise to end meeting on time and stick to it
	Schedule second meeting at workplace so people realize this is just the kickoff session
	Take good minutes of the meeting and distribute to everyone, especially those who leave early or come late
	Show video of LIFT during lunch hour next day to those who did not come
May be nervous about going there	Organize car pool from work
	Distribute clear map of house location, show way from work and back to main routes and commuter station
	Make sure no one leaves alone
	Get one of the workers to come with me on a day before meeting so that he or she can reassure folks who are nervous
	Have Kristen or Ms. Chu stop in a few days before and informally meet some of the staff

technique to his newly acquired repertoire of planning techniques, and
increased his self-confidence.

STEP 5: DEVELOPING PROGRAM DETAILS AND
PRESENTING A PROGRAM PROPOSAL

There comes a point in the program development process when all the
ideas have to be committed to paper into a coherent program proposal.

HOW CAN WE KNOW THAT THE PROGRAM WE ARE PROPOSING IS GOING TO WORK?

Planners can no more answer that question about a program they are proposing than could a counselor who recommends that a young woman be sent to a program for anorexics or a young incarcerated man be transferred to a prerelease center. The social service worker makes calculated judgments based on data collection, relevant theory, and his or her practice wisdom. All intervention plans include a reasonable amount of risk.

As a protection against overconfidence, someone in a group should play the devil's advocate—a skeptic who must be convinced that the program has a reasonable chance of accomplishing change in the direction of the goal. The devil's advocate role-play happens before the final version is set in stone. This assures that planners do not oversell their proposal and alerts them to elements in it that need more work.

ASKING HARD QUESTIONS

The mentoring committee had to be able to answer the types of questions shown in Table 5.5, which any skeptical reader of Raymond's proposal is likely to ask.

Every aspect of a plan should be open to question without the program planners becoming defensive. It is helpful for planners to write "draft" on the cover of the proposal through its first several permutations so planners do not become prematurely wedded to their ideas and prose.

Of course, the questioning has to finally end; otherwise, planners would never progress from the thinking stage to the action stage. Once convinced that program decisions make sense, it is time to commit them to a final ver- sion, knowing that the program will continue to evolve throughout its life.

THE PROGRAM PROPOSAL AND FUNDING PROCESS

Most social service agencies generate many different proposals over time. Some are for major projects and are worked on by several staff members until submitted for funding to private philanthropic foundations or governmental bureaus. These major proposals should adhere carefully to the formal outline required by each funding source. The person at the funding source who first reviews the proposal is looking for reassurance that the proposal fits the general mission of the funding group. It does not guarantee that the money will flow in, but it gives the proposal a second reading.

Table 5.5   Devil's Advocate Questions

What makes you think that the young mothers really need these community mentors? Maybe it makes more sense to fund-raise and hire another professional tutor.

What makes you think that with all the other problems they are coping with they will show up for their tutoring sessions?

What makes you think that you can attract and retain enough mentors so that the mothers will not be disappointed if they do agree to accept the help?

How can you ensure that the mentors will not bring attitudes of judgment with them that will make the young women feel worse about themselves?

How can we be sure that you will raise the funds promised?

How adequate is the study space at the house?

Is $15.00 a month a reasonable stipend for the mentor-mentee teams?

How long is Raymond going to be around to supervise the program? What will we do if he leaves during the year? Who else could fill in for him? Would it overburden the existing staff and volunteers?

Guidelines for presenting a plan in a formal proposal can often be obtained in a document called a Request For Proposal (RFP). Guidelines might also be extrapolated from the mission statement of a fund. There are literally thousands of sources of private and public funding. Descriptions of the programs these grantors are interested in funding fill large reference books in general libraries. In some large urban areas, the foundations have established specialized libraries specifically geared to help social service staff or volunteers thread their way through the funding maze. For example, in New York City there is the Foundation Library, and in Boston, there is the Associated Grantmakers. Check to see what resource is accessible.

Some public and private funding sources limit themselves to giving small sums of money to many agencies for expansion of existing services. Others underwrite the entire budget of a select few projects. For every proposed program, there is a pool of potential funders interested in that area of service. This pool is much wider and deeper than many realize. Those who hold the purse strings are just as interested in initiating programs as are the program planners. It is always worthwhile to communicate with the grant's officers. Some can provide technical assistance in conceptualizing and writing the proposal. Many will give an advisory opinion early on about the probability of obtaining their support. If they cannot provide assistance, they might suggest more appropriate sources. It is also useful to resubmit a proposal several times, especially if one has received comments about why it was rejected. A few adjustments in the proposal or a shift in the competition can often reverse a refusal.

Table 5.6   A Sample of Topics Included in a Proposal

Background of the problem being addressed

Evidence that the needs that this program will meet are not adequately filled by other existing programs

Long-term and short-term goals and objective of this particular program strategy

Specific activities that will accomplish the goals and objectives

Sponsoring agency or board that will oversee the program

Characteristics of the population to be served, estimated numbers

Eligibility criteria that will be used to accept people

Ways in which potential users of the service will be recruited, screened, and oriented

Staffing of the agency—how many of what kinds of staff, what their duties will be, and how they will be chosen, trained, and evaluated

Location of the agency and what kind of facility it will need

Ways in which this program will dovetail, complement, and work with other programs of a similar kind

Money that will be needed, how it will be used, and what other sources of funds are or might already be available

Proposed time frame for accomplishing the work of the program

Way in which the work of the program will be evaluated, recorded, and disseminated

Backgrounds of the organization or people making the proposal and their own track records and credibility

Evidence that other groups or agencies are enthusiastic about the plan and can offer support

It is recommended that planners seek out a workshop or course in proposal generation. These are often found in community education or continuing education courses. Several helpful books can guide the novice through step-by-step procedures, offering examples of well-organized proposals (see Clifton & Dahms, 1993; Coley & Scheinberg, 1990; Geever & McNeilly, 1995; Lauffer, 1997; Lefferts, 1982; Robinson, 1995; Upshur, 1982).

Even though the mentoring program was not requesting funds from a private foundation or government agency, the LIFT board insisted that Raymond's committee prepare a formal program proposal. From some recent failures in program planning by other well-meaning volunteers, the committee had realized the following: *If you do not know how you are getting there, you are not likely to reach your destination.*

Whatever the funding source or program goals and scope, most proposals require a clear description of the topics shown in Table 5.6.

The process of writing the proposal forced the committee members to make hard choices, turning vague ideas into concrete steps. After four meetings—with some help from Ms. Chu—the members had specified their goals and objectives, filled in a project activities worksheet, sketched a brief resource bank, written brief descriptions of the role of mentor, and even created a budget and evaluation plan.

PREPARING A BUDGET

The budget preparation phase, although much dreaded, was an especially useful one because it forced the committee members to tie down loose ends, turning program concepts into specific tasks with price tags attached. Next to each number, there had to be a credible explanation of how that number was arrived at. For example, to estimate how much postage they would need for a whole year for the program, they had to decide how many mailings they would send out to approximately how many people. The following boxed text shows what their worksheet looked like.

**Sample of Worksheet to Estimate Amount
of Postage for Program for 1 Year**

Subject of Letters	Quantity
Initial letters sent to potential mentors	50
Follow-up application to the responders	30
Invitations to interview sessions	30
Acceptances and invitations to training session	20
Three newsletters during year	160
Solicitation letters for donations	40
Invitations to graduation	100
Thank-yous to mentors and donors	50
Invitations to final evaluation session	20
Miscellaneous administration	50
Total	550

Therefore, 550 stamps at 32¢ each = $176; round to $180 for postage for year.

Of course, this estimate is simply a best guess. They might choose to do another mailing for some unexpected event during the year, or perhaps they will find that phone calls replace several of the letters. Although the planning committee members felt uncomfortable committing themselves to such minute detail so far in advance, Ms. Chu explained that this is precisely what she does when she constructs the LIFT budget for the upcoming year. When she estimates her food costs, for example, she has to anticipate the quantity of each kind of food that will be used for each meal for each day, week, month, and year. Obviously, before she constructed the first LIFT budget, she consulted with a professional chef and with several directors of residential facilities similar to LIFT. Now that LIFT has had several years of experience, the board can more accurately predict costs based on previous expenses and their growing knowledge of the food tastes of their residents and the generosity of their suppliers.

Funding sources understand that no one can completely anticipate expenses to the exact penny. They usually permit some shifting among the lines of a budget. The essential message of the budget process, however, is that you must create a ballpark estimate of what you will need to do your work, it has to make sense, and you have to try to live within it. This is not much different than the way one learns (through many missteps) to take care of personal expenses.

The budget part of the proposal is just as important as the narrative; in fact, it should clarify the narrative. Many planners make the mistake of asking for too little money, thinking that this will guard against a refusal. An experienced reader of program proposals, however, will perceive that what the program wants to do cannot be done for the amount requested, or perhaps the planners have overlooked funds for an activity they included in their statement of program intent.

Listing an expense in the budget that is not explained in the narrative, however, might signal to the reviewer that the writer has not done his or her homework. It is important to remember that a budget is a mathematical statement of a program plan. It is a good faith document that will ultimately be refined by experience.

Typical categories for a budget submission are presented in Table 5.7. Of course, they will vary according to the type of program and the demands of the sponsoring or funding agency (see Lewis & Lewis, 1990; Lohmann, 1980).

TABLE 5.7   Typical Items in a Proposed Budget

Staff costs
Consultant or contract services
Travel
Facility rental
Office or other equipment
Program supplies
Activity fees
Clerical
Miscellaneous expenses

THE LIFT MENTORING PROGRAM BUDGET

The mentor planning committee knew from the start the amount of money it could spend. The employee's association at Raymond's firm had pledged $2,500, a sum usually raised at its yearly charity event. Unless the mentor planning committee was willing to do some additional fundraising, that figure would be its bottom line. Therefore, the committee built its budget within the constraints of that bottom line.

For example, the committee had decided that each mentor-mentee team should attend an educational or cultural event once a month. The committee had to decide the exact amount of those stipends. The committee wanted it to cover the cost of tickets to a play or admissions to a museum. Committee members phoned the local museum to find out its least expensive rate (and the possibility of free admission) and looked in the newspapers to estimate the cost of tickets to community theater productions. On a work sheet, the committee derived the following amounts:

8 teams × 12 months of outings = 96 outings
$20 allocated for each of 96 outings = $1,920

Although $20 was a reasonable figure, it became clear that the committee could not spend that large a portion of its overall budget. Therefore, with much discussion, the committee decided that given holidays and vacations, it was more likely that there would be nine outings during the year, which resulted in the following amounts:

8 teams × 9 month of outings = 72 outings
$20 allocated for each outing × 72 = $1,440

Table 5.8   Budget for LIFT Mentoring Program

2 Computers	Donated by Larson Computers	$6,000
6 Software pkgs incl. GED	Donated by Larson Computer	180
Computer supplies	Donated by Larson Computers	200
Team stipends for outings		1,440
Retreat in fall and spring		
Rental fee for camp site	(2 × $60)	120
Bus	(2 × 83)	166
Picnic food	(2 × $100)	200
Graduation ceremony gifts,		
Refreshments & photos		200
Postage, printing		300
Miscellaneous		74
Total		$2,500

The budget planning sessions continued in this manner, with much rewriting and refiguring, until the committee managed to fit all its program dreams into the $2,500 available.

Creating this budget was a relatively easy process because the planners did not have to include any overhead costs such as office rental, heat, light, repairs, or equipment. They also had no staff costs because everyone was a volunteer. Table 5.8 shows the budget they settled on. Notice that they have listed the items that will be donated. This is often done so that planners can see exactly how much their program would actually cost if they did not receive the donations. Including these in-kind items also demonstrates to funders that the planners have tapped a variety of sources for financial support.

THE PROGRAM ABSTRACT

Proposals usually begin with a program abstract (although in practice planners write it after the proposal is finished to be sure they do not leave out any important points). The abstract affords the readers a brief overview of the whole proposal so they can decide if it fits within their overall parameters and will receive further scrutiny. Although the LIFT proposal was several pages long, the committee prepared the abstract shown in the boxed text for the board members of LIFT and the manager of Raymond's firm.

Abstract of LIFT Mentoring Program

To: The Board of LIFT

From: The Mentoring Planning Committee

Re: Request for approval of the LIFT mentoring program

We propose a mentoring program in which each LIFT resident will be paired with a team of two community mentors who have both academic and world of work experience. Sixteen mentors will be recruited primarily from retirees from the college faculty and alumni group, from retired business senior groups and employees of a high-technology computer firm.

The mentor teams will be selected after an interview with the planning committee. They will be chosen for their experience as well as for their capacity to work with young women from diverse backgrounds.

The mentors will be responsible for meeting with their mentees for at least 3 hours weekly to

- Provide tutoring as needed toward the goal of obtaining the GED as soon as it seems possible
- Provide tutoring as needed for any other courses in which the mentee is, or will become, enrolled
- Help to create a career life plan with their mentee which will include steps toward short-range and long-term work and academic goals
- Arrange for visits to appropriate academic or occupational sites and accompany her when advisable
- Orient the mentee to the process of obtaining employment or training
- Arrange for one cultural or educational outing during each of the 9 months to be jointly chosen by mentor and mentee

The mentors will be asked to make a 9-month commitment. Because each resident has a team of two mentors, it is likely that there will be continuity of relationship.

The mentors will be required to take a 5-week training program held weekly for 2 hours each week. After that, they will be expected to attend a once a month training session held at the college faculty center. They will be able to earn Continuing Education Units through Anselmy College at the successful conclusion of the first 6-month cycle. Mentor-mentee teams will attend a daylong retreat at the start and end of the program at the Ecumenical Retreat Center.

Each mentor team will be reimbursed up to $20 a month for nine cultural or education outings and for any transportation costs incurred. Mentors will be invited to dine with their mentee at LIFT before tutoring sessions.

Tutoring activities will take place in the small nook used as a basement recreation room and will be off-limits to others during that time period.

We anticipate spending $2,500 for the first year of the program for mentor stipends, training sessions, and two program retreats. A similar sum has been committed for a 3-year period by the employee's association of Larson Computers. The computers and software for tutoring and GED books will be donated by the management of Larsen Computers.

The first mentor team will start work by January. We will phase in the other teams through the end of February, by which time each LIFT resident who wishes to participate will have at least one mentor. In June, we will hold a program retreat and a graduation ceremony.

The planning committee will solicit brief weekly feedback from the mentors and mentees and will meet to evaluate the program and make adjustments every 2 weeks for the first 3 months of the pilot program. After that, they plan to meet once a month or as needed. Raymond will attend LIFT board meetings each month to report on progress. Dr. Hightower, a professional evaluator, is donating his services to conduct a program assessment in June. The committee will produce a 1-year report by the July board meeting.

We ask the board to approve the plan for the LIFT mentor program and to participate in an appreciation event to honor the mentor-mentee teams.

In addition to preparing the proposal for each board member, the committee members carefully planned their oral presentation. Although Raymond tried to convince them to choose someone else as spokesperson because he believed in sharing leadership, they felt that he had the requisite credibility and enthusiasm. He accepted but insisted that each member attend and take at least a small role, lest the board receive the erroneous impression that this program was a one-man operation.

Before the meeting, he reviewed the following skills of making a presentation that he had learned in his marketing course:

1. *Know your audience:* Whether formal or informal, a presentation always needs spade work before it happens. You need to know the background of the organization you are addressing and if possible something about the individuals to whom you will be speaking. Often, this can be accomplished by a phone call to a friend or associate and by carefully reading brochures, annual reports, and so on.

   Try to anticipate what they will expect from you and what you want to receive from them. Think through responses to the kinds of questions or objections they are likely to raise. Clearly state your objectives. Be very concrete and speak in action-oriented terms, such as

   "I am coming here to ask you to contribute X sum of money."

   "I am requesting your permission to use the auditorium for classes."

"I want to fill you in on what we have been doing but at this time have no formal request to make."

You also need to know a great deal about your own organization and have a genuine conviction that what it does is worthwhile.

2. *Plan your delivery:* Think about the method of delivery. Are you going to try to reach the audience on an emotional or cognitive level or both? Should the presentation be a formal speech or an informal conversation? Will the presenter need charts, slides, historical or statistical data, or newspaper clippings supporting your request or showing your track record and credibility?

Who should do the presenting? Should it be a combination of clients and workers, should a sympathetic board member take a role in the presentation, or would that be a potential conflict of interest? Have you left enough time before the presentation for preparing the members doing the presenting.

Any handouts you distribute should be concise, clear, and appropriately reproduced—neither too slick and glossy nor sloppy and hard to read—and should be carefully numbered.

3. *Gear your presentation to the time allotted:* Make sure that you know exactly how much time you have. When making a presentation singly or with others, have an agenda for the presenter that has a notation of the approximate amount of time that should be spent on each item and who will do the speaking. A role-play before a presentation is especially useful when co-presenting.

Also try to ascertain what else is on the agenda for that meeting. This may well indicate how receptive the listeners will be and if you can afford to go over your allotted time (adapted from Clifton & Dahms, 1993; see also . Jolles, 1993).

The chairperson of the board had already warned Raymond that there were other pressing items on this meeting's agenda. Therefore, he decided to focus his presentation on the severity of the GAP and the hoped-for outcomes of the mentoring program. He knew that in a 15-minute presentation, if he got sidetracked discussing the small details of implementation, the board members might lose sight of the need for action. He feared that a decision would be postponed until their next meeting if he did not get right to the point. He planned to hand out a diagram depicting the program structure, activities, and budget. He prepared an overhead projector transparency of the diagram to add further clarity and impact.

The board members listened intently and were impressed by the basic common sense and thoroughness of the proposal. They enthusiastically endorsed it and urged the committee to get started. Even though no funds had been requested, they also voted to allocate $100 for certificates and small gifts for each of the residents when they earned their GEDs. They agreed to sponsor the mentor appreciation event at the end of the pilot period and voted to commend the mentoring committee. They gave Raymond a round of applause.

ONTO THE NEXT STEPS

Now that the general shape of the program was committed to paper and accepted as a workable proposition, Raymond knew from his business experiences that a step-by-step plan had to be drawn up that would move the program concept toward implementation.

THE 5-MINUTE RECAP

- Most of the GAPs that a troubleshooter observes have probably already been noticed and thought about by other concerned people in the community. When that has happened, planners can start their design process by using those ideas and then tailoring them to fit their own particular population and problem.
- Program designs are always in a state of dynamic change, responding to feedback and other pressures or opportunities.
- Regardless of how skilled the planners are, they still need to systematically proceed through each of the steps of the design process. Of course, as they grow more experienced, they are likely to move through the design process much faster and with increased confidence.
- Most of the small-scale programs at LIFT are initiated by new staff or volunteers who bring with them fresh enthusiasm, energy, and time.
- Raymond, the volunteer computer programmer, has begun to troubleshoot the very inadequate LIFT education program. Careful data collection has convinced him to try to fill the GAP by organizing a mentoring program that provides one-on-one tutoring and coaching to each of the mothers.
- His planning committee members began their design process by composing a set of probing questions to use when they were inventorying other similar programs in the community.
- Their search for appropriately useful resources started out in their own backyards, where they explored the resources in their networks of friends and coworkers.
- After interviewing their own contacts first, they cast their net wider to find more agencies and people who might have expertise to offer.

- The large umbrella agencies, such as the Department of Education and the Human Services Provider's Coalition, were the first ones interviewed because they could provide a wide overview on other adult education efforts.
- These interviews generated a large amount of reality-based information that started the committee members' creative juices flowing and ultimately helped shape their program design.
- Planning meetings were made more efficient and productive through using problem-clarification and idea-generation techniques such as

  Mapping

  Task analysis

  Nominal group techniques

  Delphi questionnaires

  Gaming and other simulation techniques
- Brainstorming in small, time-limited groups that had specific questions to work on encouraged full participation and resulted in many creative ideas.
- The inventories and focused planning sessions produced an abundance of ideas that had to be sorted and ranked on the basis of practicality, attractiveness, feasibility, and other criteria.
- A few key program designs emerged that were then analyzed for their positives and negatives by utilizing a force field analysis. Then the flesh was added to the skeleton.
- The proposal written by the LIFT mentoring committee presented evidence of the need, the goals and activities that would fill it, staff, budget, supplies, a proposed work plan, and other specific details of service delivery and evaluation.
- Members planned for the presentation to the LIFT board by preparing a one-sheet program abstract and an audiovisual model for clarity.
- At meetings before the presentation, committee members rehearsed answers to the kinds of questions they anticipated being asked. They then assigned roles to each of the presenters and set time frames for each segment of the presentation.

PUTTING THEORY INTO PRACTICE

EXERCISE 1: TAKING AN INVENTORY OF PROGRAMS
IN THE LOCAL COMMUNITY

Assume that you are a member of the mentor planning committee at LIFT. Locate six people or agencies in your community that you could interview who would be likely sources of useful information on programs such as tutoring, mentoring, or coaching for teenagers or adults. (Note: If you are on a college campus, you might logically inquire in the offices that deal with foreign students, students with handicaps, students from minority backgrounds, or perhaps nontraditional students returning to school after many years, and so on.) If there is another topic of concern to you, choose that one and do the same research to ferret out possible agencies or experts.

Choose one of those people or agencies and ask them to give you an interview so that you can learn about their program and about any other programs of which they are aware. Conduct the interview in person or by phone. Prepare a list of questions that will gain as much insight into the process of mentoring as is possible.

Write about the material you have collected, and end your report with a set of reflections about what you have learned. If you were put in charge of designing a mentoring program for a group of young adults who needed extra help finishing high school, what did you learn from this interview to avoid or replicate in your own program design?

To what extent do you think the person you spoke with might be a valuable resource for your program? What factors entered into your assessment of his or her potential as a resource? If you visited the agency, what impressions did it leave you with?

EXERCISE 2: BRAINSTORMING

To attract volunteers to your mentoring program (or any other program you have decided to work on), you will need an eye- and ear-catching title (like the ones that commercial advertisers use to attract the public to their products).

Divide into groups of four, and in a 5-minute brainstorm exercise come up with a written list of at least 15 possible titles for a mentoring program. Each member of the group should try to contribute at least 5 possible titles. There is to be no judgment of each other's suggestions, and each person should build on what has already been proposed. You are by no means limited to acronyms, but remember that acronyms such as LIFT (Let Infants and Families Thrive) or FATHER (Forging a Trusting, Healthy, Energetic Relationship) can be powerful emblems of a program. The overall word chosen should reflect the goals of the program. Each individual letter within the word represents another word that further explains what the program is all about.

After 5 minutes, each group reports its suggestions. All are written on a large paper or board so that they can be clustered and duplicates can be eliminated. All the group members then quickly vote on each suggested title. Those with scant support are immediately crossed off, whereas those that garner widespread approval are raised higher up on the list.

The process of eliminating and combining elements of a few titles in various combinations continues until only three remain. One of them is finally chosen. In actual practice, choosing the title is delayed for a few days while members work on refining it to its final form.

This exercise can be repeated by brainstorming a slogan or logo for the mentoring program.

If brainstorming is done individually, take 10 minutes of undisturbed time and, with total concentration, write down everything that comes into your head. Then go back over the list, crossing out names that you reject immediately and rewriting others that have potential. Surprisingly, the brainstormer will get closer and closer to a workable title in this fashion. Then the list of five or six possible titles can be "slept on" and shared with others for feedback and further refinement.

In both forms of brainstorming, it is important to set an overall time limit to this process. Eventually, planners settle on one idea, even if it is not "perfect." If they do not do this, the "baby" is held in limbo, waiting to assume an identity and a life of its own.

CITATIONS AND SUGGESTIONS
FOR FURTHER READING

Gardner, J. W. (1964). *Self-renewal: The individual and the innovative society.* New York: Harper & Row.

These books are a pioneering model for the resource phone books now found in many areas of the country:

Human Service Yellow Pages of Connecticut. (1996). Boston, MA: George D. Hall.
Human Service Yellow Pages of Massachusetts. (1996). Boston, MA: George D. Hall.
Human Service Yellow Pages of New York. (1996). Boston, MA: George D. Hall.
Human Service Yellow Pages of Rhode Island. (1996). Boston, MA: George D. Hall.
Jolles, R. L. (1993). *How to run seminars and workshops, presentation skills for consultants, trainers and teachers, planning the program, selling your message, captivating your audience.* New York: John Wiley. This is a very readable book full of many creative ideas that can be used for a wide variety of adult learning, training, and orientation programs.

FOR AN OVERVIEW OF THE ELEMENTS
NEEDED FOR CREATING A PROGRAM

Clifton, R. L., & Dahms, A. M. (1993). *Grassroots organizations: A resource book for directors, staff and volunteers of small, community-based nonprofit agencies* (2nd ed.).

IL: Waveland. This book provides a brief and very readable overview of the process of mounting a program. It is a good book to start with.

Kettner, P. M., Moroney, R. M., & Martin, L. L. (1990). *Designing and managing programs: An effectiveness based approach.* Newbury Park, CA: Sage. This book is useful before starting the proposal process. It has an especially strong section on setting goals and objectives.

Liebert, E. R., & Sheldon, B. E. (1974). *Handbook of special events for non-profit organizations.* New York: Association Press. Although old, this book offers program ideas and concrete information about the elements that go into mounting a wide variety of program events.

Upshur, C. C. (1982). *How to set up and operate a non-profit organization: Guidelines and procedures for incorporating, raising funds, writing grant proposals.* Englewood Cliffs, NJ: Prentice Hall.

TECHNIQUES THAT HELP
TO FOCUS PLANNING SESSIONS

Lauffer, A. (1982). *Assessment tools for practitioners, managers and trainers.* Beverly Hills, CA: Sage. This book provides an excellent presentation of techniques that focus the planning meetings, with examples of their use. These techniques can be used through each of the phases of the planning process described in succeeding chapters.

Osborne, A. F. (1957). *Applied imagination* (Rev. ed.). New York: Scribner. This is the classic on brainstorming theory and practice.

Van Gundy, A. B. (1988). *Techniques of structured problem solving* (2nd ed.). New York: Van Nostrand Rienhold.

White, S. (1981). *Managing health and human service programs: A guide for managers.* New York: Free Press. This book has an especially good section on brainstorming.

GUIDELINES FOR PUTTING THE PROPOSAL TOGETHER

Coley, M., Soraya, M., & Scheinberg, C. A. (1990). *Proposal writing.* Newbury Park, CA: Sage. This is a well-organized and jargon-free guide to step by step preparation of a program proposal.

Geever, J. C., & McNeill, P. (1995). *Guide to proposal writing* (Rev. ed.). New York: Foundation Center. This is a small but useful pamphlet from a major source of information about private grantors.

Lauffer, A. (1997). *Grants etc.* Thousand Oaks, CA: Sage.

Lefferts, R. (1982). *Getting a grant: How to write successful grant proposals* (2nd ed.). Englewood Cliffs, NJ: Prentice Hall.

Robinson, A. (1995). *Grassroots grants, an activist's guide to proposal writing.* Berkeley, CA: Chardon Press.

GUIDELINES FOR THE BUDGET-MAKING PROCESS

Lewis, J. A., Lewis, M. D., & Souflee, F., Jr. (1991). *Management of human service programs* (2nd ed.). Pacific Grove, CA: Brooks/Cole. See especially Chapter 5 on budgeting to meet program needs.

Lohmann, R. A. (1980). *Breaking even; Financial management in human service organizations.* Philadelphia: Temple University Press.

FOR SOURCES OF FUNDING

Each of the following books provides useful overviews of the types of governmental or foundation grants or private donations one might seek and the trade-offs inherent in each. They also help the seeker of funds to understand the motivations of potential donors. Although some are clearly aimed at readers seeking major grants, each offers some insights that can be creatively adapted for funding the small-scale program or single event. In Chapter 6, the reader will find further resources for nongrant fundraising.

Annual Registry of Grants Support. (1995). New Providence, NJ: Bowker.
Directory of grants. (1996). Phoenix, AZ: Oryx Press.
Gronbjerg, K. (1993). *Understanding nonprofit funding: Managing revenues in social services and community development organizations.* San Francisco: Jossey-Bass.
Howe, F. (1991). *The board member's guide to fund raising: What every trusteee needs to know about raising money.* San Francisco: Jossey-Bass.

The Internet lists grant award programs under the title of each of the federal government agencies.

6

MICROSCOPING
Translating Goals Into Small, Systematic, Sequential Tasks and Setting Up Systems to Accomplish Them

He who would learn to fly one day must learn to stand and walk and climb and dance: One cannot fly into flying.

—Friedrich Nietzsche

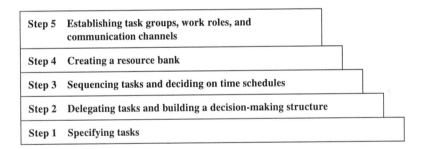

Step 5	Establishing task groups, work roles, and communication channels
Step 4	Creating a resource bank
Step 3	Sequencing tasks and deciding on time schedules
Step 2	Delegating tasks and building a decision-making structure
Step 1	Specifying tasks

Ask the workers at Let Infants and Families Thrive (LIFT) House about their worst program planning screwups and each can describe a nightmare come true.

Kristen describes her worst planning gaffe as follows:

I'll never forget how relieved and proud I was when I finally mailed the 400 invitations to the LIFT open house. Then my mother called. She said she had just received her invitation, it looked great, but May 7th was Tuesday not Wednesday. I couldn't figure out how to fix my mistake. We had already spent $200 on printing and postage and it was too late to print and send out a corrected flyer.

I anticipated that some of the invited guests would call the house to clarify the date. But what about the others? Some folks might show up on Tuesday and some on Wednesday, according to how they interpreted my mistakenly written date.

I decided there was no choice. I had to run an open house on both Tuesday and Wednesday night for whoever showed up. It was double work, the momentum was dissipated and I came off looking very flaky.

But it taught me a lesson: No flyer leaves the office until at least three sets of eyes have reviewed it. I also tacked up a checklist of items to remember when creating a flyer.

I also learned from that experience that when you do goof up, despite your best efforts, you have to retrieve it somehow and go on.

Ms. Chu describes her planning blunder as follows:

I have to admit that after raising five kids while being a full-time worker, I prided myself on my organizational skills. But the day I was going before the city council to plead for the boarding house license that LIFT required before we could renovate the house, I left a crucial folder in my car. My husband had driven me to the meeting and then taken off on a business trip. So there was no way I could retrieve my overhead projector transparencies.

Luckily, I did have handouts with all the vital data. But using the overhead projector made it so much clearer when I presented our case. Because of my carelessness, I started off the presentation annoyed at myself and even at my poor, innocent husband. It shook my self-confidence.

They granted us the variance we needed so I guess I did okay. But now I have learned to gather everything I am going to need the night before a big meeting and then put everything together in my briefcase. If I need to take anything with me that doesn't fit inside it, I pile the stuff in front of my entrance door so I'll fall over it.

My kids enjoyed teasing me since I've yelled at them plenty of times for the same kind of carelessness with their homework.

Inevitably, mistakes creep into our work in the most unexpected ways. The following poem hangs on the bulletin board in the LIFT office as a goad to Raymond, the computer freak, who puts too much faith in his machines:

I have a spelling checker
It came with my P.C.
It plainly marks four my revue
Miss stakes I cannot see
I've run this poem threw it
I'm sure your please to no

Its letter perfect in its weigh
My checker told me sew

Understanding that to err is human, how do we try to minimize the kind of program disasters just described? In this phase of the planning process, we must adopt the obsessive-compulsive stance of the competent accountant. We become list makers, double checkers, and all-around nags. That does not mean we act rigidly, however, destroying everyone's creativity and sense of freedom to create and learn. Genuine freedom comes only with structure—the two are interdependent, not mutually exclusive (Conrad & Glenn, 1983).

In the previous phase of program development, we chose our overall program strategy. Now, we jettison all the could-have-been-ideas from our list. Perhaps we will return to them at another time. Now, however, we begin translating our program concept into specific short-range goals and tasks, spelling out the marching orders. Using our pad and pencil, computer, date books, clocks, directories of resources, and the networking contacts gathered during the previous phases, we create lists of tasks and resources. Now, the mind-set of the planner is neat and orderly, leaving as little as possible to chance.

The best "umbrella," in case our parade gets rained on, is a well thought-out and mutually agreed on action monitoring plan that can be used from the moment a GAP is identified and continues until the program, follow-ups, and evaluation are completed.

THE ACTION MONITORING PLAN

The pioneering work of Drucker (1974, 1985) underscored the need to monitor worker performance to make sure everyone is on track when intervening. Monitoring can also add to knowledge of the relationship between program effort and outcome (Alter & Evans, 1990). (This will be discussed in further detail in chapter 8, which examines the tasks of program evaluation and dissemination.)

Although the research and theory on management techniques have been drawn primarily from the business sector and human service work is much more affectively based, we can still try to achieve some uniform standards of performance (see Bard, 1971, for an excellent assortment of forms that can be adapted for monitoring performance in a human service setting). By careful record keeping of each program goal and the daily activities that aim to implement it, program implementation can be made more realistic. We can see to what extent our work activities are accomplished according to the schedule we initially anticipated, and then we can make sensible adjustments. How much time does it take to design, produce, and mail out a set of flyers? How much lead-up time is needed to apply for and receive all the necessary permits for our annual block party? Are there ways we can more efficiently do both tasks without controlling an individual worker's style or increasing his or her stress? Rather than being a whip, when used properly frequent systematic monitoring raises the probability that feedback will be positive. Because small errors or misjudgments are caught quickly, readjustments can be made that might save the planner some grief later on down the line (Christian, 1984).

Behind every successful monitoring plan lies a philosophical attitude that is supportive to the process. Luckily, the folks at LIFT House realize that although they are hardworking and thoughtful, they are fallible, overworked human beings. As the stories of program goof-ups illustrate, they also have created an atmosphere of flexibility so they can make their "lemons" into lemonade. Words such as *feedback* and *monitoring* form an integral part of their vocabulary.

In their agency culture, monitoring of work is not just for the staff and clients. The board members also commit themselves to keeping descriptive records that relate back to the baseline of their goals. The more that staff, clients, and board members are involved in setting the goals and understanding the activities needed to achieve them, the more ego involvement and ownership there can be in helping to achieve them. At LIFT, no plan is activated before a feedback system is in place. It cannot be started later on in the development process because then it is likely to be seen as intrusive. Worse still, if a monitoring plan is suddenly begun, it can be viewed as a vehicle for placing blame for any failures that have already happened.

It must be recognized that every new or expanded program, every change in the normal way of work, can be perceived as a threat to somebody's security. It behooves one to look as closely at what planning will do to the people within the organization as one does at what planning will do for the constituency (Conrad & Glenn, 1983).

PAULO PLANS A HOMELESSNESS AWARENESS DAY AT HIS COLLEGE

After living and working at LIFT for two semesters as a college work-study student, Paulo has become a strong supporter of its programs.

He has also found himself getting very annoyed by the callous attitudes some of his classmates have about people who are homeless.

He tries to understand the root causes of their attitudes. Many of his fraternity brothers are working at several part-time jobs to pay for their education. He can understand that they might resent the fact that the young mothers of LIFT receive aid from Aid to Families with Dependent Children for their living expenses and receive help finishing high school or getting training. They ask, "Why should I bust my back to pay for my own education and see my family's tax money used to support teenagers who have allowed themselves to become pregnant and then can't support their children?" This is a tough question!

Paulo thinks he has come to understand some answers. He knows how easy it is for a young woman to end up pregnant and without resources to care for her child, in a situation similar to those of the women at LIFT House. He realizes how often men, including his friends, walk away from (or feel pushed away from) their parental role.

In his sociology and politics courses, he has learned how difficult it is to build support for affordable housing in a free enterprise economy. Realizing how complex the dual issues of homelessness and young parenting are, he wants to challenge his classmates to grapple with the hard questions. If they continue to accept negative stereotypes, they will make uninformed choices at the ballot box.

He has also long wanted to encourage more volunteerism on his campus, especially among his fraternity brothers. Given these dual goals—understanding the social issues of homelessness and promoting volunteer action—he has conceived of the idea of holding a formal homelessness awareness program on his campus.

He told Kristen what he was thinking, and she encouraged him to write his program ideas down on paper. She also encouraged him to present his ideas widely and seek out others who might help him.

Therefore, Paulo sat down at his computer and sketched out his plan. He took it to LIFT House and showed it to everyone whom he could get to sit still. He incorporated a few of their suggestions and then presented it at the Inter-Fraternity Council. One of his fraternity brothers, an officer in the Student Government Association (SGA), offered to carry the proposal to their next meeting. Paulo also made an appointment with Mr. Aronian, his sociology professor, who he thought would be enthusiastic about the idea and have excellent contacts for speakers. Paulo asked him to be the faculty sponsor. Mr. Aronian accepted and suggested that the chaplain from campus ministry might also be a coadviser. Together, they could offer advice, support services, and give credibility. Their names on

Table 6.1   Homelessness Awareness Week at Siego Community College:
             Major Components of the Program

The Student Government Association will declare the week of May 9th as campuswide Homelessness Awareness Week. During this week, we will bring a wide variety of speakers to campus who can share insights about the problems of homelessness from many different perspectives.

We will also arrange opportunities for students to volunteer their time and money to aid groups that sponsor programs to alleviate the ravages of homelessness.

The steering committee will perform the following tasks:

1. Compile a list of appropriate speakers willing to talk about homelessness from a variety of perspectives.
2. Contact all faculty members to inform them of available speakers and arrange the details of guest speaking assignments in classes during the week.
3. Arrange for speakers to give informal talks in the dorms for one night during the week.
4. Serve a "banquet" in the student cafeteria of a lunch that is affordable on a typical daily welfare budget. A speaker will tell of experiences living on welfare and the food concessionaire will donate the total cost of a regular lunch to the citywide food pantry.
5. Organize a teeter-totter-thon fund-raiser in which participants solicit monetary pledges for the amount of continuous time they can rock on a teeter-totter set up in the campus quad to raise money to buy baby equipment for LIFT House.
6. Present an award during the Walk for Hunger recruitment drive on the quad to the college president for his sponsorship of the annual walk.
7. Arrange for campus and community media coverage of class and dorm speakers and for interviews with four college students who have experienced homelessness.

---

the flyer might reassure faculty members and staff that there would be adequate follow-through.

In Table 6.1, an overview of the program that resulted from the input Paulo solicited is shown. The program was presented to the SGA steering committee and unanimously accepted.

Starting as one individual with a perception of a GAP and a vision of how it might be filled, Paulo soon found he had connected with many others who shared his vision and could expand on it. Without realizing he had been doing it, Paulo had begun connecting with others who might form a group, and he was forging valuable coalitions with groups that commanded both resources and respect.

On the one hand, Paulo was excited by the growing, contagious enthusiasm for Homelessness Awareness Week. On the other hand, he worried a little that "his" project was getting away from him. He realized with a shock that he was encountering one of the inherent dilemmas of participatory democracy: When one asks people for their ideas, and really listens to them, one cannot control the outcomes of the decisions that will be made! He found this to be a startling and humbling revelation.

STEP 1: SPECIFYING TASKS

Now that the plan was accepted, Paulo thought he would feel a sense of relief and pride. Despite all the resources and labor that had been promised, however, he could not shake the feeling of being totally overwhelmed. Kristen, noticing his hesitation, assured him that everyone at LIFT had felt exactly the same way before they started a new project—the mountain of tasks that lay ahead always appeared too high to scale.

Kristen calls this the "who, me?" syndrome. Inside each inexperienced planner is a voice that keeps repeating, "Who, me . . ."

- Get the board of selectmen to change a zoning rule?
- Sign a mortgage on a 12-room house?
- Plan a reception for 80 people?
- Design a playroom for infants?
- Ask a faculty member to plan a class at my suggestion?

Kristen told him that the most important skill in this phase of the planning process is the ability to break down the big tasks into a series of smaller ones. One must learn to walk one step at a time! She also suggested to Paulo that once the tasks were broken down into small, interconnecting pieces, they could be assigned to the committee members. As coordinator, Paulo's job was to delegate tasks and then check back to see how they were progressing. The coordinator's role is to conduct the orchestra, not to play all the instruments. Table 6.2 shows the first task list that Paulo created.

Remembering that he had to keep breaking tasks down into smaller and smaller units of work, Paulo examined one item on his list (Table 6.2), Task 5—locate and arrange speakers for classes—to see what small steps lay within it. When the time came to assign each task to a different person, Task 5 is the item that he might take on himself. Table 6.3 shows what his task list looked like. It would be useful for him to plot his work and could also serve as a sample for the other committee members.

Table 6.2   Major Tasks That Need to Be Done for Homelessness Awareness
                   Week—List 1

---

1. Assemble a planning committee for the Homelessness Awareness Week.
2. Book a place on the quad for the fund-raiser.
3. Book a room in case of rain.
4. Choose a time for the ceremony and book the president.
5. Locate and arrange speakers for classes (try for 10 classes).
6. Contact all faculty and ask if they will have a speaker, and then schedule them.
7. Print flyers and posters for banquet and fund-raiser.
8. Get publicity articles into the school newspaper.
9. Give budget to the student government for funding.
10. Arrange for desk, phone, and supplies in SGA office.
11. Organize Dining Services for the Hunger Luncheon.

STEP 2: DELEGATING TASKS AND BUILDING A
DECISION-MAKING STRUCTURE

Once tasks were broken into smaller units and he understood that he did not have to do everything himself, Paulo could relax slightly. He had found a few people to whom he could delegate some specific tasks. He began helping them create their own task lists. During the first few weeks, however, everyone seemed to be coming back to him, asking questions or seeking approval, or he would not hear at all from someone and had no idea how he or she was coming along or if that person needed to change direction. He realized he needed some structure to get everyone together and remove himself from being the spoke in the middle of the wheel.

He needed to create a think tank for pooling ideas, monitoring progress of delegated tasks, and arguing out any changes in direction. More important, Homelessness Awareness Week had to keep engaging the spirit and energy of a few hardy souls. By sharing responsibility for the whole program with this group, he could garner their allegiance and energy in return. Also, if others could see the program in its entirety as well as in its parts, then maybe they would be willing to coordinate it next year.

There are no formulas that dictate the type of decision-making structure that is best for all programs. Whatever design is chosen, it should be committed to paper. If it is not articulated, structure, like a fast-growing vine, will still grow. A covert or informal structure, however, can be confusing and demoralizing. No one is sure who is in charge, although inevitably a few people seem to be pulling the strings or pushing their agendas. This can lead to what Freeman (1972) dubbed, "the tyranny of structurelessness."

The techniques suggested for creating and operating an effective decision-making structure in the large established agency can be adapted for the small-scale group and onetime event. By starting small, but starting clear, a reasonable governing structure that is right for the current stage of development can be created. When they began LIFT, Ms. Chu and Kristen consulted with established programs, attended a workshop on board structuring, and read several how-to books on delegating and structuring (see Conrad, 1983; Fram, 1995; O'Connell, 1976).

Paulo decided his planning group should be composed of the following:

- The president and a few other officers of the SGA
- Professor Aronian and the chaplain
- Three fraternity brothers he was close to and several other members who would be more marginally involved
- His girlfriend
- Raymond and the staff members of LIFT (who could act as consultants but would not be available for the spade work on the campus)

The first meeting of the planning group was set. Paulo composed an agenda. The first item of business would be making sure that all the major tasks were delegated to an individual or a group. Raymond tried to prepare himself for the critical job of delegating tasks by suggesting a basic rule of thumb that he had learned when doing the mentoring planning: The principal program planner needs to assess the skills, interests, and follow-through potential of each of the people who have taken on tasks in a project.

From social events that Paulo had worked on with his fraternity brothers, he knew who he could trust to do what they said they would and who might say "yes" when asked but were not likely to complete a task in a timely fashion. He also knew who in his fraternity had specific skills and interests. He did not know, however, how to realistically anticipate the work output and follow-through of the chaplain or the sociology professor. Both were notoriously overcommitted, which could mean that they juggled many balls well, but it might also mean that a student project would be shoved onto their back burner. Both had good reputations among the other students, however. That was a good sign. The SGA representatives were totally unknown quantities, which was a bit worrisome.

Raymond suggested the following other two rules of thumb that would come in handy:

Table 6.3   Task List for Task 5: Locate and Arrange Speakers for Classes

---

1. Ask Kristen, Ms. Chu, and Professor Aronian for names, addresses, and phone numbers of good speakers in the following categories:
   Homeless families and parents
   Homeless veterans
   Self-help groups of homeless people
   Someone from Spare Change, the newspaper published by the homeless
   Political action coalitions of the homeless
   Advocates for affordable housing
   A shelter director and a volunteer
   A legislator who works on these issues
   A college student who has been homeless
2. Draft letter to speakers with description of Homelessness Awareness Week and suggested topics and times for class presentations. Print it and mail it.
3. Draft letter of confirmation to the ones who agree, check it, reproduce it, and mail it.
4. Make follow-up phone call to each speaker to provide name of professor and class level, room location, and time. Mail confirmation with campus map and invitation to Hunger Luncheon.
5. Make final follow-up phone calls to make sure speakers received detail packet.
6. Send final schedule of speakers to campus newspaper.
7. Book audiovisual equipment if needed by speakers.
8. Find out if speakers need parking spaces or cab fare; arrange if needed.
9. Arrange escorts to classes to introduce speakers to professors.
10. Return audiovisual equipment
11. Write, reproduce, and mail thank-you letters to speakers and to professors.
12. Ask professors to fill out brief evaluation form on student reactions to the speaker.
13. Compile feedback and write list of suggested speakers if week is repeated next year.
14. Write letter to student newspaper, thanking speakers, professors, students, and so on.

- One should double-check the progress of committee members whose past follow-through has been weak or who are unknown quantities more often, especially during the early period of the planning process.
- One should avoid assigning the most pivotal tasks, those on which everything else rests, to those whose previous follow-through has been weak or who are unknown quantities.

At the first meeting of the Homelessness Awareness Week planning committee, Paulo pasted on the wall a blown-up version of the list of the 11 major tasks. As each person volunteered to serve as a coordinator, Paulo listed his or her name next to his or her task. Table 6.4 shows what this list looked like.

By the end of the meeting, Paulo had firm commitments from several people. He asked each coordinator to fill out a form he had prepared,

Table 6.4 Major Tasks That Need to Be Done for Homelessness Awareness Week and the People in Charge of Each

1. Assemble a planning committee for the Homelessness Awareness Week	Paulo
2. Organize the teeter-totter-thon fund-raiser	Fraternity—Ric in charge
3. Book the quad and a room in case of rain	SGA, Marcia, VP
4. Organize award presentation to the president	No one (try Sam A)
5. Locate and arrange speakers for classes	Doris, Felix, and Prof. A
6. Contact faculty and ask if they will have speaker, then schedule them	Prof. Aronian
7. Print flyers and posters	No one (try Delta Tau)
8. Get publicity articles into the school newspaper	No one (try PR Club)
9. Give budget to the student government for funding	SGA treasurer, Myra
10. Arrange for desk and supplies in SGA office	SGA adviser, Ms. Orlando
11. Work with Dining Services on the Hunger Luncheon	The chaplain and Women's Center

which would help them enumerate each of the smaller tasks within their overall task. He distributed copies of the detailed work list he had composed for Task 5 (Table 6.2) to use as a sample.

A few major tasks were still not assigned. Paulo resisted the impulse to say, "Oh well, I'll do that one myself." That can be a prelude to leader burnout. He also resisted the impulse to pressure a genuinely reluctant committee member into agreeing to take on a coordinating role. He realized, however, that many initially refuse when asked to take a leadership role but relent with gentle urging and genuine promises of support. Sometimes, assigning two people to a task makes it less cumbersome and ensures that the task will get done. Ultimately, a genuinely unwilling or overwhelmed coordinator can be worse than an empty slot.

Someone suggested that the college public relations (PR) department or student club might be willing to take on the publicity tasks. Because Paulo's group feared that the PR department might not be responsive to a request coming from a student, Professor Aronian agreed to ask the PR director for assistance.

That night, Paulo tried his hand at composing the other 10 detailed task lists. A few days later, he distributed them to those coordinators who had not returned their lists. He suggested that they could incorporate his list into the ones that they were in the process of composing. He felt the need to start the wheels moving. He was pleasantly surprised by the thoroughness and timeliness of the task lists of two of the coordinators. Others were late or never did turn them in. He wondered if he had insulted any of the coordinators by doing some of the task list drafts himself. He also realized, however, that everyone on the committee had many other things going on in their lives and the project might not be the most pressing item on their personal agenda. At this point in his life, the project was at the top of Paulo's list. Within the next 2 weeks, he had assembled all the lists, enlarged them on his computer, and hung them on the wall over the project desk in the SGA office. Finally, each task had one or more coordinators, and there was a detailed list of tasks staring down at all of them from the wall in the SGA office.

Paulo told Raymond that although the work to be done was much clearer now, he was still overwhelmed by the huge amount of it that lay ahead. Raymond suggested that now that Paulo had seen all the work laid out before him, this might be the time to decide that some parts of the program should be eliminated. The plan might be too ambitious for the human resources currently available. It is no disgrace to trim back a plan to a more manageable size, especially if it is done early on in the planning process.

At the next planning committee meeting, Paulo suggested the elimination of the poverty luncheon from the week's activities. The chaplain spoke up with conviction, assuring the members that he and his committee had a positive response from the food service manager. They had the event under control.

Perhaps another event was a candidate for cutting back. Paulo suggested a process the group could use to make that determination. Each coordinator should refer to his or her task list, marking with a highlighter the most pivotal tasks, the ones on which the whole event would depend. For example, if a large enough inside space could not be booked for the teeter-totter fund-raiser in case of rain, or if the tent could not be rented for a reasonable fee, then it should be canceled. By listing the tasks in order of their importance and logistical sequence and deciding on a reasonable deadline for completing them, a determination could be made regarding which activities were feasible.

After that meeting, Paulo sensed that the commitment to the event was growing and that a structure was emerging. In the next several weeks, each time he looked at the chart on the wall and panicked, he reminded himself of the following rules of successful delegating:

- Remind yourself and everyone else that you are willing to be the orchestra leader, but you cannot be a one-man band.
- Ask each member to take over a main task or some of the smaller items within the task.
- Assess the resources available, prioritize tasks, and cut back early if necessary.

- Check regularly with the members to find out what has been accomplished and what barriers they are encountering.

Ms. Chu warned Paulo that he had taken on a complex, often thankless role as overall coordinator of the week's activities. As the person at the top of the delegation hierarchy, the buck stops with him. To some extent, however, he had limited control over the planning process. This is a role that requires much subtly and tact. He must encourage and advise the members when they are having difficulty completing a task while avoiding giving the impression that he does not trust their judgment and hard work.

If you ask a dozen planners what is the single hardest part of mounting an event, they will undoubtedly answer in one voice: Getting people to follow through on what they have promised and keeping myself from doing all the work, in my way, of course!

STEP 3: SEQUENCING TASKS
AND DECIDING ON TIME SCHEDULES

The committee members had taken on responsibilities for pieces of the work and had highlighted the most critical tasks. Many of those were completed. Accordingly, they decided to retain all the activities they had originally proposed.

Then things slumped again, however. When Paulo called the task coordinators to check on whether a speaker for a class had been contacted or audiovisual equipment reserved, he heard the following responses:

"Oh yeah, I'm gonna do that next week."
"I'm waiting for xyz to call me back."
"Wait until midterms, finals, my comps, etc. are over"

The clock kept on ticking, however, and days were passing too quickly. Time schedules rule our lives in modern society. Fight it though we might, it is still a fact that

- Newspapers have deadlines for copy and advertisements.
- Permits to use a room or close off a walkway have to be applied for a specific number of weeks or days before an event.
- It takes a certain amount of time to draw a check to pay a vendor.

The speakers Paulo wanted to attract probably had calendar books that were rapidly filling up with meetings. The longer the students waited to book them, the less chance they had of fitting a specific speaker into a class time slot and the less chance there was that faculty members would reserve one session of their course to discuss homelessness. The committee members had 4 months to plan every detail. At times, that seemed like so far in the future that they had no reason at all to worry. The next day, however, it felt as if the date was approaching too quickly and little had been accomplished. Paulo also sensed the moment of the dreaded "point of no return" that every coordinator worries about. Activities can be relatively easily eliminated or scaled back in the opening phases of program development. Once commitments to people have been made and money has been expended, however, the freedom to turn back is lost. A program cancellation late in the process can be costly in money as well as in the reputation and credibility of the planners. Every planner remembers the parable of the boy who cried wolf.

With the realistic pressures of time, the planner has to find a comfortable position somewhere between being a compulsive worrier and a laid-back procrastinator, appropriately concerned about time but not frantic. Paulo needed to know when he could say "We are on target, we're doing fine" or "We had better spend more time doing x, y, z or we are in trouble."

He also needed a system that encouraged each of his committee members to monitor his or her own progress without waiting for a prod or pat on the back from him.

CREATING A TASK-TIME FLOWCHART

Professor Aronian, an old hand at planning programs at the college, understood that the coordinators needed to have a realistic estimate of how they were progressing. Therefore, at their next committee meeting, he showed the members how to create a task-time flowchart. This device places each task into a time grid, showing when it should be completed, who is responsible for it, and if it has been completed.

Some organizations call these charts timetables, work plans, PERT charts (PERT stands for *P*rogram *E*valuation *R*eview *T*echnique), or Gannt charts (after Henry L. Gannt, who studied planning and work flow in business organizations in the early 20th century) (see Frame, 1995; Lewis, Lewis, & Souflee, 1991; Schaefer, 1987; Upshur, 1982). No matter which format a particular agency chooses, they are all highly effective visual devices. They tie together the work that needs to be accomplished, the personnel available to do it, and the deadlines for completion.

Each of the committee members can create a task-time flowchart for his or her specific assignment. The overall coordinator of the project can create a master chart that incorporates each aspect of the program. If that master chart is kept up to date, in a central place, everyone can easily see what has been done and what tasks remain. At each planning meeting, there is a record indicating which tasks to concentrate on, or perhaps some that have not met their deadlines, need logistical help or reinforcements. Table 6.5 shows the chart that Professor Aronian helped the committee create for Task 5 (Table 6.2) of Homelessness Awareness Week.

Ms. Chu was very impressed when she saw the task-time flowcharts that Paulo's committee created for each of the major tasks. The charitable foundation that she applied to for the funding of LIFT had initially rejected her proposal because the reviewers did not see evidence that she knew enough about how to organize a complex agency. When she resubmitted the proposal 6 months later, she had added a series of detailed task-time flowcharts. These demonstrated that she had a realistic grasp of the work that needed to be done and the personnel and time it would take to get the project off the ground. Just as important, the act of creating the charts clarified the start-up process for her committee, highlighting areas that were poorly conceptualized.

Although the new chart on the wall above Paulo's desk helped him take a quantum leap forward out of muddle and anxiety, Ms. Chu felt she had to warn him that life is only orderly on paper. Few, if any, timelines actually proceed as written. They represent the planner's best estimate of how long a task should take. In the real world, most tasks are likely to take twice as long as one thinks. Pleasant surprises of offers of assistance and strokes of good fortune, however, might speed along other tasks.

Task-time flowcharts, like budgets, create broad guidelines. Each time an event is repeated, the charts come closer to representing the realities of mounting a specific program. For example, far into the planning, the committee realized that it had set the date for Homelessness Awareness Week too close to finals and graduation. It was not a major stumbling block, but the committee was turned down by some professors who would have booked a speaker but had to use the remaining class sessions for review before exams. The committee also lost the involvement of some seniors who were too stressed or distracted to take on a planning role. A recommendation to move the date up would be noted in their final report.

Table 6.5   Task-Time Flowchart: Homelessness Awareness Week

Task 5: Locate and arrange speakers for classes (goal, 10 classes)
Assigned to Doris and Felix, assisted by Paulo and Prof. Aronian

Task	To Be Done	By	Comments (X = Completed)
1. Get suggestions of speakers	Feb. 1-15	D & F	
2. Draft letter to speakers	Feb. 15-17	D	
Reproduce them	Feb. 18-19	F	
Mail	March 20-28	F	
3. Draft confirmation packet	March 25-April 5	D	
Reproduce	April 6-11	F	
Mail			
4. Reserve audiovisual equipment	April 11-15	F	
5. Follow-up phone call #1 to speakers & profs.	April 30-May 3	P, D, & F	
6. Follow-up phone call #2 to speakers & profs.	May 7-8	P, D, & F	
7. Arrange for parking spaces	May 8	D	
8. Print master schedule and distribute	May 8	F	
9. Arrange escorts	May 9	D	
Homelessness Awareness Week Speakers Come	May 15-19		
10. Return audiovisual equipment	May 15-19	F	
11. Write thank-you letters	May 20	D	
Reproduce	May 21	F	
Mail	May 23	F	
12. Create evaluation form for profs.	May 9	Prof. A	
Reproduce	May 11	F	
Distribute	May 12	F & D	
Collect and analyze	May 17-26	F, D, & Prof. A	
13. Write letter to student newspaper	May 20	P	
Mail	May 17	P	
14. Complete evaluation report	June 3	F, D, & Prof. A	
Party for Committee at Paulo's House	Saturday, June 11th	All members	

STEP 4: CREATING A RESOURCE BANK

Every action plan needs to draw on a rich bank of resources—the people, agencies, and objects that might provide goods, services, labor, and advice. All participants in the planning process bring their unique resource banks with them, providing entry into their extended network of contacts.

Helping people identify and access their resources is a skill necessary in all social service interventions. Caseworkers encourage clients to tap into their network to locate others who can provide emotional sustenance. They try to help clients revive long-dormant skills or hobbies that might be a source of social contacts, employment, or pleasure. They use their own skills in finding resources to locate open slots in day camps and empty beds in residential services. The worker's abilities to play a musical instrument, drive a van, or secure a piece of equipment at reduced price are often relied on by his or her's agency (Maguire, 1983).

Most people have talents and creative energy that they use in one sphere of their lives but never thought could be of use in others. In his very energizing book, *Revolution of the Heart* (1995), Robert Shore, the founder of Share Our Strength, a national organization that funds hunger-relief projects, tells how he marshals the resources of a wide range of people to fight hunger. He does not concentrate on asking for donations of money, but instead he asks people to share their skills, talents, and experience to raise money from others (many of whom have little interest in his charitable cause). When people contribute their unique abilities, their contribution is not dependent on their net worth, cash flow, or the approval of their employer. What they are giving is at their core and, once tapped, it unleashes lasting energy and commitment. Thus, in Shore's projects, chefs donate their skills by teaching low-income parents to create nutritious meals. Their employers might be asked to donate a percentage of their restaurant's profits during one highly publicized evening a year. Writers and poets (who are often unable to make generous financial contributions) have been asked to contribute to an anthology; the proceeds from the book sale are then donated to hunger relief.

Shore has successfully demonstrated that most people want to be part of something that is larger than themselves. He has found that every collaboration that taps into a person's creative skills and talents will spawn another one that could not have been foreseen. He underscores the point that being able to give something tangible, something you are proficient at, forms a bond that transforms the lives of both the giver and the receiver.

Workers whose business is the recruiting and retention of volunteers in nonprofit programs make similar points about the transforming experience of giving. They discuss the kinds of motivations that attract and bond volunteers to social agencies where they donate their money and time. They agree that finding a good match between a volunteer's interests and a job description of a task that needs to be done is one of many skills that can be successfully employed (Fischer & Schaeffer, 1993; Ilsley, 1990; Kouri, 1990).

DOING A RESOURCE ANALYSIS

Each activity needs to be analyzed so that the planners can ascertain the following:

- The exact resources they will need
- The resources they already possess
- Where they might locate the resources they need but do not have
- Ways to make do without the resources they cannot find

Table 6.6 shows the resource analysis chart Paulo created when he first started planning Homelessness Awareness Week.

Because Paulo is a college student organizing an event on a college campus, he has access to the resources of the various academic departments and support programs. To these, he adds his own ability to systematically "hustle" from sources beyond the campus. From sponsoring community service events for his fraternity, he has developed a database file of the fast-food franchises, supermarkets, food and soft drink companies, and civic-minded individuals who are likely to donate specific items if asked. In his file, he notes how their contributions can be accessed. Some chains require several weeks' notice, and requests must be in writing on a nonprofit agency letterhead and sent to corporate headquarters. Each company he deals with has a slightly different system. He keeps track of when he made his last request so that he does not go back to the same well too frequently.

He also has gathered up the addresses of warehouses and food clubs that sell at discount and the shops that sell day-old or used products. For example, some of the bakeries in his town will allow him, at the end of the workday, to pick up the rolls and cakes that have not sold. Obviously, he has to exercise caution in what foods can safely be recycled.

Even workers at the most poorly funded agency, however, utilizing their skills of networking and persuasion, can locate a surprisingly wide array of free or reduced-cost resources. Once they identify the GAPs between what they need and what they have, they brainstorm possible sources. Kristen, for example, wanted a VCR that she could use just for parent training sessions. This was a luxury item that LIFT could hardly afford. The VCR did not need to have all the advanced features, it did not even need to record, but it did need to be dependable. After many refusals from large appliance shops, she thought of the idea of asking VCR repair shops if they had an older machine that had been repaired but never picked up. She knew that this often happened because she had once done this with

Table 6.6   Resource Analysis for Homelessness Awareness Week

Resources We Need	Resources We Have	Possible Sources
1. Photocopy & fax and supplies	Student government office	
2. Postage	Money from SGA to buy	
3. Phone, e-mail, & message machine	Use ones in SGA office	
4. Computers (2)	Paulo has one at home	Maybe Prof. A
5. Laser printer	In Dean's office	
6. Person to design poster	Ira (in Fraternity) is graphic arts major	
7. Teeter-totter	Physical Education Dept.	
8. Tent	YMCA might lend one	
Helium tank for balloons	Chem. Dept.	
9. Sound system	Drama Dept.	If not, Aras supply
10. Audio visual equipment	AV office	
11. Plaque for president		Purchase for $29 at
Plaque for Frat.		Fosters in Belmore
12. Food for Hunger Lunch	Cooked in college kitchen; cost donated by concession	
13. Parking for speakers	SGA budget will pay for guest parking at college garage	

a vacuum, the repair cost of which was almost as much as the cost of buying a new one. On her sixth attempt, she hit pay dirt. The repair shop owner gave her both a repaired VCR and an old but serviceable TV to use with it. Understanding that a small-business person operates on a thin margin or profit, she told the manager of the TV shop that if he donated one of those unclaimed machines, she would acknowledge it with a donation receipt he could use for his taxes. Of course, she also mentioned the name of his shop in the next LIFT newsletter and invited him to LIFT's next open house.

In the back of her mind, she has a plan to ask him someday to teach VCR repair to one of the residents, if that "just-right candidate" for such training ever came to live at LIFT House.

Other staff and volunteers, by asking their friends and relatives for contacts, and by tapping the goodwill and self-interest of local merchants, have managed to obtain the following:

- The consulting services of a skilled gardener who is Kristen's uncle
- New living room furniture that was used in a department store display window and was slightly sun faded but otherwise very acceptable

- Receiving free passes twice a month to movie theaters by writing to the headquarters of a large chain
- Gift certificates for paper goods from a volunteer whose husband manages a store
- Rewiring of the electrical circuits by members of the electrical union
- Used athletic equipment from a local adult softball league
- The loan of sleeping bags from the college outing club
- Free haircuts from the local beauty school
- Prepared food for holiday celebrations from a cooking school that is managed by the wife of one of the volunteers
- General Educational Development books donated by students at the local community college who have passed the test and no longer need them
- Two computers and much software from Raymond's employer

Table 6.7 shows a copy of a resource bank form that was used by Gardenia for her camping trip. It was sent home to family members, volunteers, and friends of LIFT. Of course, each resource form is adapted to fit the special project that one is seeking resources for.

MONEY AS A PRIMARY RESOURCE

Before they agreed to cosponsor Homelessness Awareness Week, the SGA required that Paulo submit a proposed budget—his statement of the anticipated costs of the total program. He had to go through the same process that Raymond did when he drew up the proposal for his mentoring program. Paulo had to nail down each of his anticipated expenses for each activity and to put a reasonable and defensible price tag on each one.

It seemed to Paulo that this was a useless exercise because virtually everything he needed to run this program was going to be donated by a campus department or agency. Sometimes, a program such as Homelessness Awareness Week can be mounted with very few direct outlays of money. It is a very rare program, however, that costs absolutely nothing. Although it might appear that all of a program's resources are free of charge, someone is absorbing its costs. Program planners need to make telephone calls, mail letters, and photocopy or print flyers, brochures, and booklets. We often want to take pictures at our events, and film and developing costs can mount up. Virtually every program incurs some expenses for transportation, refreshments, or program supplies.

Even if planners are fortunate (and skillful) enough to get every service and item donated, they still have to keep track of how much money is being expended on the program. The planners need a realistic estimate of

Table 6.7   Sample Resource Questionnaire

Resource Form
Topic: Camping Trip

1. Which of the following pieces of equipment do you have that we could use?

    Equipment   *Quantity*   *Condition*
    Lantern
    Stove
    Tent
    Sleeping bag
    Canteen
    Knapsack
    First aid kit
    Cooler
    Guitar (or other small instrument)
    Sports equipment: (describe) _____

2. Which of the following do you, your family, or close friends have that we might use for advice or help?

    I know someone who is:

    1. An experienced camper _____

    2. A medical person (doctor or nurse) _____

    3. An accountant (for budgeting) _____

    4. A guitar player _____

    5. A cook or dietitian _____

    6. Other _____

3. What type of transportation do you have access to?

    Type   *Size or Seating Capacity*

    Car _____   _____

    Van _____   _____

    Bus _____   _____

    Boat _____   _____

4. What other talents or equipment might you be able to provide?

    _____

    _____

    _____

how much it would cost to mount a program in case the next time they are not able to get every service and item donated.

The SGA was aware that if it did not require a budget projection from every event it sponsored, there would be no way for it to know whether it was staying within the limits of its own yearly budget. Every agency has a finite limit to how many papers can be photocopied in 1 year and how many letters can be mailed out. The SGA was not giving the homelessness planning committee carte blanche to their postage account, they were simply letting them use a fair share of it.

Paulo protested, quite rightly, that for some items he could not establish a cost. What does a teeter-totter cost to rent? Therefore, he skipped a few of the costs of some items. He did find out what a tent rental cost, however, in the event it turned out that one was not available on campus.

After filling many worksheets with mathematical equations, the following are the anticipated expenses of Homelessness Awareness Week:

Estimated Expenses for Homelessness Awareness Week

Postage	$71
Photocopying	52
Art and clerical supplies	48
Phone (toll calls)	20
Plaques: 2 at $36	72
Food for hunger luncheon: 60 at $1	60
Miscellaneous expenses (travel-related, etc.)	15
	$318

PIGGYBACKING ON AN ESTABLISHED PROGRAM IS AN EXCELLENT WAY TO FUND AND ADVERTISE A SMALL-SCALE PROGRAM

Often, a small-scale program can reduce both its potential expenses and its risk of failure by piggybacking on an already established event. The Homelessness Awareness committee did this by using classes as the venue for speakers on that subject. If the committee had started from scratch, reserving a room on campus during an evening and recruiting an audience, it would have meant costly printing and much time and worry in attracting students to hear the speakers. Nothing destroys the morale of a new group quite as much as a sea of empty seats when a speaker has donated his or her time. By piggybacking on the classes, the committee members assured themselves an audience at little cost. The small expenses incurred by the speakers were likely to be absorbed by the academic departments because this was a legitimate extension of class work.

When piggybacking on a closely related event, one does risk "preaching to the already converted." Most of the professors who ultimately invited speakers on homelessness to their classes were from the social sciences. Many of the students enrolled in the host classes might have already been exposed to materials about this complex issue. It was less likely that a professor of a science course was going to invite a guest speaker on the topic of homelessness. Although it would be better to attract majors from disciplines far afield from the subject, this is a trade-off that must be made.

By gaining SGA sponsorship, Paulo was able to piggyback onto its resources. The dining services and Office of Religious Life, also recruited as sponsors, were willing to absorb the small costs of the "poverty banquet." Most of the speakers work for, or are affiliated with, advocacy groups that regularly do public speaking, and so they required no exorbitant speaking fees. Because Paulo's fraternity had taken on the coordinating of the teeter-totter fund-raiser, it would provide the manpower and any small expenses would be absorbed by the fraternity.

The trade-off inherent in relying on other groups for funding and energy is twofold. First, it is much harder to guarantee the quality of the event. These other groups have their own agendas and organizational problems that can affect the quality of their output. Paulo had several ideas about alternate plans if these groups did not come through as they promised. The second trade-off is that if the event is a success, the credit is spread widely. Often, the planning committee's work is barely noticed. This does not help their own group-building efforts. Conversely, the blame for mishaps still can devolve on the original planners, although they had very little real control. This is a cost-benefit analysis that each group should make after a realistic appraisal of the positives and negatives. A force field analysis might help make a reasoned decision.

The committee also piggybacked on other events to advertise the Poverty Luncheon and the Teeter-Totter Fund-Raiser. It got permission to set up an informational table at the Drug-A-Hol Fair sponsored by the campus counseling center. A band on the campus quad (paid for by the counseling center) helped attract a large crowd. The committee members keyed their publicity to the impact of alcohol on homelessness. They also requested that students abstain from buying beer for the day of the Poverty Luncheon and donate the money they saved to LIFT. On a chart, they drew several bottles of beer, added up the cost, and equated that cost with the cost of a day's diapers or formula for a homeless child. They asked students to sign pledge slips for both events. The pledge slips became raffle tickets for a certificate for a dinner for two at an expensive local restaurant (which was donated by the owner, who was a friend of Raymond's).

RAISING MONEY FROM FUND-RAISING EVENTS

In chapter 5, some of the techniques of proposal writing were discussed and some of the resources useful in applying for grants to fund small-scale programs were mentioned. Many small-scale programs, however, are funded through some form of direct solicitation of donations. These solicitations range from the omnipresent bake sales and raffles at the shopping mall to the $500-a-plate socialite dinner dance mounted by the boards of social service agencies. Many of these events—for example, Girl Scout cookie sales, walks for hunger and multiple sclerosis, bike rides to support research in AIDS, and rock concerts for famine and flood relief—are often recurring events that are an integral part of community life. Each of these events takes a different amount of lead-up time and labor, and some, after they outgrow their grassroots organizers, are run by paid staff.

Most of the planners of small-scale programs do not try to compete with the large-scale fund-raising operations of the professionals. The field of charitable solicitation has become so specialized that whole books have been written on how to target specific populations of donors. There are, however, several useful books that describe fund-raising events in a cookbook fashion (Brakeley, 1993; Gronbjerg, 1993; Howe, 1991; Jencks, 1987; Leibert, 1974; Prince & File, 1994; Shaw & Taylor, 1995).

Although the numbers these authors toss around and the rather manipulative tone they often adopt can be disingenuous, much can be learned from the research they have done on the why, how, and who of soliciting donations. The kind of fund-raising events they describe can also be modified to fit the neighborhood small-scale agency. The books by Brakeley (1993), Gronbjerg (1993), Howe (1991), Jencks (1987), Leibert (1974), Prince and File (1994), and Shaw and Taylor (1995) describe the following types of donations:

Annual giving appeals to members, friends, and so on as pledges or dues

Mass appeals through mailings and advertisements

Program grants for a specific purpose from foundations, government agencies, corporations, churches, clubs, or civic associations

Single fund-raising events—awards dinners, dances, raffles, plays, walks and runs, yard sales, flower sales, logo T-shirt sales, selling advertisements in commemorative books, and so on

Employee matching-donation programs of companies

Soliciting specific donations of equipment or services

Asking for in-kind contributions of facility, labor, and so on

The literature stresses that the fund-raising plan should include a way for even the most altruistic giver to get something in return for "doing good." Because the motivations, interests, and needs of the givers are bound to vary, there should be several possible rewards built into the fund-raising strategy. Incentives might include the following:

- The opportunity of repaying a personal or loved one's "debt"
- The good feeling that comes from doing good
- Public approval, status, or positive exposure from doing good
- Fun and comradeship from doing good
- Business goodwill garnered from doing good
- Some kind of quid pro quo, such as a tax deduction, letter of commendation, a promise of reciprocal support in their projects, and so on

Experienced fund-raisers also stress the importance of realistically estimating the amount of money, time, and personnel that will be needed to mount a fund-raising campaign versus how much might conceivably be raised through specific events. Projecting this ratio takes the same skills used in projecting a budget and estimating resources.

To do this, solid data on how much up-front and hidden costs of an event might be are needed. The data must be matched against the best projection of an achievable goal. The goal can only be estimated by each member of the committee being honest about how much time and energy each can give and to what extent each has the network, opportunity, and personality necessary to raise funds in that particular way. Asking for money is never easy, and many people find it downright unpleasant unless they have a high predictability of success. Although a novel idea such as the teeter-totter-thon might be seductive, a tried-and-true bake sale or car wash might still be the event that is most likely to succeed for a particular group. There is actually something very comforting in putting on a fund-raiser that has a formula to follow and results that are consistent. On a college campus, for example, one can never run out of patrons for a food sale. In certain towns, a chowder cook-off, a square dance, or cow chip bingo, if well organized, always helps the cash flow, unless the "market" has already been saturated with similar events, in which case it may be time to tackle the novel fund-raising idea.

Finally, events should also offer an opportunity to educate and inform the donors about the issue one is working on, albeit it might be a very cursory introduction. For example, when folks stop at a fund-raising table to purchase a homemade brownie, they might also find the following:

- An agency banner or poster and a stack of agency brochures
- An attractive display of photos of the agency at work
- A stack of brochures or a handout describing what the agency does
- A listing of job descriptions of volunteers or a wish list
- A sincere "thank you for helping us send kids to camp"

STEP 5: ESTABLISHING TASK GROUPS, WORK
ROLES, AND COMMUNICATION CHANNELS

Using both intuition and knowledge culled from much of the small-group research, we know that by working in small groups, as opposed to working on our own, we gain the momentum that comes from sharing and elaborating on ideas (Hare, 1976). Narrowly focused task groups with specific, time-limited tasks provide the planners the practical advantages of multiple skills and energy as well as a division of labor.

Of course, groups can also slow down and frustrate the efficient planning process as individuals struggle to make decisions and carve consensus. Too many people and too much interaction can also lead to task confusion and dispersion of responsibility. Worse still, members' varied communication styles, and personal issues that are extraneous to the group's task, can intrude on the group's achievement. Therefore, in forming task groups, as in all other phases of the planning process, the initial organizer of the project weighs the trade-offs of using a task group for a specific set of activities rather than going it alone (Fatout & Rose, 1995).

The coordinator also needs to think about how members can be motivated and monitored so as to complete a task in a manner that builds morale and encourages continued collaboration. As in most other areas of life, members of task groups will function more effectively if there is an appropriate reward structure to encourage interdependence (Haines & McKeachie, 1982).

At the first meeting of the planning committee for the Homelessness Awareness Week, several members urged that the core group be expanded. Paulo resisted, reasoning that they could move more efficiently with a limited number of people. Just setting the date for a meeting with the co-ordinators, given their complex schedules, was a feat of organizational genius. Instead, he urged the coordinators to recruit their friends to form task groups. More people would be involved in the work of mounting each aspect of the program, but only a small cadre need be concerned about the progress of the entire event.

To establish a series of small task groups, the coordinators needed to be clear about where the job of one began and where the next one took up. At the second meeting, Paulo arrived with brief written job descriptions, or mission statements, for each of the task groups. He assured the members that these were just drafts, useful to start the ball rolling. One of the members protested that this felt overly bureaucratic. Paulo persisted, having learned from previous projects that nothing damns the planning process more than spending hours working on a task only to discover that another group has already done it, or, worse still, finishing a series of tasks only to realize that they are not necessary. If the committee members knew what the parameters of their roles were before they started brainstorming and delegating tasks, perhaps frustration might be avoided. Of course, tasks might need to be changed along the way, and jobs that were not initially anticipated were likely to emerge. It was the coordinators job to keep the job descriptions current with information flowing in all directions.

AIDS TO COMMUNICATION FLOW

No task group can function without sound communication (Henry, 1992). Because all the planners were members of a college community, they were likely to share common understandings and word usages that could facilitate their communication. An interdisciplinary team or a group composed of people of varying cultural or socioeconomic backgrounds often experience inscrutable sets of professional jargon and the subtle or contradictory meanings of phrases and actions.

The coordinator of every planning project is also challenged to find ways in which the members can intersact to clear up confusions and carve out their own program-based common language. Paulo was fortunate. Not only did his group share a "language" and set of expectations but also members shared a physical space that allowed them to communicate rapidly and in a fair amount of detail with all the members. Everyone could be tracked down on the campus by cornering them before or after a class. All had access to the Internet on campus, to the bulletin boards in the SGA office, and to the weekly college newspaper.

Paulo still needed additional aids to keep the information flowing without driving himself ragged in the process. Raymond suggested the following three methods to keep the information flowing in the needed directions:

1. Establish simple data-retrieval systems.

   Paulo printed out and distributed lists containing the names, addresses, and phone, fax, e-mail, beeper numbers, or all four of each of the members of the steering committee and (as many as he knew) each of the members of the task groups. One of his fraternity brothers set up a label program on the computer so minutes and last-minute notices could be quickly sent to planners. When it came time to send out each of the four sets of letters to the list of speakers, this avoided the frustration of running around looking for lost zip codes. It also avoided hand addressing four sets of envelopes. The time spent up front always seemed to pay off farther down the line.

Paulo then distributed to each coordinator (with hard copy and on e-mail) and posted on his wall in the SGA the following separate lists:

Faculty who had agreed to have a speaker come to class

Speakers who agreed to come and the students who would be introducing them

Students who volunteered to participate in the teeter-totter fund-raiser

Everyone connected with putting on the Hunger Luncheon

Merchants who were donating goods or services to any of the events

No one's memory could be counted on to hold all the bits and pieces of information collected during the planning process. Paulo had the bad habit of writing notes in the margins of newspapers and on the backs of envelopes, then throwing them away during weekly cleanups. Therefore, he established an index card file with each of the names in the database. He kept it on his desk so that whenever he finished speaking to someone he could grab his or her card and make a note about what had transpired. For example, "George would be willing to be an escort for two speakers on Tuesday," "No, Sue Grogan wasn't available to speak but she suggested Joe Kiley," and "Martha had a great source for discount T-shirts, here's the telephone #." Having the file box filled with notes on his desk reassured him that, if he was not available, someone else could note and retrieve the information. The file cards would also form a legacy to be passed on to those who would plan a similar event next semester.

2. Keep meetings short and focused and use the phone in-between times.

Although meetings should be kept to a minimum, those that do occur should be used to maximum advantage. They can be enormously effective forums for information sharing and joint decision making. They also build commitment to a program. Meetings can also cut down on the feelings of being alone and overburdened that program coordinators often experience. Obtaining maximum attendance involves the following necessary steps:

Surveying the members' schedules before picking a time

Letting everyone know in advance what will be done at the meeting and what they need to think about beforehand

Setting and keeping to a realistic starting and ending time

Notifying and then reminding members by mail, by phone, and in person of the date and location of the meeting

Sticking to an agenda and reaching closure on critical issues

Conducting the work of the meeting in a positive way, regardless of how many people actually show up

In between meetings, one can solicit members' votes by phone when a quick decision needs to be made. Sometimes, a three-way conference call can be arranged, avoiding having to set up a meeting. Paulo also used his voice mail as a source of accurate updated information. Each day, he changed his own message, counting down days to the event and mentioning tasks that were due that day. He also left messages to his committee members on their voice mail.

3. Take clearly focused minutes and make sure they are well circulated.

Although at first Paulo thought it was overly bureaucratic, he soon discovered that if there were no accurate meeting minutes, each member left the room with his or her own perceptions of what had transpired. Participants were often unsure about the tasks they had agreed to do and the time frames. Paulo asked a friend to take notes during the meeting while he was busy chairing, but he always did the final rewrite of the minutes. These minutes became the lifeline of the group. If someone was absent or drifting off during a discussion, he or she could catch up on what work had been accomplished and what decisions had been made. Paulo had been warned that most students probably would not give the minutes more than a cursory glance, so he kept them short and to the point. He used boldfaced heads such as the following:

- **This is what we each agreed to do, by a certain time**
- **This is what we decided to do or voted on this issue**
- **This is when and where we will meet next**
- **Think about this for the next meeting**
- **Call me if you find out . . .**

Because the minutes were such a vital part of the planning process, Paulo e-mailed them and then personally delivered a hard copy to the key members' mailboxes. He even taped them onto the members' dormitory or office doors. He also sent minutes to a campus VIP list to keep them posted on the project's progress and keep the program high in awareness. Finally, a copy of the minutes was hung on the bulletin board of the student government office and in his fraternity house.

Although it might seem like overkill, or even rather insulting, human beings are surprisingly predictable when it comes to absorbing information. Often, something critically important has to be said, read, heard, and repeated several times to solidly take root. When one encounters the highly organized person who is insulted at being reminded three times about a speaking commitment, one must smile winsomely and say "Forgive me for being a bit compulsive, and thank you for being so on top of things."

The minutes of meetings take their place alongside the databases and file cards in the program archive. As the mound of paper grows, so too might the self-confidence and excitement of the planners. Each new task completed is checked off on the task-time flowchart, and another piece is fitted into the giant jigsaw puzzle that will, very soon, become a full-blown program with all its whistles and bells.

THE 5-MINUTE RECAP

- Even the most experienced planners can relate horror stories of times when they jeopardized the outcome of a social program by carelessly overlooking or mismanaging a major task in the planning process.
- Although to err is inevitable, one must try to leave as little to chance as possible by translating concepts into specific short-range tasks and spelling out each step needed to complete each task.
- No plan should be activated until a careful feedback system (also called an action-monitoring plan) is designed and is understood and accepted by all the players in the planning process.
- Paulo, the college student who works at LIFT, is coordinating a Homelessness Awareness Week at his college. It will include the following:

    Experts on the topic as guest speakers in classes and in evening dorm discussions

    A luncheon "banquet" of a meal possible on the typical welfare food allocation

    A fund-raising event on the campus

    Recruitment of volunteers for the citywide Walk for Hunger

    A presentation of a recognition award to the college president for his support of efforts to fight homelessness

- Paulo's program-planning efforts illustrate the techniques described in this chapter.
- This program is beyond the time, energy, or expertise of Paulo, so he recruits a planning group of interested individuals and groups on the campus.
- Breaking a program into its component parts is the first step in the program-specification process. It moves the planners into action by cutting through the immobility that can result from feeling overwhelmed by the enormity of a plan.
- After the main tasks are listed, a second list is then composed of the smaller tasks within the larger ones. Each list describes progressively smaller units of work.
- Once these lists have been made, the overall tasks are delegated so that each task has a coordinator who appears to be a person who will dependably follow though.
- Each coordinator can then recruit other workers for his or her own network. The optimal size of the task group is determined by the complexity of the assignment (or mission).

- Each of the tasks on the lists needs to be logically sequenced, set in a reasonable time frame, and then visually represented in a task-time flowchart.

- Each task group analyzes the resources it needs for the program and then creates a resource bank to see who can fill its needs.

- Although many programs can be conducted on a shoestring budget, some funds, equipment, or clerical support are almost always required.

- The planners try to estimate their expenses as accurately as possible and then list all the sources that might provide funds.

- The planners' resource needs might be met by piggybacking onto an already existing program that has resources or by conducting fund-raising campaigns.

- After task groups have been established, each group needs an articulated description of its role within the total planning endeavor.

- Channels of communication among task groups and between the overall leader and task group coordinators need to be established. With constant feedback, the planning and implementation process can be readjusted as needed.

- Communication flows freely in all directions when simple data-retrieval systems are established; meetings are short and focused and respect the members' life constraints and skills; and clear, brief minutes of decisions and assignments made are circulated after all meetings to act as a reminder and reveal any duplications or omissions.

- As tasks are successfully done and checked off the master list, the confidence and excitement of the planners creates a momentum that further commits them to the ultimate completion of the program.

PUTTING THEORY INTO PRACTICE

EXERCISE 1: PROGRAM PLANNING GOOF-UPS
AND THE LESSONS THEY TEACH

Interview at least two people who have taken a leadership role in planning a small social program or a onetime event for a group. On a college campus, that person might be found in the counseling program, the religious life or resident life office, or student activities office. In the community, that person might be the social chair of the American Legion, the coordinator of the Red Stocking Christmas Drive, organizer of The Walk for Birth Defects, and so on.

Create a list of open-ended questions about how the work was organized and delegated in the weeks leading up to the actual event, what went well, what the person believes were the major omissions in the thinking and planning work of the committee, and what the person learned from them.

EXERCISE 2: CREATING TASK LISTS

You have been asked to create an all-day awareness program for the members of a Girl Scout troop and their families. The topic can be self-chosen or it might be one of the following:

AIDS awareness

Protecting the natural environment

Understanding the problems of immigrants in the community

Understanding physical handicaps

Raising the glass ceiling for women in the professions

Sensible dieting and healthy body image

The program is to include the following:

• Speakers on the topic that the young people can relate to
• A short dramatization of a critical issue that the group can then discuss
• A luncheon
• A sport or relaxation exercise
• A video appropriate to the topic

Each program component will have one person assigned to be its coordinator.

Choose two of the previously mentioned program components. Briefly describe what each of your components might include and then compose a task list for each.

Compose two more lists that break each of the individual tasks down into smaller units of work.

EXAMPLE: if you are in charge of the video portion of the program, your list of tasks might include the following:

Deciding on a general focus for the video and finding out how much time will be allotted

Locating a source that has several videos on that topic for your age group

Reviewing a few so you can make a first choice and an alternate

Thinking of some provocative questions to ask after each has been shown

Finding out what it costs and arranging to obtain the money

Seeing if it is available when needed and then reserving and picking it up

Checking to make sure it plays well

Securing and bringing a working video player

Deciding whether an extension cord will be needed

Setting up the machine in the best spot for viewing

Returning the video

Writing a statement about how well it was received

EXERCISE 3: SPECIFYING TASKS AND RESOURCES AND MAKING A TASK-TIME FLOWCHART

You are coordinating a luncheon for 18 scouts and their families (average two guests per scout). Both an indoor and an outdoor fireplace are available and it is near a town with restaurants. You also will have a van, so you could carry prepared dishes if the luncheon is to be a potluck. Decide on a menu. Next proceed to the following:

1. List all the tasks that would be involved in putting on the lunch.

2. Sequence these tasks and put them in the form of a task-time flowchart (remember that the event will not end immediately after lunch is over—some follow-up tasks will need to be completed).

3. Do a resource analysis of what you will need for the lunch. Be very specific in listing both the foods and ancillary equipment you will need.

4. Explore your own resource bank. What you might be able to get donated and what you might obtain from your friends and coworkers (use your real situation)?

CITATIONS AND SUGGESTIONS FOR FURTHER READING

AIDS TO STAYING ON TRACK

Some of the following sources will also be useful for completing a wrap-up evaluation, which will be discussed in Chapter 7. The thoroughness and appropriateness of the ongoing assessment tools will influence the usefulness of the final program evaluation.

Alter, C., & Evans, W. (1990). *Evaluating your practice: A guide to self-assessment.* New York: Springer.

Bard, R. (1971). *Program and staff evaluation.* Washington, DC: Education Training & Research Sciences. Books in this series were developed during the War on Poverty to be helpful to community action agencies. It is still useful. It has many samples of charts that can be used by clients, staff, and board members to assess progress toward goals throughout the program development process.

Drucker, P. (1973). *Management: Tasks, responsibilities, practices.* New York: Harper & Row.
Frame, D. J. (1995). *Managing projects in organizations, how to make the best use of time technique and people.* San Francisco: Jossey-Bass. Although written primarily for a business course, this text is accessible to the social service program planner and adaptable for social programs. It provides good examples of the use of PERT and Gannt charts and sensitive material about the human side of project management.
Lauffer, A. (1982). *Assessment tools for practitioners, managers and trainers.* Beverly Hills, CA: Sage. This book provides a useful description of several forms used for monitoring, and it is especially useful for writing job descriptions.
Lewis, J. A., Lewis, M. D., & Souflee, F., Jr. (1991). *Management of human service programs* (2nd ed.). Pacific Grove, CA: Brooks/Cole. This book provides a good discussion of designing an organizational structure and examples of timelines and PERT charts.
MacGregor, D. (1965). *The human side of enterprise.* New York: McGraw-Hill.
Schaefer, M. (1987). *Implementing change in service programs, project planning and management.* Newbury Park, CA: Sage. Chapters 3 and 4 on identifying resources and Chapter 5 on scheduling activities are especially useful for this phase of the planning process.
Winston, S. (1991). *Getting organized* (Rev. ed.). New York: Warner. This is a very basic and general book on personal organization that might be useful for a planner who has a tendency to be scattered in many aspects of personal and professional life.

CHART-DESIGN SOFTWARE (FROM LAUFFER, 1997)

The chart-design software programs listed are relatively easy to use and inexpensive. Many of these products can help planners think through, keep track of, and ultimately assess each aspect of the planning process. Having appropriate charts in a form that can be modified, updated, and retrieved can improve every facet of the planning process.

Prices, manufacturers' addresses, and detailed reviews of the following computer software are found in many popular computer magazines:

1. ViSiO 3 and ViSiO SHAPES (Shapeware Corporation) includes organization charts, flowcharts, network designs, maps, project management software, and useful clip-art. ViSiO 3's project management software creates easy-to-read Gannt charts and simple PERT-style charts. ViSiO SHAPES can help to draw virtually any kind of chart or map. A "connector tool" and other innovations make it easy to locate appropriate types and lengths of connections between shapes.

2. ManagePro (Avantos Performance Systems) is a project management tool that focuses on the people behind the project. Its goal planner section includes such standard tools as Gannt and PERT charts. The People/Team Planner is useful in assigning tasks and relating them to others on the staff. This software demonstrates staff activities graphically.

3. For more comprehensive (and costly) project scheduling and management programs, consider Microsoft Project Version 4 for Windows (Microsoft

Corp.), CA-SuperProject (Computer Associates International), Time Line 6 (Simantec Corp.), Sure Track (Primavera Systems), or Proiect Scheduler 6 for Windows version 1.5 (Scitor Corp).

4. Three popular and inexpensive flowchart programs for Windows include Flow Charting 4, an easy-to-edit program in which you can design your own shapes for specific applications (Paton and Paton); CorelFlowl-2 (Corel Corp.); and ABC Graphics (Micrografx).

5. Useful MacIntosh programs include Microsoft Project 4 for the Mac (see Windows description under Number 3) and TeamFlow 3.1 (CFM Inc.), which focuses on tasks to be performed and people assigned to perform them, including PERT and other planning and tracking systems.

SETTING UP GOVERNING STRUCTURES

Conrad, W. R., Jr., & Glenn, W. E. (1983). *The effective voluntary board of directors.* Athens, OH: Swallow Press. Although directed at members of volunteer boards of nonprofit organizations, this book offers many easy-to-adapt techniques for keeping committee members clear on what their mission is and how they relate to other volunteers and staff. This will be particularly helpful if the program becomes an ongoing organization.

Fram, E. H. (with Brown, V.). (1995). *Policy vs. paper clips: Selling the corporate model to your non-profit board* (2nd ed.). WI: Families International.

Freeman, J. (1972). The tyranny of structurelessness. In A. Koedt, E. Levine, & A. Rapone (Eds.), *Radical feminism* (pp. 285-299). New York: Quadrangle.

O'Connell, B. (1976). *Effective leadership in voluntary organizations: How to make the greatest use of citizen service and influence.* New York: Association Press.

O'Connell, B. (1985). *The board member's book: Making a difference in voluntary organizations.* New York: Foundation Center.

SECURING RESOURCES

Kretzmann, J. P., & McKnight, J. (1993). *Building community from the inside out, a path towards finding and mobilizing a community's assets.* Evanston, IL: Northwestern University, Neighborhood Innovation Network. (Distributed by ACTA Publications, 4848 N. Clark St., Chicago, IL 60640)

Maguire, L. (1983). *Understanding social networks.* Beverly Hills, CA: Sage.

Shore, W. H. (1995). *Revolution of the heart: A new strategy for creating wealth and meaningful change.* New York: Riverhead Books. This book presents an innovative series of ideas on locating sources of funding and other types of human resources for program development from a planner who has started a nationwide network of groups to fight homelessness and hunger.

AIDS TO FUND-RAISING

Brakeley, G. A., Jr. (1993). *Tested ways to successful fund raising.* Printed by University Microfilm International, 300 N. Zeeb Road, Ann Arbor, MI.

Gronbjerg, K. (1993). *Understanding nonprofit funding: Managing revenues in social services and community development organizations.* San Francisco: Jossey-Bass.

Howe, F. (1991). *The board member's guide to fund raising: What every trustee needs to know about raising money.* San Francisco: Jossey-Bass.

Jencks, C. (1987). Who gives to what? In W. W. Powell (Ed.), *The non-profit sector: A research handbook.* New Haven, CT: Yale University Press.

Leibert, E. R., & Sheldon, B. E. (1974). *Handbook of special events for non-profit organizations.* New York: Association Press. This book provides excellent concrete examples of how to use public outreach events to increase the resources of a program. There are many ideas for fund-raising events and useful checklists and samples of forms that aid in every aspect of planning an event. This is a rare find for the novice planner.

Prince, R. A., & File, K. M. (1994). *The seven faces of philanthropy: A new approach to cultivating major donors.* San Francisco, CA: Jossey-Bass.

Shaw, S. C., & Taylor, M. A. (1995). *Reinventing fundraising: Realizing the potential of women's philanthropy.* San Francisco, CA: Jossey-Bass.

WORKING WITH GROUPS AND KEEPING CHANNELS OF COMMUNICATION OPEN

Ephross, P. H., & Vassil, T. V. (1988). *Groups that work.* New York: Columbia University Press.

Fatout, M., & Rose, S. (1995). *Task groups in the social services.* Thousand Oaks, CA: Sage. This is one of the few books in the professional literature that brings to bear social service principles to the organization and conduct of time-limited, focused task groups.

Haines, B., & McKeachie, W. (1982). Cooperative versus competitive discussion methods in teaching introductory psychology. *Journal of Educational Psychology, 58,* 386-390.

Hare, A. P. (1976). *Handbook of small group research* (2nd ed.). New York: Free Press.

Henry, S. (1992). *Group skills in social work, A four-dimensional approach* (2nd ed.). Pacific Grove, CA: Brooks/Cole.

Jorgenson, J. D., Scheier, I. H., & Fautsko, T. F. (1981). *Solving problems in meeting.* Chicago: Nelson-Hall. This is a very basic beginning book for those who have not conducted meetings and need an organizational format to start off with.

Moore, C. (1994). *Group techniques for idea building* (2nd ed.). Thousand Oaks, CA: Sage.

Nelson-Jones, R. (1992). *Group leadership, a training approach.* Pacific Grove, CA: Brooks/Cole.

Seaman, D. F. (1981). *Working effectively with task-oriented groups.* New York: McGraw-Hill. This book provides a quick overview of some of the problems that time-limited, task-oriented groups can encounter and some useful suggestions for getting unstuck.

Tropman, J. E. (1996). *Effective meetings, improving group decision making* (2nd ed.). Thousand Oaks, CA: Sage.

7

ACTING AND REACTING
The Program in Action

Whatever you can do, or dream you can, begin it.
Boldness has genius, power and magic in it.
         —Johann Wolfgang von Goethe

Murphy's Law: Anything that can go wrong, will!
Sullivan's amendment to Murphy's Law: Murphy was an optimist!

Step 4	**Ending an event. Doing immediate follow-ups**
Step 3	**Making in-process adjustments**
Step 2	**Drawing the map and marching orders of the event**
Step 1	**Nurturing and sharing leadership**

The first three quarters of this book has described the multitude of tasks that precede the implementation of a program. Months of collecting data, brainstorming ideas, making choices, and double checking each detail precede the moment when

- The doors of the center finally open and the first program participant enters
- The agency director steps up to the microphone and says "welcome" to the audience at the conference
- The bus doors close and 15 eager teens begin their long-awaited trip

It might seem as if this obsessive attention to detail for such a long time before a program actually happens robs the event of spontaneity and creativity. That is the reverse of what actually occurs, however. In practice, creativity thrives in an atmosphere carefully structured so that the potential of each participant is allowed maximum expression. On the day the program begins, well-orchestrated cooperation will enhance, rather than constrict, each person's initiative. Confusion simply dissipates energy.

By readying all the materials you will need in carefully labeled stacks and reviewing your "to-do" list the night before a program, you can avoid a sleepless night. So, too, can having a person assigned to be in charge of a well thought-out snow or rain cancellation plan. Having committee chairs arrive an hour early at the program site and posting a legible chart describing the days events, an equipment checklist, instructions for volunteers, maps to the rooms, and signs in the hallway can avoid many two-aspirin headaches during a conference.

To see how careful attention to details ensures a smooth-flowing event and leads to client and staff growth, this chapter follows the planning process used by Gardenia, the foster grandparent who has been working at Let Infants and Families Thrive (LIFT) since it first opened its doors.

GARDENIA ORGANIZES AN OVERNIGHT CAMPING TRIP

While brainstorming program goals at the annual staff and board retreat, Gardenia suggested a weekend camping trip for the young mothers. She thought that if it was planned for late in the spring, it could act as an incentive and a release after the stress of final exams. Some of the staff thought it was too labor-intensive an activity. Others felt that these very urban young women had few camping skills and would be uninterested in this activity. More important, all their babies would have to be cared for while they were away. One LIFT board member thought it was far too expensive for the bare-bones recreation budget.

Gardenia, however, persisted. She had grown up on a farm and had wonderful memories of nights spent under the stars camping out with her large family. She argued that in preparing for such a trip, each young woman could practice the systematic planning skills she would need when she was on her own. Its very uniqueness would be a challenge. She promised to spend much of her time working with the residents to raise the money for the trip and prepare for it. Ms. Chu volunteered to spend the weekend of the camping trip at LIFT overseeing the care of the babies.

Finally, Gardenia's enthusiasm convinced everyone to include it in that year's list of special events. Kristen volunteered to go on the trip with Gardenia.

STEP 1: NURTURING AND SHARING LEADERSHIP

A program concept often begins its life as the "child" of one dynamic person's commitment and energy. That person becomes the program catalyst, articulating a vision and gathering in others to form a board or task force to transform the vision into an actual program. Optimally, the leadership role of that initiating planner will evolve as the program moves through each of the phases of the development process. As tasks become more clearly delineated, other planners—staff and clients—should be assuming progressively more responsibility for the completion of tasks. By accomplishing small successes along the way, those who were less involved at the beginning of the process often grow in their skills, confidence, and ownership of the program.

As momentum develops, the coordinator continues to delegate and check on the progress of tasks while consciously providing opportunity for other members to initiate ideas and take on leadership roles. If that central person cannot yield some of his or her control or if the members resist buying into the program's goals and vision, however, the catalyst is likely to become overburdened. From feeling that all the weight rests on his or her shoulders, he or she might become resentful and eventually suffer burnout. Worse still, the program can turn into a narrowly conceived "one-person show," sparsely attended or poorly received by both the other planners and the target group.

This process of leadership rotation or diffusion is just as necessary in a small planning group as it is in a large social agency. If leadership is too fixed and centralized, then only those people in charge really understand the whole picture and how each task fits into it. Leadership tasks and roles should be rotated often enough so that hardening of the bureaucracy cannot set in but not so frequently that the group flounders for lack of expertise. Leadership rotation is a developmental tool for everyone involved in the system. Clear statements of exactly what constitutes successful task completion and an atmosphere that allows failure without shame help this process along. Aldridge, Macy, and Walz (1982) stated,

Perhaps the most important aspect of leadership turnover is that it allows the administrative group to be recycled, to re-experience other roles and functions of the agency. An agency is tightest and experience is greatest when the workforce appreciates the roles of all coworkers and remains connected to the clients being served. (p. 99)

After 3 months of planning, however, there was little evidence of leadership-sharing for the LIFT camping trip. For the first several months, it was Gardenia's enthusiasm and hard work that kept it afloat. She booked the campsite, organized the fund-raising event, and located a van and a driver. The young women at LIFT needed to be prodded to complete each task. This worried Kristen. She was convinced that Gardenia was drifting into "doing for" rather than "doing with" the residents. Therefore, at the next staff meeting, Kristen proposed that the trip be canceled for lack of participant follow-through and enthusiasm. Clearly upset, Gardenia countered that she would work harder to motivate the group members. Then, Ms. Chu jumped into the debate, suggesting that the young women did not need more pep talks. Signs of apathy in a group's planning tasks might be the symptoms, not the causes, of underlying problems. She said that when one perceives widespread apathy, the coordinator should be asking some tough questions about the program. For example,

1. Does the program seem unimportant or less important than other issues or projects on the group's agenda?
2. Do they really want the program but have worries about their ability to pull it off or be comfortable once there?
3. Do they have adequate preparation or the skills necessary for planning or implementing this program?
4. Do they feel a sense of their own power in shaping the program?
5. Are there tensions among members or a lack of communication that is distracting their efforts?
6. Have they had past failures with this kind of planning which have made them overly cautious.
7. Were there a few specific members who did not want to participate, who might be inhibiting other members' energy and interest?
8. Was the potential payoff or reward of this program sufficient to motivate them? (Seaman, 1981, pp. 59-67)

Before making any decision about the future of the trip, the women needed to grapple with these questions. The staff members then did some talking about the guidelines they should follow in choosing any project or program.

Gardenia and Kristen met with the group the next evening. They asked the women to answer a series of questions or come up with suggestions about the trip, first in writing and later to be reported on by Gardenia after examining their slips of paper. Then their opinions would be discussed with the whole group. Therefore, as they sat sprawled around the living room, each woman concentrated on writing down her answers on a short questionnaire that Kristen had prepared. Using this technique, sometimes called a nominal group technique (Lauffer, 1982), brought out much information in a short period of time. It allowed the women to express themselves without being pressured or embarrassed. In a larger group, it might also afford individuals anonymity. In this small society in which everyone knew each other so well, it was unlikely that they would have that protection.

Most of the young women at LIFT House have led lives with little predictability or order. They are used to feeling like passive recipients—life simply happens to them. Therefore, they were surprised and flattered that Gardenia and Kristen were taking their feelings and suggestions seriously. Because of this clear sense that they were being respected, they felt free to express their ambivalence and, in the end, they decided they really did want to go. Therefore, the trip was declared definitely on, and the next several days were a whirlwind of catch-up activity.

Because Gardenia realized that leadership roles must be consciously nurtured, she decided to focus her energies on the following:

- Assessing each member's special skills and interests and then assigning a task or teaching role based on those strengths
- Taking a dry run or walk-through of the activity in advance to decrease insecurity
- Coaching before the event to teach needed skills
- Anticipating potential problems and discussing strategies to deal with them
- Making constant feedback a part of the ongoing process

ASSESSING EACH MEMBER'S SPECIAL SKILLS
AND INTERESTS AND THEN ASSIGNING A TASK
OR LEADERSHIP ROLE BASED ON THOSE STRENGTHS

People are more likely to agree to take on a leadership task when the work to be done is clearly specified and they feel confident that they will have the support they need to accomplish it. Gardenia encouraged the women to articulate their special attributes that could be used in the planning and implementing of the program. When one of them resisted

Table 7.1   Assignment of Tasks for LIFT Camping Weekend (According to the Members' Special Skills)

Cindy had excellent computer skills so she was asked to produce the letters of reservation and reconfirmation and the lists of equipment and groceries. With Paulo's help, she learned to use a graphic program and created attractive banner and flyers for the fund-raiser and thank-you cards for the donors. She was also put in charge of producing the final report.

Marie was the most articulate and most dramatic of the group. Because of her comic flair and singing voice, she was asked to take charge of the evening's activity around the campfire.

Lao, painfully shy and only speaking hesitant English, had an artistic flair. She was asked to do the table setups, take photos, and decorate a gift T-shirt.

Karen, the group's athlete, was assigned to conduct the morning aerobic exercises and organize a Frisbee or softball game.

Carmen, acknowledged to be the diplomatic peacemaker, was put in charge of getting everyone to quiet down at night. She was also the official "double checker" after cleanups were completed. She would chair the feedback sessions on the planning meetings.

Susan was the unanimous choice for chief cook. She took leadership in figuring out and gathering the food and equipment needed for each meal.

---

taking on a particular task because she was too unsure of herself to volunteer, Gardenia led the other residents in an effort to "draft her." Table 7.1 shows how the major roles were divided.

TAKING A DRY RUN OR WALK-THROUGH
OF THE ACTIVITY TO DECREASE INSECURITY

Once everyone had a major assignment, the group needed to brainstorm what specific things had to be done to complete each assignment and how to go about securing what was needed. The women complained that they still did not know enough about the campsite to make intelligent decisions. How big was the refrigerator in the main house? Was there a field large enough for a baseball game? Exactly what were the sleeping arrangements like and was there a place to plug in a hair dryer? Gardenia realized they were right. When she took her family on its first camping trip, it was total chaos because she had not taken the time to prepare them for what they could expect and what was expected of them. From this experience, Gardenia should have remembered the importance of going through a dry run or walk-through before any new activity or program. Regardless of the nature of the facility that will be used—a conference room or a playground—the way a program is conducted will be dictated by the constraints and resources of the facility.

If one plans to use media and has not checked on the location of the outlets or brought along an extension cord, a program can be seriously hampered. Only a foolhardy planner would trust to fate the condition of the oven or the state of repair of a handicapped ramp. If someone on the committee has not seen them firsthand, both are potential program glitches.

Taking a trip to the campsite with two of the women (Carmen and Lao) and talking to the park ranger was the first part of this group's dry run. After Carmen and Lao returned, they showed the others a sketch of the campsite and described the facilities and program options. The women could now replace their suppositions and apprehensions with the following reality:

They would sleep in beds and not on the ground, as some of them had feared.

There would be hot showers and a place to plug in a hair dryer.

There were some young men in a campsite nearby.

The lake was shallow, clean, and inviting.

Having a firsthand account of the site and activities readied them to finalize their equipment list and prepare a blow-by-blow plan for the weekend. They were excited about the idea of a boat ride with the ranger. It did not cost extra and the two nonswimmers in the group would have a way to get into the water. The campgrounds, however, did not provide life vests, so the women added those to their equipment list and decided to try to borrow them from the college outing club.

The women also found out that there was an 11:00 p.m. quiet-time curfew, which put a damper on their plans to stay up all night. Knowing that they were unlikely to want to go to bed that early, they decided to bring decks of cards and, instead of a boom box for their tapes, they would use cassette players with earphones.

WHEN IT IS NOT POSSIBLE TO VISIT THE FACILITY IN ADVANCE OF CONDUCTING A PROGRAM

If it is not possible to visit in advance the site that one will be using, one must brainstorm a long list of questions and, via a phone call or in writing, obtain specific information. When, for example, one is running a trip, conference, or fair, it is critical to have accurate answers to the kinds of questions shown in the boxed text.

Sample of Questions to Ask Before Using a Facility

How accessible is the room or site to public transportation and what is the parking situation?

How large is the facility, is there more than one room or space available. Can someone from the facility send a map of the facility?

What activities are going on simultaneously in the adjacent spaces?

How many and what kind of tables and chairs are there, and how mobile are they?

What kind of stage or platform is there? Does it have sound or projection equipment built in? Can the facility's equipment be used, or will it have to be rented?

Where are the electrical outlets and is there sufficient power for the equipment that will be used?

What kind of handicapped access and facilities are there?

Does the facility allow food to be brought in? Are there any limitations on the type? Is alcohol allowed? Can we sell it? Will we need a permit?

Can we use the refrigerator or stove? How large are they and what condition are they in? Can we have food delivered in advance?

If we are providing child care, is there a space we can use and is there any play equipment we can use?

Will there be a maintenance person available?

Is there a phone and or fax we can use while there? What is the number? What are the limitations?

Who will have the key?

If neither a sneak preview nor an accurate set of answers can be obtained, one might arrange to arrive at the facility far in advance of the time the event is scheduled to begin. Then, one can reorganize the room, change plans, and decide how to deal with any unanticipated shortcomings.

The volunteers who were caring for the LIFT children also had to have a dry run. Each young mother was required to have a 30-minute interview with Ms. Chu and the volunteer who would be caring for her child (even if the volunteer was her child's father).

Gardenia composed a checklist of items regarding the habits, likes, and dislikes of the babies. The checklist structured the interviews, ensuring that each volunteer knew as much as possible about what the baby needed. Sharing this information helped reassure the mothers, some of whom had never spent a night away from their babies. This thorough preparation was also vital for volunteers such as Paulo, who had never been a "weekend parent" to an infant.

COACHING BEFORE THE EVENT TO PRACTICE NEEDED SKILLS

In the 2 weeks before the trip, Gardenia spent time with each of the young women to find out exactly what kind of help each needed. Susan, the woman in charge of the food committee, had written down the menu ideas that had been brainstormed. Now she was unsure of which ones to choose, the quantities needed, and what would fit their very tight budget. Gardenia offered to go with her to a food warehouse to estimate the cost of alternative menus. After that, they met with the chef at a local restaurant who had given classes to low-income women on using economical foods in creative ways.

Finally, they called one of the volunteers who does a lot of camping to find out about the limitations of the cooking equipment they had borrowed. Gardenia showed her how to itemize the lists of food needed for each menu and then insisted that she make the final choice. Taking leadership means taking risks, but always within the limits of good data.

One by one, Gardenia went through the same process with each woman. Although their tasks seemed very simple at first glance, many of these young women came from homes in which there had been scant budgeting and little order. Few had the luxury of being members of clubs or school groups that had planned dances and parties, and none had ever camped. To move from what was familiar to a new challenge, each needed a different amount of support at different moments. That is what coaching is all about—helping people see what the next step is and then holding their hand as they take it.

ANTICIPATING POTENTIAL PROBLEMS AND SUGGESTING STRATEGIES TO DEAL WITH THEM

At one late-night meeting the week before the trip, Kristen and Gardenia brainstormed with the women a list of the types of conflicts or tensions that might arise during the trip. The following is their list of what-ifs or potential problems:

What will we do if someone does not do her job or refuses to help others?

What will we do if anyone brings along pot or beer?

What will we do if Gardenia or Kristen get sick and cannot come?

What will we do if one of the babies gets sick and the mother has to go home?

What will we do if it rains, if we get bored, or if there are too many bugs?

Gardenia and Kristen started the meeting by making it clear that they were not going to assume the role of the policeman or group mother on the camping trip. As staff members, however, they were representing LIFT. The behavior of one member could ruin the trip for everyone else and make it impossible for the next group to return to the campsite. None of these potential problems had simple solutions, but everyone had to give her opinion about how each issue should be handled. One of the situations was role played. Kristen took the role of the camper who would not go to bed at night, did not want to get up in the morning, and was damned if she was going to clean up on her one weekend off. Kristen really got into her role, and there was much hilarity as each young woman tried her hand at improving Kristen's attitude. Although it was a caricature, the role-play did make some points in a very powerful way. Cindy, a LIFT House member, wrote down the possible solutions, several of which seemed very feasible.

By the end of the meeting, Kristen and Gardenia were convinced that the members had begun to make a commitment to the success of the trip.

STEP 2: DRAWING THE MAP AND
MARCHING ORDERS OF THE EVENT

When the date of the trip finally arrived, the planners at LIFT were excited and ready to take off. Now they could begin to see the "payoffs" of all the decisions they had made and the time they had invested leading up to the trip. The planning was hardly over, however. As she prepared still one more list, Kristen pointed out that, "as the date on the right-hand side of the time line gets closer, the divisions of time become smaller and the tasks are more detailed."

Time and task flowcharts at LIFT House are not simply dust collectors decorating a wall. As items are completed, they are checked off and new lists are generated. In March, when Gardenia started organizing the trip, the units on her chart were months. As the date came closer, the units became weeks and then days. The day of the trip and during the whole program, the time units on the time line were collapsed into hours and minutes.

The task and time flowcharts for the camping trip evolved as follows:

1. Tasks to be done during the 4 months before the trip (Table 7.2)
2. Tasks to be done during the 3 weeks before the trip (Table 7.3)
3. Tasks to be done the day the trip leaves (Table 7.4)
4. Tasks to be done each of the hours on the Saturday and Sunday of the trip (Table 7.5)

Table 7.2   1: The Major Tasks to Be Done During the 4 Months Before
the Trip

Staff: Coordinators—Gardenia and Kristen To Be Done By:

Task	March	April	May	June
Book campsite _____ K _____				
Secure van _____ K _____				
Reserve place for bake sale _____ G _____				
Arrange for driver _____ K _____				
Round up equipment _____ G _____				
Organize child care _____ K _____				
Hold bake sale for $ _____ G _____		5/13		
Shop _____ G				
Cook _____ G				
Practice camp skills _____ K _____				
Leave on trip _____ G,K _____			6/16	
Rain date _____			6/23	
Do follow-ups _____ G,K _____				
				End by July 30th

Notice that in the first plan (Table 7.2), each of the leaders took overall responsibility for a task, but as planning progressed the work was more widely dispersed among the group members. Experienced group workers understand that program leadership requires a subtle sense of knowing when to act because the client is not able to and when acting would rob the client of an opportunity to practice an important skill.

PREPARING AN AGENDA FOR AN EVENT

Even after a program has been designed and tasks have been broken down and delegated (Table 7.2, 7.3, and 7.4) many small decisions being still must be made about the allocation of time and responsibility during the actual event (Table 7.5).

To make sensible choices, this group had visited the site and made three follow-up phone calls to the administrator and the park ranger to clarify the parks resources and rules. They understood what options for the program there were at the campsite and the trade-offs of each one. Had one of the mothers not been able to go, had the blackflies been on a rampage, or had the van been late in either direction, they would obviously continue to refine their plan.

Table 7.3   2: Tasks to Be Done During the 3 Weeks Before the Trip

Staff: Gardenia, Kristen, and Ms. Chu

Members: Cindy, Carmen, Lao, Marie, Susan, and Karen
Time frame: May 22-June 16

Tasks:

Done by:	M22-28	M29-J3	J4-9	J10	J11	J12	J13	J14	J15	J16	Coord.:

Campsite details

Reconfirm campsite
Check on key to lodge
Take reserve form
Take map of camp

Travel tasks

Reconfirm van
Reconfirm driver
Get map
Pick up van
Gas up
Load van

Child care arrangements

Reconfirm volunteers
Reconfirm nurse
Complete baby instruction forms
Check baby supplies
Purchase if needed

Finances

Draw check for food
Cash petty cash check for
driver and G

Program supplies

Pick up tents, stove, cooler
Pick up sleeping bags
Buy batteries
First aid kit
Sports equipment
Cellular phone

Food

Make up menu
List of cooking implements
Preshop for prices
Buy staples

Table 7.4   3: Tasks to Be Done the Day the Trip Leaves

Staff: Gardenia, Kristen, Ms. Chu, and Larry (the driver)
Members: Cindy, Carmen, Lao, Marie, Susan, and Karen

6:00 a.m.	Check weather, decide to go or postpone	G, K, & Ca
	If postpone call campsite	G
	Call van driver	G
	Call all child care volunteers	Ch
	Inform mothers if cancel	Ca
If it's a go:		
9:00 a.m.	Leave to pick up perishables	Ka & G
	Remind Larry to pick up van before 3:00 p.m.	G
	Get extra car keys, gas up car, check map	K
2:00 p.m.	Pack coolers	Ka
2-3:00 p.m.	Van arrives	
3:00 p.m.	Pack van Checklist:	G, C, & L
	Sleeping bags	
	Coleman stove	
	Lanterns	
	First aid kit	
	Sports equipment	
	Cooking utensils	
	Paper goods, charcoal	
	Food and coolers	
	Case of soda	
	Cellular phone	
	Campsite reservation	
	Petty cash	
	Camera and film	
	Cassettes and player	
3:00 p.m.	Ms. Chu, Raymond, Paulo, Doris, Enrique, and Eileen meet with mothers for last-minute reports on children. Review mothers' instruction sheets and check child care supplies	all
	Mothers make final decision if they can go on trip	
4:00 p.m.	Residents in lobby with bags	all
4:30 p.m.	Finish loading van	all
5:00 p.m.	VAN LEAVES FOR CAMP WELLMET	
	Kristen leaves in own car, at same time or waits for any latecomers	

Table 7.5   4: The Tasks to Be Done Each Hour on Saturday and Sunday
                   of the Trip

Staff: Gardenia, Kristen, and Larry (the driver)
Members: Cindy, Carmen, Lao, Marie, Susan, and Karen

Friday:

Leave LIFT at 5:00 p.m.		*Coord.*
6:30-7:30 p.m.	Arrive at campsite, check in with Mr. C.	G
Set up tents while still light		L, K, & all
Sandwiches, chips, and hot cocoa for dinner		G & S
Build fire		K
Marshmallow, cocoa, and stories		M
Quiet by ll:00 p.m.		L & C

Saturday:

8:00 a.m.	Set up Coleman stove, put on coffee/tea	K & C
8:00-9:00 a.m.	Breakfast—milk, cereal, juice, bread, p & j tea, and coffee	S & M
9:00 a.m.	Phone call to LIFT	G
9:00-10:00 a.m.	Clean campsite, dishes, etc.	all
10:00 a.m.-12:00 p.m.	Hike to Mt. Greylock with ranger	
Lunch back at campsite—hot soup, tuna sandwiches, chips, & juice		S & L
Free time until 4:00 p.m.	Optional aerobics, softball, & frisbee	Ka
4:00 p.m.	Boat ride on Lake Cochee	
7:00 p.m.	Barbecue at campsite; hamburgers, hot dogs, baked beans, fruit, cookies, & juice	S & Ka
8:00 p.m.	Campfire with marshmallows and stories	M & L
9:00 p.m.	Campsite sing-along	
11:00 p.m.	Quiet down	C & S

Sunday:

8:00 a.m.	Set up Coleman stove, put on coffee/tea	S & L
8:00-9:00 a.m.	Breakfast—milk, cereal, juice, bread, p & j tea, and coffee	S & L
9:00-10:00 am	Clean up camp site	
10:00 a.m.	Ride to church with Kristen	K
	Call Larry to wake him up,	G
	make sure he has van,	

Table 7.5   Continued

10:00 a.m.-12:00 p.m.	Free time—optional aerobics, sports, etc.	Ka
1:00 p.m.	Lunch—sandwiches, cold cuts, chips, cookies, & juice	S & C
Close down campsite		K in charge
2:30 p.m.	Load van	All; Larry in charge
3:00 p.m.	Leave for home	
Pick up ice cream along the way to have sundae party for volunteers		G & M
4:00-4:30 p.m.	Arrive at LIFT	
Van gets returned—with full tank of gas—leave keys with night watchman		Larry
	Drive Larry home	K
Perishable food unpacked		all; S in charge
Sleeping bags and tents put in front hall		L

STEP 3: MAKING IN-PROCESS CHANGES

When one examines the scheduling shown in Table 7.5, it appears incredibly rigid for a leisure-time activity. Of course, the initial choices of activity and schedule are only educated estimates of the participant's interest and attention span and the activities' saliency and engagement. At a workshop or conference, it often turns out that the speaker needs much more time than has been allotted or the audience is clearly restless. Like the captain of a ship, the planner watches which way the wind is blowing and tries to make small midcourse adjustments wherever possible. Some activities or tasks can be quickly reorganized according to the mood of the participants and unforeseen events. Other events have no latitude. In every schedule, there are *absolutes*—time frames that must be closely adhered to—and *optionals* that can more easily be adjusted. It is important to recognize the differences between the two, making adjustments where possible and simply accepting the inevitable when there is no room to maneuver.

ABSOLUTES

Absolutes are activities and time frames to which an agenda must adhere. If an engaging speaker is given more time or a disastrously boring panel is shortened, like dominos leaning against each other these schedule changes might bump every other event in the day off schedule. Thus, an in-process shift might irritate the kitchen help, the maintenance crew, and every other activity leader and participant.

Absolutes can also be those activities that are part of the rules or requirements of the host organization or of a cooperating agency. In some cases, one might be penalized for a last-minute shift in the program. On the LIFT camping trip, for example, the times for the departure and the return to LIFT had to be absolutes. Because the van was borrowed from the owner of a local flower shop who needed it back at a specific time for his business, it had to be returned promptly. If a rented van is returned late, for example, it can incur an overtime charge that someone—often the staff—has to pay.

After the LIFT women decided to include the boat ride and hike with the ranger in their agenda, they were locked into time slots. The curfew of the campgrounds also locked them into a time when their campfire had to end. They were still stewing about a curfew on their big night out, but that was, as Gardenia pointed out, "the way it had to be." It was a trade-off they had to make.

Similarly, the volunteers who had committed themselves to taking care of the babies had to arrive at LIFT House before the mothers could leave for the weekend. Conversely, the mothers had to return at the time they promised so that the volunteers, who graciously gave up their weekend, could return to their families and social plans. If a promise to a volunteer is broken or a donor is treated with a cavalier attitude, one risks getting turned down the next time one asks for help.

These young women will need to adhere to tight time schedules when they enroll their children in a day care program or go to the clinic for a doctor's appointment. Although they are apt to fight against these limits, if they do not meet their commitments, they might be penalized as neglectful parents. Gardenia used the discussion about the time schedule to underscore this point.

The sensitive planner tries to build a schedule that incorporates activities that need to stick to a prescribed schedule both with less structured periods when individual proclivities can set the pace.

OPTIONALS

Optionals are those items on an agenda that have built-in flexibility. If on the trip the women attend the campwide sing, for example, and are clearly bored, there is no point in prolonging the misery. They can quietly slip away.

Those who want to stay can do so. If on Sunday morning the impulse to go to church has dissipated, then the young women can sleep in a little longer. The cooking committee, for example, cannot simply decide to skip a meal, but members are free to make last-minute changes in the menu within the constraints of what they have brought with them or can find locally.

Whenever one plans any event, one needs to build in optional time for participants to unwind, reflect, and relate to each other in their personal way. Many conferences, for example, schedule informal roundtable talks. These are the times for participants to caucus or simply trade war stories with others who share a special interest. There may also be times to seek out and share coffee with friends. Even a 2-hour meeting should have a small portion of time set aside for members to catch up with each other. This can often be done by planning a refreshment break during the meeting or having refreshments set out before the meeting begins so those who want to chat informally can come early. For some wisdom on pacing seminars and workshops, see a useful book by Robert Jolles (1993).

THE QUICK RETRIEVAL

Although the planner strives for predictability, he or she is a flexible person with the capacity to make the quick retrieval. When the unexpected happens—for example, the speaker does not show up or the sound system stops working—the planner needs to make the proverbial lemonade out of the lemons he or she has been handed.

For example, whenever a planner has invited speakers who are un-known quantities—generally a risky business—the planner must try to minimize disaster by sending them guidelines in advance to gear their talk. By collecting written questions from the audience during a break or in advance of a presentation, the planner might help the speaker stay focused on the interests of the audience. If during the question time, none are forthcoming, the planning committee members jump into the vacuum with a few questions they have in reserve.

When we take a group to a place that we know very little about, we might discuss in advance the possible need for a fast retreat. Sometimes, we can shift to a more engaging activity that we had not anticipated. At one of the LIFT fund-raising dinners, for example, the singing group that had promised to entertain was sidetracked by an outbreak of the flu. Their disorganized manager misplaced the phone number of the hall that LIFT had rented. As the clock kept ticking and the tables were cleared, it became apparent that the stars of the event were among the missing. The evening was saved by a board member who took over the microphone and hosted a spontaneous amateur hour of such ineptness and hilarity that members of the audience still remember it fondly. Sometimes, these "fast saves" turn out to be serendipitous gifts. Although no one would wish them to happen, those unanticipated rainy-day programs can be memorial events that bring out our finest moments of creativity and humor.

DAMAGE CONTROL

Of course, no matter how creative one is at the fast retrieval, disasters might still happen that really cannot be turned around. For example, perhaps the van had broken down on the way back from the camping trip or a baby had taken ill and her mother had to rush back to LIFT House.

From her years of raising a large family, Gardenia has become proficient in damage control. Now, her skills have been enhanced by the acquisition of the cellular phone she brought along. If the van had broken down and could not be returned on time, an abject apology and progress reports from the garage might have helped to mollify the flower store manager. A call to the house would have warned the volunteers that the mothers would be late. No one would be happy about it, but they could at least adjust their own plans with family and friends.

If the planner has had a track record in the past of being scrupulous about keeping commitments, most disasters will probably be forgiven. Each disaster can become the base on which one then builds more creative backup plans in the future.

SWITCHING LEADERSHIP STYLES DURING AN EVENT

Years of group dynamics research in laboratory studies suggest that a democratic or participatory style of group leadership is most productive. That is certainly what Kristen was assuming when she raised her concerns about Gardenia taking on too much leadership. There are times, however, when the other two styles of leadership, laissez-faire leadership and autocratic leadership, are actually more appropriate to the demands of the particular situation.

For example, had there been a downpour, a forest fire, or a life-threatening bee sting during the camping trip, it would have been inappropriate for Gardenia to use a participatory democratic leadership style. Those crises demand a more authoritative style. Gardenia would more likely have told the women what immediate steps needed to be taken and who should do what. A crisis situation calls for clear, centralized leadership.

If a speaker or a caterer does not show up, if the video camera does not work, or if a developmentally delayed client is acting out, the coordinator of that segment of the program must decide what to do and everyone else should, in all but the most extreme cases, go along with that decision. Later, when the dust settles, the other members of the committee can debate the correctness of the actions taken. When the emergency has passed, members should return to participatory decision making.

The ability to shift leadership styles to match events in the environment is called situational leadership. There is significant research that indicates that this type of leadership has great value for the long-term survival of a program (Hare, 1976).

Using a laissez-faire leadership style in which the organizer allows participants in a group to succeed or fail solely on their own initiative so that they may learn from the results of their actions, can sometimes be the appropriate choice. It is, however, difficult to decide when to use it. The LIFT staff members have many protracted debates trying to decide how actively they should intervene when they believe one of the mothers is about to make an inappropriate or self-defeating decision. Although failure can be an excellent learning opportunity, it can also shatter fragile self-confidence. It is particularly a problem when one's actions could have a negative impact on others. With the mothers from LIFT House, each act they take has ramifications for the lives of their infant children. The LIFT staff members are convinced that a laissez-faire leadership style should be used only after much soul-searching consultation. The staff members believe that LIFT House members should be warned in advance that both their successes and their failures will be solely their own responsibility.

STEP 4: ENDING AN EVENT AND PERFORMING IMMEDIATE FOLLOW-UPS

Just as one tries to visualize the opening setting of a program, so too should one try to sketch a mental picture of a program's ending. Terminations can often color an entire event, influencing the way participants will judge its overall effectiveness. A program must officially end with a bang rather than petered out with a whimper! Nothing dampens the spirits of the exhausted organizers more than watching their audience drift off, one person at a time, before the program is officially over. If the scheduling of the event is set within realistic time limits, if it is consonant with the attention span of most of the participants, and if it engages the participants' interest, there is less likelihood that this will happen. If it does occur, it is a message that one needs to fine-tune the pacing next time.

Some groups create their own ritualized closing procedure for ending a meeting or event. Ten minutes before the time the event is to end, perhaps everyone joins hands for a prayer or friendship circle, evaluates what has transpired, or reviews the details of their next encounter. Other groups, such as the Boy and Girl Scouts and specialized support groups such as Alcoholics Anonymous, use a prepackaged closing ceremony, perhaps adding their own variations.

No matter which format is chosen, closure activities might include the following:

- Some form of public acknowledgment or appreciation of those who have worked on this program or made some type of other significant contribution.
- A brief time for participants to raise further questions or give brief immediate feedback to the organizers and each other.
- A wrap-up talk or summation given by an especially engaging speaker who reviews what has transpired and looks to future programs or tasks.
- A recognition that ending an especially successful or emotionally involving program can be painful for some or all of the participants. Members may need some time to grieve the ending or let go of each other in a way that looks to the future (Garland, Jones, & Kolodney, 1973; Wayne & Avery, 1979).
- Choosing of the schedule and content for a follow-up session or some other related event and the soliciting of participants to form new committees or work groups.
- A mutually agreed on plan stating who will dispose of equipment and return the facility to its prior state, deposit money, clean up if necessary, wait until the last participant leaves, and contribute to whatever final paperwork or accounting is necessary. People will usually agree to stay through the aftermath of a program but will become resentful if they are left "holding the bag"

ENDING THE LIFT CAMPING TRIP

LIFT has a tradition of giving innovative presents to its friends and members when they leave the house or do something out of the ordinary. People vie with each other to come up with original presents. Gardenia's camping trip was no exception. Before they left the campsite, the residents presented a bright red T-shirt to Gardenia. Lao had used her skills in calligraphy to print "I'm not getting older, I'm getting tougher" across the back. Each of the women signed her name on the shirt with a textile marker.

Kristen then surprised the campers by presenting each one with a shirt that read, "I survived the LIFT camping trip." The shirts had been an unexpected gift from Ms. Chu on behalf of the board members. Kristen had decided to save them and end the weekend with a flourish. After the thank-yous had been said, the women began packing, cleaning up, and loading the van, goaded on by Carmen, the diplomatic straw boss.

In the van on the way home, Gardenia reviewed the list of immediate follow-up steps that the women had composed before they left. Some tasks, such as washing out the equipment, unpacking the leftover food, and airing the sleeping bags, had to be done that night. The van had to be filled with gas and returned. No matter how much they moaned about sore feet and wanting to be with their children or promised to do it all in the morning, Gardenia held firm. They would meet in the LIFT common room at 9:00 p.m. to do the essential closing up tasks.

They returned to LIFT House at the end of their weekend, only 30 minutes late, with all the equipment they had taken and with no mishaps worse than sunburn, hoarse throats, and a very weary volunteer. Their reunion with the babies was noisy and cheerful. The ice cream they had brought for the volunteers was received with pleasure by the exhausted weekend parents.

Kristen had warned Gardenia that one can lose momentum when an event is over and the participants are basking in the glow of their achievements or licking their wounds about their disappointments.

Gardenia resisted her impulse to take care of the final details herself, although it would have been easier for her in the long run. She knew that developing the patience and persistence to follow through on a plan is a skill each young mother would need when she strikes out on her own. She reminded them that Sunday was the last day of this camping trip, but it was the first day of the next one.

After Larry and Kristen returned the van and the mothers put their little ones to bed, everyone reassembled in the living room to begin the tasks that needed immediate attention and begin thinking about the longer range follow-ups that are described in Chapter 8.

THE 5-MINUTE RECAP

- The largest part of this book has described the data collecting, brainstorming, and list making that precedes the moment when a program begins. This is similar to how planning time should be allocated when actually creating a program.
- The obsessive attention to preparation might appear to risk robbing the program of spontaneity. Preparation, however, enhances the potential for cooperation, creativity, initiative, and satisfaction.

- To understand how the attention to detail facilitates a smooth-flowing event, we follow the work of Gardenia, the foster grandparent at LIFT House, as she prepares to leave and triumphantly returns from a camping trip with the young mothers.

- Although a program is frequently initiated by the energy and commitment of a central person, during the planning process leadership should evolve until it is shared among all the group members.

- Although group members might be hesitant to take on leadership roles at the beginning, small successes can build their self-confidence and skills.

- In Gardenia's project, this was not happening. There were continuing signs of member apathy, so several hard questions about its goals and its method of organization had to be asked and answered.

- Gardenia had not realized that the leadership skills of each member must be consciously nurtured by the following:

    Assessing each member's special skills

    Taking a dry run through the activity to increase confidence

    Coaching to teach skills needed for the project

    Anticipating and discussing potential problems and strategies to handle them

    Making constant feedback a part of the ongoing process

- After a frank discussion, both LIFT members and staff were convinced that the program was still desirable and feasible.

- With renewed energy, tasks were articulated and then delegated to the mothers according to the special skills and interests of each of them.

- Members composed a list of their questions about the site and a few visited it in advance to seek answers. If a visit had not been possible, a letter or phone call could have secured the information they needed to prepare for the trip.

- At meetings before the event, the leader and members asked "what-if" questions to prepare themselves to deal with conflicts or crises that might occur.

- As the date of the event drew near, new task and time charts were created with greater specificity and progressively smaller units of time.

- Initial charts covered a period of several months, whereas later ones covered periods of several weeks and days. The final chart divided up the minutes within a single day during the trip. This became a working agenda for the event itself.

- An agenda for an event is an educated guess about the time needed for each component. Sometimes, the time allotted can be readjusted to meet the demands of the moment because the component is *optional*.

- Other components of a program cannot be readjusted. By their nature, they leave no room for adjustment. These are called *absolutes*.

- Like dominoes, many absolute program components depend on the completion of the previous components; thus, a change in one could reverberate negatively throughout the day.
- Although striving for predictability and attempting to anticipate problems, the planner must be flexible enough to make a quick retrieval or do damage control when a totally unexpected situation threatens the successful outcome of a program.
- Usually, participatory leadership is the most productive of group cohesion and involvement, but crises often demand a shift from participatory to a more directive style of leadership.
- The termination of an event includes the following:

    Acknowledgments and appreciations

    Wrap-up or summary when appropriate

    Strategies to work through the negative as well as positive emotional impact that endings can have on planners and participants

    The setting of a schedule of follow-up events

    A plan for returning the facility and equipment to their preprogram state

    Reflections on longer range projects suggested by the event

PUTTING THEORY INTO PRACTICE

EXERCISE 1: PATTERNS OF LEADERSHIP AND METHODS OF ROTATION

Choose one agency or nonprofit group and study the shape and history of its leadership patterns. If you are on a college campus, the group you choose to study might be a student council, environmental action group, fraternity, sorority, an academic department, and so on. If you choose a community group to study, it can be any small-scale association or social agency, such as a community residence, a gardening club, or neighborhood association.

Ask to interview a person whose position of formal authority is near the top in the group so that he or she knows about its history and inner workings. This person might be a staff coordinator or president. Optimally, the respondent should have been with the group at least 2 years and be in a position to make decisions about the group's activities and work plan.

Create a list of questions for the interview that will help you to understand and record how decisions are usually made in this group and the ways in which members are oriented to their leadership roles. To help you begin your list, the boxed text provides some suggested questions.

After asking a question, it is useful to ask for an example that might illustrate a statement that the interviewee has made.

Sample questions:

What are the formal leadership positions in this group and who reports to whom?

How do positions usually get filled (hired by board, appointed, or elected; if so, by whom)?

How long do incumbents fill these positions and how is turnover achieved? How content are you with the amount and quality of rotation of leadership roles?

Does the group have job descriptions for each leadership role? Are they written? To what extent are members aware of them?

How are members prepared to take on leadership positions? Are there any training sessions? Do former leaders train their replacements?

How are new members brought into the group and what methods are used to encourage feedback and leadership from them?

EXERCISE 2: DRAWING THE MAP AND
MARCHING ORDERS OF AN EVENT

You work for an afterschool recreation center and have been assigned the task of coordinating Halloween activities for young teenagers. After discussions with the members of the teen youth council, the members decided that they would

conduct a Saturday workshop with the younger children in which they would be helped to make their own costumes;

organize games and serve traditional refreshments of donuts and cider on the day of Halloween to both the youngsters and the teens;

have the teenagers take the youngsters trick-or-treating in small groups around the neighborhood to show off their costumes and raise money for the United Nations International Children's Emergency Fund (UNICEF)

have a dance for the teen volunteers after the youngsters have been escorted to their homes.

Begin by brainstorming a list of tasks that will be needed for each of the four components of this total program: the pre-Halloween workshop, games and refreshments, trick or treating, and the teen dance.

For each of the components, create the following four task-time flow-charts that list each unit of work to be done in the left-hand margin and the time frames for their completion across the top of the page (a few sample tasks include booking of space, sending home and obtaining signed parental permission slips for the youngsters, writing for UNICEF materials, etc.):

> Task-time line 1 should cover major tasks to be done 3 months before the event.
>
> Task-time line 2 should cover tasks to be done 1 month before the event.
>
> Task-time line 3 should cover the period of 1 week before the event.
>
> Task-time line 4 should be the time line for the day of the event, beginning a few hours before the event starts and ending at least an hour after it is officially over.

EXERCISE 3: TERMINATING AN EVENT

Think about how the first three components of the Halloween program could be ended on a positive note. Design a closing activity for the youngsters and teens that might last for 10 minutes before the children are escorted home.

Create a list of the immediate follow-up tasks that you would require from the teenage planners when the Halloween program has ended.

EXERCISE 4: DAMAGE CONTROL

If it rains so heavily on Halloween day that trick or treating will not be possible, what might you do as a backup activity? Describe three alternative activities you could have planned in the event that this small disaster might occur.

What might you do in advance to ensure that no child wanders off during trick or treating? In case a child does wander off from the group, what might you do?

CITATIONS AND SUGGESTIONS
FOR FURTHER READING

Aldridge, T., Macy, H., & Walz, T. (1982). *Beyond management: Humanizing the administrative process.* Iowa City: University of Iowa Press. This provides a still-relevant antidote to many of the business-oriented management systems now designed for health and human service agencies.

Hare, A. P. (1976). *Handbook of small group research* (2nd ed.). New York: Free Press. This book describes much of the pioneering work on the theory and practice of communication and productivity in small groups.

NURTURING PARTICIPATION AND LEADERSHIP

An essential element in nurturing leadership is conducting a participatory meeting that facilitates communication and shared decision making. The following sources discuss many of the necessary skills.

Duffy, T. K. (1995). The check-in and the go-rounds in group work: Guidelines for use. In L. Schulman (Ed.) (with Boston University School of Social Work Group Work Faculty), *Readings in differential social work practice with groups.* New York: American Heritage.

Garland, J. A., Jones, H., & Kolodney, R. (1973). A model for stages of development in social work groups. In S. Bernstein (Ed.), *Explorations in group work.* Boston: Milford House.

Jolles, R. L. (1993). *How to run seminars & workshops, presentation skills for consultants, trainers & teachers.* New York: John Wiley.

Jorgenson, J. D., Scheier, I. H., & Fautsko, T. F. (1995). *Solving problems in meetings.* Chicago: Bowker.

Seaman, D. F. (1981). *Working effectively with task-oriented groups.* New York: McGraw-Hill.

Tropman, J. E. (1980). *Effective meetings, improving group decision making.* Beverly Hills, CA: Sage.

Ulshak, F. L., Nathanson, L., & Gillan, P. G. (1981). *Small group problem solving: An aid to organizational effectiveness.* Reading, MA: Addison-Wesley.

Wayne, J., & Avery, N. (1979, January). Activities for group termination. *Social Work, 24*(1), 58-62.

8

FOLLOW-UPS AND EVALUATIONS
Closing O-ne Program Loop and Opening up the Next

The reward of a thing well done is to have done it.

—Ralph Waldo Emerson

Life is lived forward, but understood backward.

—Søren Kierkegaard

Experience is the name everyone gives to their mistakes.

—Oscar Wilde

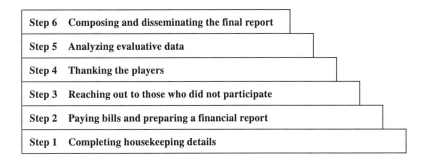

Step 6	**Composing and disseminating the final report**
Step 5	**Analyzing evaluative data**
Step 4	**Thanking the players**
Step 3	**Reaching out to those who did not participate**
Step 2	**Paying bills and preparing a financial report**
Step 1	**Completing housekeeping details**

Many planners draw their task and time flowcharts so that they end on the day of the big event. Some add a few days for the debriefing, during which they can share reactions. Then the dust settles, the desire to rehash the program dissipates, and they turn their attention to the next activity or go on a well-earned vacation. Many tasks remain, however. The official "end" of an event cannot be declared until several weeks, perhaps months, after the event.

Every event has its unique follow-up tasks, but most fall into one of the six steps in Figure 8.1. Although listed in a ladder formation, many of these tasks are likely to be occurring concurrently.

KRISTEN COMPLETES A SERIES
OF PARENTING SKILLS CLASSES

For the reader to see how these follow-up activities appear in the real world of small-scale planning, I will follow Kristen as she completes her first cycle of parenting skills classes. The 8-week, 2-hour classes were held in a conference room of a nearby general hospital. Twenty parents were enrolled. The classes were open to Let Infants and Families Thrive (LIFT) mothers and fathers as well as to new parents from the local community. The classes were free, and the small program expenses were paid for by a grant from The Right Start Foundation, which funds activities that enhance family life.

Kristen wrote the proposal to obtain the grant in collaboration with a nurse practitioner from the hospital. The parenting sessions, taught with much discussion and hands-on exercises, included the following topics:

- Infant exercise and nutrition
- Responses to medical emergencies
- CPR and first aid training
- The developmental stages of the first year of life
- Discipline and behavior management techniques
- Time management and stress reduction for new parents

Each parent was given a variety of pamphlets and videos on issues of infant care as well as a kit that included basic emergency, nonprescription medications.

Combining education as well as the opportunity for group support, each class included a time for the parents to discuss issues that were not on the agenda. Members were encouraged to stay for refreshments and 30 minutes of informal conversation after the meetings. Each participant who completed the course was awarded a certificate and was invited to choose one toy from a catalog of educational baby toys. A local TV talk show host presented the certificates at the graduation and gave a short, comical talk about the ups and downs of her first year of parenting.

During the enrollment interviews, the participants were asked what two or three topics they especially hoped would be discussed in the course. They also completed a short questionnaire about their knowledge and attitudes toward several areas of infant health and parenting roles. During the last class, they were asked to reflect on how well the initial topics they suggested had been covered, and they completed the questionnaire for a second time. They also spent 30 minutes in three small groups discussing and rating each of the units of the course. These verbal interchanges were taped by the group leaders with the participants' permission.

When Kristen recruited the nurse practitioner to co-lead the group sessions, she promised to take full responsibility for the details of program administration. Therefore, Kristen, with help from the hospital social worker, recruited and interviewed prospective participants, booked the guest speakers, obtained the audiovisual equipment, and purchased the books and toys to be used. She also completed all the necessary paperwork. Because the series of classes had ended, Kristen was in charge of all the follow-up details.

STEP 1: COMPLETING
HOUSEKEEPING DETAILS

Although it seems obvious, Kristen had forgotten how much time and thought went into the mundane acts of housekeeping at the end of a program. Surprisingly, many planners diminish the impact of an otherwise successful event by relaxing their attention to details too soon after the program ends. This is the time, however, when the planners most need to carefully implement a set of tasks that restore the facility to the same, or even better, condition than it was at the beginning of the program. This is the time when the equipment that has been used (especially those items that were borrowed) is examined and returned promptly to its source.

With the parenting program, this was a particularly critical set of tasks. When she first proposed the idea of the classes at the hospital, Kristen had requested permission to use the doctors' conference room for the eight sessions. This room was quite elaborately furnished and very formal, with chairs arranged in straight rows facing a lectern and head table. It was the only space in the hospital, however, that was private and lent itself to rearranging the chairs into the informal circle she visualized. It also had cabinets that could be used for storage of her materials so she would not have to carry the books and other teaching tools with her each week. She soon discovered, however, that the hospital ground's director was very hesitant. He worried about having an outsider use this facility because he would be held accountable for its condition. After much cajoling, he finally gave her permission to use it and to store her handouts and posters in one of the cabinets that lined the walls. He also reluctantly agreed to permit her to bring refreshments to each class. He would not budge, however, on the issue of allowing her to have full-scale refreshments on the evening of the graduation because his staff would not have time to clean the room before the doctors used it early the next morning. She let the issue drop, resolving to convince him that she was trustworthy before renewing her request.

On the first night of the class, before she rearranged the chairs into a large circle, she drew a quick sketch of how they were initially positioned so that each week at the end of the class, the participants could replace them exactly as they had been.

After four sessions of monitoring every detail of the nightly cleanup, she returned to the ground's director and asked again about having a light supper at the graduation reception. This time, she pried from him a reluctant permission. Therefore, after the graduation reception ended and the participants and guests left, Kristen and two of the parents from LIFT stayed behind and removed every trace of the reception. They had carefully hung and carefully removed the LIFT banner and their poster board collages of the babies and parents that had made the room look appropriately festive. They emptied the wall cabinet of the papers, markers, catalogs, and posters that had accumulated during the 2 months of the program. Then, Kristen retraced her footsteps down the hall and out the front door to remove the handwritten signs with arrows that she had taped up in the corridors to ensure that the guests could find the class graduation ceremonies.

After years of running programs, Kristen had learned through some painful experiences that the final cleanup should be double checked by the person in charge of the event. Given the maintenance supervisor's obvious lack of enthusiasm, Kristen knew that she had no latitude for even the slightest sign of sloppiness. If he had gotten any complaints about the state of the room from the doctors who met there, he would quite understandably have refused her request for the next set of classes.

For the graduation reception, Kristen had borrowed a camcorder so there would be a visual souvenir of the wonderful event. When she arrived home that night, she made certain that the equipment was working just as it had been when she borrowed it. If anything had been wrong with it, she planned to bring it to a repair shop on her way into work the next morning. Gardenia had gone through similar steps the night the mothers returned from the camping trip. She had immediately made sure that the van and borrowed sleeping bags were in the same condition as they were before the trip.

As the program supervisors, Kristen and Gardenia were aware that the buck stopped with them and any goof-ups redounded badly on their competence as professionals.

STEP 2: PAYING BILLS AND PREPARING A FINANCIAL REPORT

No matter what project they work on, the staff members at LIFT are self-conscious about the way they spend and account for program funds. As members of a nonprofit organization, the board members remind them constantly that they are always accountable and always in the public's eye. Whether funded through a foundation grant, government program, or the donations of private citizens, they can be monitored at any time. Because of the current period of retreat from social program funding, the pressure to spend every penny wisely and responsibly has escalated. Any implication that they are benefiting themselves or squandering funds jeopardizes their already shaky financial support.

LIFT has gone through a legal process to incorporate as a 501(c)(3) agency. This special status exempts it from paying state and local taxes. Most important, its status as a nonprofit organization allows contributors a deduction on their taxes for any money or equipment they donate to LIFT. Thus, LIFT can get more for the money it spends and can attract more private contributions, helping the agency to be less dependent on grant income (Upshur, 1982, pp. 5-8).

EVERY EXPENSE MUST BE
RECORDED AND ACCOUNTED FOR

When Kristen planned the closing ceremony for the parenting classes, she worked with five volunteers from the parenting class, all of whom were responsible for different tasks, such as preparing refreshments or buying film, decorations, books, and certificates. She tried to get each of the committee members to anticipate their needs before they purchased supplies so that she or Ms. Chu could issue a check, or she asked the vendors to bill LIFT so the accountant could send the payment. Checks make the best permanent record of moneys expended.

Inevitably, however, Kristen still needs to use cash, and cash expenses are the hardest to keep track of. Despite the best anticipatory planning, there is always a need for small outlays of funds—for example, an occasional cab fare or a last-minute container of milk. When these purchases are made, she reiterates the urgent need for people to bring back a receipt. Although LIFT staff are always given a small sum of petty cash funds to use the day of a program, they frequently find themselves having to use their own money for expenses. They run the risk of not getting reimbursed for these small purchases if they do not compulsively collect receipts. There is no way the bookkeeper can keep track of what has already been spent and what remains unless staff adhere to this rule. There is a tendency for both staff and volunteers to let small out-of-pocket expenses slip by unreimbursed. They view this as their contribution to the program. Although this is well-intentioned, it is a disservice. It leads the residents to think the program has funds which it may not actually have on any other occasion. It also makes it almost impossible to estimate what a program has actually cost for budgeting purposes. It would be much more useful if anyone who wanted to contribute did so directly to the program or contributed at a LIFT fund-raiser so that the income and expenditures can be tracked.

WHEN THE MONEY SPENT IS MORE
THAN THE MONEY ALLOCATED

When all the receipts were located and the last of the bills from vendors paid, Kristen made up her final financial accounting on the classes. For this program, the final accounting was relatively simple. There were a minimum of out-of-pocket purchases and, because of the nature of the activity, there were few unforeseen expenses. For several programs she had organized in the past, however, even before the financial wrap-up was completed, she realized that the figure in the outgo column was larger than the figure in the income column. The shortfall occurred because of any one of the following reasons:

- The initial prediction of expenses was unrealistically low.
- The money or donations that were expected never materialized.
- There was an abundance of unanticipated or emergency expenses.
- There was a lack of communication among the planners.

- There was inconsistent recording of financial commitments as the program occurred, so no one realized they needed to reassess the expenditures (Howe, 1991).

The financial accounting achieved two purposes. First, it alerted Kristen to the reality that she needed to find an additional source of funds to finish paying off the debts that the program had incurred. Second, an analysis of the reasons for the shortfall helped her to propose changes in the way the program should be planned or implemented if it were to be repeated.

STEP 3: REACHING OUT TO THOSE WHO DID NOT PARTICIPATE

When analyzing the effect of a program immediately after it is finished, planners often focus much of their attention—and sometimes their intense disappointment—on "the ones that got away." They are the people who were targeted for the service but did not come, those who committed themselves to being there but never did show up, or those who came a few times but did not return. Inevitably, and understandably, most programs experience some amount of fall out of attendees. To planners, the program they are presenting takes center stage in their lives, but it is simply one of a series of competing demands on someone else's time or interest.

When the program has been especially well received and smoothly run, inadequate attendance is particularly frustrating to the planners, especially when they too are volunteers. After the emotional dust settles, however, they can be helped to realize that by analyzing the reasons people do not come they can also learn information that might reshape and improve their next attempt at mounting a similar program.

In addition to learning what barriers might have existed that planners did not account for, they also keep trying to reach out to the target audience, if not with one particular program then perhaps in some other way. Therefore, the following list presents follow-up tasks for nonattendees:

- A phone or mail survey to find out what barriers stood in the way of their participation
- Sending out minutes or material they missed with a note that brings closure to the program
- Inviting them to another program or discussing with them other ways to reach the initial goals if applicable

When the program a planner is analyzing is one aimed at large numbers of attendees—perhaps a conference or a mass rally—the planner cannot realistically call everyone who did not attend. The planner can, however, target a few people who had indicated interest to get a sampling of their reasons for not attending.

Regarding the parenting classes, there was a small, defined population that made it relatively simple to perform a nonattendee follow-up. When Kristen returned to her office the day after the graduation ceremony, she examined the list to see who had either dropped out early on or had not shown up for the "graduation." Her plan of action was to call them and tell them that she had missed them without making them feel guilty or defensive. Two couples and one single parent fell into that category. After her phone call to the first couple, she decided that their daily lives were just too hectic to take the time for so many classes. Both sounded interested, so she said she would send them written materials on the program and inform them when the next classes were organized. She made a note to think about having a shortened series of classes for one cycle.

The husband in the second couple indicated that his wife did not feel she understood enough of what was being said because her native language was Creole (she had recently immigrated from Haiti). Kristen made a note to give more thought next time to translating the written materials into Creole and perhaps having at least one or two sessions in Creole. Perhaps she could conduct a separate class session in the Vietnamese language. There was a steadily growing population from both those countries in the hospital caseload. She thought the foundation grant's officer would be empathetic to their special situation and would be likely to grant additional funds.

After the phone conversation with the single mother, Kristen still did not understand why the woman had not come to the graduation, especially because the woman had been a faithful participant until the last session. The woman seemed preoccupied and did not want to talk. Kristen wished her well and promised to mail her certificate of completion. She also said that if at any time the woman just wanted to talk, she should feel free to call Kristen at LIFT House.

Kristen decided not to phone the hospital administrators who, although invited, had not appeared. She felt that her call might be interpreted as putting undue pressure on these busy people. She did, however, write them to say that she had missed them and understood that they were undoubtedly busy with hospital duties, and she enclosed their certificates of appreciation.

STEP 4: THANKING THE PLAYERS

It is an absolute rule of thumb in planning that you cannot thank too many people too many times. Although most people who help in the development or implementation of a program do not do so to garner gratitude, they will notice when their help is taken for granted for too long. Although you might never return to ask them for their services or resources again, the next planner who does may get a negative reaction and wonder why. Because social service agencies rarely have all the funds they need to do the things they want to, it is likely that most people who control resources will be asked over and over again for help.

Early in the development and implementation of the parenting classes, Kristen started keeping a database on her computer of everyone she met along the way who had contributed their wit, wisdom, or concrete assets to the parenting classes. It was an extensive list that included the professionals from whom she obtained materials, speakers, secretaries, maintenance workers, and the merchants who had donated their services or goods.

A few weeks before the course was completed, Kristen asked Lao to use her computer graphics skills to design a personalized thank-you card. Kristen let Lao choose the type style and layout, but she asked her to incorporate a photograph of the collage of the babies into the design. Kristen is convinced that the thank-you note created for each program should reflect in words and pictures the unique qualities and memories that all the recipients of the notes helped to create.

Although it was time-consuming, she hand signed all the cards, and on some of them she added a brief note, personalizing the "thank-you." She also had two blowups made of the card. She posted one on a bulletin board in the lobby of the hospital so that any staff member to whom she had not sent a thank-you note would also be thanked. The other blowup she framed and hung on a wall at LIFT House. Each of the residents who graduated from the course autographed it. It stands as a permanent reminder of the seriousness of purpose of the residents and the centrality of the children in the programming that LIFT House performs. It also gives Kristen a sense of her own efficacy when she has a bad day.

STEP 5: ANALYZING EVALUATIVE DATA

At the close of the graduation ceremony, the parents and guests milled around—few were eager to leave a group of people with whom they had shared many supportive moments in the past 2 months. There was much hugging and they crowded around Kristen and the nurse practitioner, saying fond goodbyes and telling them how much they had grown in their sense of security about being competent parents. These kinds of feelings and statements are music to the ears of hardworking planners when they complete a major project.

Anecdotal statements alone, however, are not sufficient to evaluate a program. They will certainly not be enough to convince the board of the hospital to repeat or expand the parenting program or to convince the foundation to fund it again. For sponsoring agencies as well as for one's own growth, one needs to apply systematic research methodology that refines the kinds of questions asked to help assess both the operation and the impact of the social program just completed.

Conducting a reasonably objective evaluation of how a program worked is a complex but achievable goal. Measuring the degrees of change in each participant's attitudes and actions in a statistically verifiable way, however, may not be completely satisfying. Every individual receives an intervention in a slightly different way according to his or her personality, characteristics, and life situation. As fraught with idiosyncrasy and outside influences as the process may be, however, it is of critical importance to the future programs.

Although we are discussing program evaluation in the last phase of the program development process, the thinking that goes into the evaluation process and the designing of evaluation strategies began, as you will remember, in the very early stages. As soon as the planners decided on their primary goals and strategies, they were beginning the evaluation process.

The evaluation techniques they choose serve many purposes and will be used in a variety of ways. Primary among them are the following:

- To demonstrate to the funding sources or sponsors of the program that the planners are serious about using the resources they have been given in the most sensible and efficient way
- To provide ongoing feedback to the coordinators and other planners so that adjustments in time and task schedules can be consistently and realistically adjusted as the process unfolds
- To provide a systematic way to collect and review the thoughts and feelings about the program from both participants and planners
- To improve elements of the program if it is repeated
- To expand the program development skills and insights of the planners
- To document the program's successes and shortcomings

- To add to the basic knowledge in the field of social service intervention (Abels & Murphy, 1981; Alter & Evans, 1990; Anspach, 1991; Rossi & Freeman, 1985; Smith, 1990)

Often, the planners are responsible for designing, administering, and analyzing evaluation techniques and documents. Occasionally, however, especially with larger programs funded by grants, an outside evaluator is brought in. Assessment of the program's strengths and weaknesses can be both helped and hindered by the use of an "outside expert." On the downside, if a program's funding hinges on the results of the evaluation, staff might feel it is in their best interest to gloss over problems that might alarm the funding source. An outside expert, however, can also encourage staff members to be more honest. The stranger is not a part of the daily life of the agency. Staff might feel protected against possible retribution if they express negative feelings—especially about the management of the agency.

Evaluation techniques, regardless of who performs them, can be divided into approximately two categories, although in actual practice they are on a continuum and often overlap. The *process* or *formative* instrument focuses on soliciting feedback on the program itself so as to improve the functioning of the ongoing program development process when repeated. The *product* or *summative* evaluation attempts to measure how successful the program was in achieving its initial goals in both the short term and the long term.

One might logically assume that a supportive and constructive planning process automatically leads to a successful outcome. The reverse might also appear to follow: A destructive or nonsupportive planning process will hinder a program from achieving its goals. Often, it does work out this way but not every time. For example, a cooperative and productive planning team can still produce a flawed program through their own miscalculations because of circumstances beyond their control, or both. It is like the situation in medicine in which "the operation was a success but the patient died!"

If the planning process was overly competitive and interactions among the planners were destructive, however, the event could still be well received by the public. The goal achievement from a professional perspective, however, is somewhat diminished. For the long-term health of the planning group, despite apparent success, it matters both how work is done and what, in fact, is achieved. A flawed planning process might eventually destroy the effectiveness of work in the future. Planners juggle a multiplicity of goals.

USING PROCESS OR FORMATIVE EVALUATION TECHNIQUES:
THE ONGOING USE OF EVALUATION TECHNIQUES

When they began their collaboration, Kristen and the nurse practitioner agreed on a format for their ongoing process evaluation. They decided to meet at the same time each week for 30 minutes, during which time they would focus on specific feedback from the previous session, make any refinements in their original plan, and assign tasks for the upcoming session. They promised each other that if one of them was forced to cancel a meeting, they would replace the face to face contact with a scheduled, uninterrupted 30-minute phone call. By setting the time aside to reflect, they could keep the channels of communication open between them and increase their understanding of the needs of each of the group members. Those insights would shape the planning for the next session. They committed themselves to being honest with each other, even if that meant they might not always be "polite." to each other.

The notes they took at each of their meetings were reviewed at the start of the next meeting. In that way, the items that did not get done could be discussed again and a readjustment could be made. Evaluative feedback was elicited with questions, mostly open-ended ones such as the following:

I wondered what you were thinking about how I intervened in the discussion last week. I wondered if I talked too much?

Do you think I was too rough on George when he started that stuff about fathers having to teach their daughters to be obedient? It really pushed my buttons.

A week after the program ended, Kristen and her co-leader held an overall summative evaluation. In an hour-long debriefing, or postmortem session, they discussed how they had worked together and how well each session of the course had been received. They examined their original proposal to assess where they started from and how far they had come. They also shared their professional opinions on what impact they thought the program had on the attitudes of each of the participants. Then, they wrote a summary for the final report. The report also included a description of the amount of time each had spent weekly and the way in which the parenting class program affected their other job assignments—Kristen's at LIFT House and the nurse's at the pediatric clinic.

During each parenting session, the participants were also involved in ongoing process evaluation. Sometimes, 10 minutes were set aside at the end of the meeting to solicit the participants' thoughts on what had just transpired. Often, however, new ideas need to simmer for a while. It is also difficult to state an honest opinion when a guest speaker is sitting in the circle or tempers are still hot from a debate. Therefore, at some sessions, the leaders chose to open the meeting with 10 minutes of critical reflection on the previous week's program. They phrased open-ended and semistructured questions and used the go-around approach. Starting at one point in the circle, they asked every other person to answer a few questions. They kept a tight rein on the time, however, because a lively discussion could sidetrack the plan for that evening, during which the topics to be discussed were also important. The following are some of the evaluative questions they asked:

What did you like best about the video we watched, what did you like least?

How close to your reality was the role-play we did? How useful was the discussion that followed it?

Someone suggested having a potluck supper at the last session, what are your thoughts on that idea?

PRODUCT OR SUMMATIVE TECHNIQUES: CREATING A WRITTEN ASSESSMENT OF PROGRAM QUALITY

For every program that LIFT sponsors, a final evaluative report must be produced. Staff use an evaluation report outline that can be adapted to the specific shape of their specific program. This form asks the planners to primarily assess input and process measures. Output or product is also assessed to the extent that is possible. The following sections discuss the steps in their assessment process.

Step 1: Breaking the Program Into Its Component Parts

The program participants are likely to sum up their responses to a program in a global sense, with statements such as "It was great, I loved it all!" or "It was a waste of my time or money!" These assessments might make the planner feel proud or cause consternation, but they do not tell the planner exactly which parts of the program worked well and should be repeated and which ones should be improved. In addition, global statements about programs are bound to be inaccurate. There is rarely a program that is all good or all bad.

To avoid glib generalizations, a planner must compose an evaluation by breaking the program into its component parts. Then, each part is put under a microscope. Some components are standard to almost every program—for example, all programs have a time schedule, a facility or location, and some types of activities. Each program, however, is bound to have a few unique parts. For example, some serve refreshments, some distribute materials, some involve transportation, and so on.

The following are the component parts of the parenting education program. Kristen used this list to compose her evaluation:

- Scheduling—when and for how long the class met
- Outreach techniques—strategies used to attract participants
- Facility—location, auspices, and room used
- Interaction—techniques used to encourage interaction, the leader's role in facilitating it, and the members' openness, articulateness, and so on
- Program—content or topics chosen, guest speakers, audiovisual aides, and so on and ways in which they were presented
- Written materials—articles, tapes, and videos that were used and distributed
- Leaders—how appropriate they were, the quality of their work, and so on
- Special events—graduation ceremony
- Overall atmosphere—level of comfort in expressing ideas and usefulness of the experience both in knowledge and in support
- Follow-ups—aids used to facilitate continued interaction, other activities that are spin-offs, and so on

Step 2: Soliciting Specific Information About the Strengths and Weaknesses of Each Component

To find out what she would do differently if she held the classes again, Kristen developed some specific questions. She composed her instrument so that it would be reasonably short and easy to complete but would not be so constricting that it kept participants from expressing their unique ideas and opinions.

Kristen wondered if she should make the evaluation instrument anonymous. On the one hand, if one of the parents had major questions that needed to be answered or strong negative feelings about what had transpired, she would like to be able to follow up on them. If any of the class members—especially the residents of LIFT House—felt they might be punished by her for having negative feedback, however, it is obviously unlikely that accurate opinions would be obtained without a guarantee of the safety afforded by anonymity.

She finally decided to let each class member make his or her own decision about signing the form or leaving the name line blank.

There are no formulas to follow in choosing for or against anonymity. Each organizer has to make this decision about confidentiality and anonymity based on the degree of sensitivity of the nature of his or her program and how the decision he or she makes might conceivably affect the honesty and quality of the answers solicited.

It needs to be stressed before administering a program evaluation that all planners grow from feedback; therefore, participants give planners a gift when they are honest. In turn, the leader has an obligation to consider their feedback seriously. Of course, the leader does not have to accept every suggestion made or vibrate to every negative criticism.

Step 3: Field Testing the Evaluation Instrument

After composing her first draft, Kristen "field tested" it by administering it to the LIFT residents who were in the class. Using their suggestions about clarity, content, and style, she fine-tuned it and produced her final copy.

Participant Evaluation of Parenting Classes

We want to make these classes as valuable as is possible and we know that they can be improved. We value your opinions, so please don't worry about hurting our feelings, tell it like it is!

I. Class Scheduling:

(frequency)—This class had 8 sessions. How many times would you have liked the class to meet?

_____ #_____ #_____

more times   less times   the same

(duration)—These classes lasted for 2 hours. How long do you think each class should be?

_____

(time of day)—We held these classes on a midweek evening. What time period do you think these classes should be?

_____

II. Out Reach:

How did you hear about this class? _____

Did you notice the advertising flyer in the pediatric waiting room? _____

Did you read the add in the *Daily Mirror*? _____

Did you hear our announcement on station WPIX? _____

What other ways can we use to tell young parents about the parenting classes?

_____

_____

III. The Facility:

We decided to hold these classes at the hospital and want to know how you think this worked out.

How did you get to the hospital? _____

How convenient was that for you? _____

What were the good things about having the meetings at this hospital? _____

_____

Any reasons you didn't like having the class here? _____

_____

Where do you think we should have it next time? _____

I suggest you hold the classes at _____ , (use hospital conference room again)

_____

IV. The Group Members:

This class was open to any young parents who used the hospital. We want to know if being open to everyone worked for you.

How do you think the other class members helped you learn? _____

_____

How do you think they got in the way of your learning? _____

_____

Mark the number of your overall level of comfort in this particular group

very comfortable   very uncomfortable

1   2   3   4   5

Why do you think that was? _____

_____

V. The Topics and Resource Materials:

There are so many issues to discuss about being a parent that we had to make hard choices on what to include and what to leave out.

For me, the most useful topics were _____

The least useful topics were _____

The topic I would like to talk more about is _____

The materials (written and videos) that were the most useful to me were _____

_____

_____

VI. The Instructors and Guests:

The things I liked the most about the instructors were _____

The things I liked the least about them were _____

The guests:

Which ones stand out in your memory as being most useful (by name if you can remember them _____

_____

VII. The Graduation Ceremony

If you were in charge of planning the next one what would you do the same and what would you change?

Do the same _____

Change _____

VIII. Overall Feelings About the Course:

If you had a friend who was becoming a parent would you recommend this course?

yes _____ or no _____ or with reservations

What would you tell him or her about it? _____

_____

IX. Follow-Ups:

Would you like additional meetings? If yes, how often? _____

We are willing to send out a list of the members' names and addresses as some of you might want to stay in touch.

Would you be willing to share your name and address with others in the class?

yes ____ no ____

Anything else you'd like to tell us? _____

_____

Step 4: Administering the Evaluation Form

Kristen knew both from reading the literature on research and from her past experience that if she handed the questionnaire out and left it up to the participants to return it, she would probably receive very few. Therefore, she decided to provide a few minutes during the last session for everyone to complete it.

She was sensitive to the fact that the sheer length of the questionnaire might be frightening to many of the participants, especially those for whom reading and writing did not come easily. To eliminate discomfort, she projected an image of each page on a large screen, using transparencies and a projector. Then, she read each question aloud, allowing a few moments for the members to record their answers. Although it looked long and detailed, it took only 15 minutes to complete. The members who missed that class or skipped over too many of the questions received a follow-up phone interview.

How Much Detail Is Needed?

The amount of information an evaluation questionnaire asks for is often determined by the newness of the program or of the leaders. It often is influenced by the likelihood that the program will be repeated. After Kristen completes many full cycles of the parenting course and readjusts the content and style several times, she will probably be much clearer about what works and what alternative arrangements are possible. It is likely that she will be far less dependent on the quality of feedback she gets from the participants. No matter how experienced the leader is with a particular program format, however, he or she must keep on soliciting evaluation. There is always a new idea, and one might become complacent if one does not take the time to ask the consumers what they think about what is being offered and what they want that is not being offered.

The thoroughness of a written questionnaire also depends on the opportunities the program has offered for verbal feedback as it progressed. For the camping trip, for example, Gardenia used a much less formal evaluation device. During the trip and especially on the way home in the van, the young women dissected every aspect of the experience they had shared. Because they interacted after the trip on a daily basis, they would keep on evaluating the program in many rich and informal ways.

Of course, no matter how much verbal feedback there has been, LIFT policy dictates that there be a written record of the details and strengths and weaknesses of each program. Gardenia brought a copy of the LIFT House program report to a posttrip meeting and together the group filled it in. When the young women resisted what they viewed as bureaucratic busywork, Gardenia pointed out that the next camping trip might be led by another volunteer with a whole new group of residents. They would need that written evaluation to benefit from the wisdom of the first group.

Other Methods of Evaluation

Many other techniques can be used to find out in what ways and to what extent the program has met its initial objectives in a variety of dimensions. The main outcome variables for training groups are participants' performances in targeted skills. With Kristen's program, that would mean the targeted cognitive and emotional areas of parenting that the program dealt with.

Research on the impact of various human service interventions is a vital and expanding area in the professional social service field. It is still quite primitive, however, and is beleaguered by many uncontrollable variables. It is also often limited by scarce time and human resources. When planners have had the commitment and been given the resources to build solid research expertise into their initial proposal, they have been well rewarded with solid insights on the utility of one intervention as opposed to others (see Alter & Evens, 1990).

Optimally, one could assess outcome by using the two-group method. For example, one offers a series of sessions to one group (the experimental group) and then identifies a similar group (control group) of young parents who have not taken the course. By comparing their knowledge and attitudes in the selected areas of parenting that the course covered, when the sessions begin and end, one could see if the experimental group had achieved greater knowledge, insight, and self-confidence. Kristen had neither the skill nor the resources to do this, but she realized it was an important omission in her design. Perhaps next time she could enlist help from the faculty of the local college.

Therefore, she settled for a reasonably simple single-group, pre- and posttest model design that examined selected areas of knowledge and attitudes and left the judgment about self-confidence to the participants' own estimates.

Pre- and Posttesting Program Impact

Assessing impact can, of course, be completed only when a program has terminated. When one assesses change, one is comparing a quality, generally attitudes or behaviors, with that same quality after experiencing the stimulus of the program intervention.

Kristen thought for a long time about how she might be able to assess the impact the parenting classes had on the attitudes, knowledge, and self-confidence of the parent participants. She was comfortable composing questions that would test the acquisition of simple factual knowledge about infant health and nutrition, but she was keenly aware of how difficult it is to asses change in qualities as global and diffuse as attitudes and self-confidence in relationship to parenting. She also knew that the kinds of changes found in a pencil-and-paper instrument administered immediately after the close of a program might not translate into actual changes in behavior. Often, the test is given while the participants are still feeling the first glow of enthusiasm from the group experience. What happens when that wears off? Similarly, she knew that learning and change are not linear processes. A person can be exposed to a set of stimuli at one time but not act on new insights he or she has gained until much time has passed. Finally, she knew that it is hard to pinpoint exactly what subtle interaction of stimuli from the intervention as well as the rest of a person's experiences are responsible for any change that does occur. She warned herself before analyzing the data not to overgeneralize any positive findings. She prepared herself not to feel deflated if there was not evidence of dramatic changes, however.

She constructed a 20-item questionnaire and at the first class and at the last class, she asked the class members to complete it. It was her hypothesis that after attending the eight sessions, class members would increase their ability to accurately answer some factual questions about nutrition and emergency first aid, would increase their understanding of the range of available options in disciplining their child, and would generally feel more secure in their parenting role. Constructing questions to tap the first two areas of change was relatively straightforward. She never did decide, however, how to assess growth in self-confidence other than to simply ask the participants to rank their feelings of security in being a parent at the first class and at the last class. The text box provides a sample of the pre- and posttest questions.

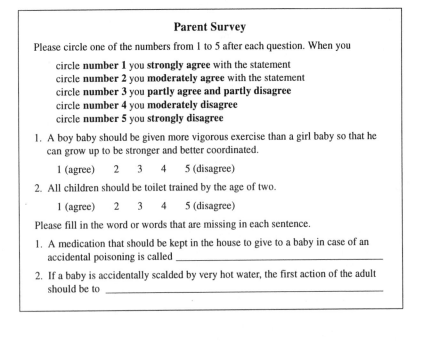

Parent Survey

Please circle one of the numbers from 1 to 5 after each question. When you

    circle **number 1** you **strongly agree** with the statement
    circle **number 2** you **moderately agree** with the statement
    circle **number 3** you **partly agree and partly disagree**
    circle **number 4** you **moderately disagree**
    circle **number 5** you **strongly disagree**

1. A boy baby should be given more vigorous exercise than a girl baby so that he can grow up to be stronger and better coordinated.

    1 (agree)   2   3   4   5 (disagree)

2. All children should be toilet trained by the age of two.

    1 (agree)   2   3   4   5 (disagree)

Please fill in the word or words that are missing in each sentence.

1. A medication that should be kept in the house to give to a baby in case of an accidental poisoning is called _____

2. If a baby is accidentally scalded by very hot water, the first action of the adult should be to _____

STEP 6: COMPOSING AND
DISSEMINATING THE FINAL REPORT

Composing and disseminating the final program report is the part of the development process that is the most likely to be neglected, even by the most competent planners. It feels so anticlimatic! The months of following up every detail and the exhilaration of the event itself have come and gone. Equipment has been tucked away, and the eager postmortems have been held. Now, most of the active planners turn their attention to the next project. The lack of an impressive final report—that shows the work in all its complexity and richness—can come back to haunt the planner. A final report can be a profoundly political document.

If Kristen hopes to repeat or expand the parenting classes, she will need to "show off" the positive aspects of both the process and the product of the first effort and demonstrate how the next classes might even be better. Simply knowing that it went well is not enough. Perhaps the LIFT board would rather have her invest her time elsewhere or perhaps the hospital administrators have other uses for their space.

A COMPREHENSIVE AND ATTRACTIVE FINAL REPORT
STATES THE CASE FOR THE ALLOCATION OF TIME
AND RESOURCES AS NO OTHER ARGUMENT CAN

An impressive report need not be an onerous chore. If the program organizers created and then carefully maintained a sensible filing and recording system and the evaluation process began at the inception of the program development, the final report should virtually write itself.

In addition to a four-page narrative describing each of the components of the parenting program and summarizing the evaluative comments and recommendations of participants and staff, Kristen's final report included the following:

1. The original proposal for the parenting course
2. The advertising flyers and press releases about the course
3. Samples of letters of understanding and memos to the hospital staff and guest speakers
4. The budget with income and outgo tallied
5. Samples of the course materials distributed
6. Copies of each the evaluation questionnaires
7. Articles about the program that appeared in a local newspaper and in the hospital newsletter

8. Selected photos and memorabilia, including two thank-you notes and a poem written by a grateful participant

Raymond designed an attractive cover for the report and had 10 copies put into a spiral binder. Kristen sent them, along with a personally addressed thank-you letter, to

- The chair of the board of LIFT
- The president of the hospital
- The director of the hospital pediatric clinic
- The LIFT liaison from the Department of Social Services
- The coteacher
- The president of the two foundations that are giving grants to LIFT

One of the bound copies was put in the file cabinet in Kristen's home, ready to be pulled out and proudly shared if in the future she applies for a job at another social agency or decides to return to school for an advanced degree. That report can also accompany her next grant proposal as a concrete example of her track record. Blowing one's own horn—when one has earned it—is a perfectly appropriate professional activity. In a period of downsizing, it may also be a survival strategy.

Finally, Kristen made several copies of the abstract and short narrative conclusion of her report and sent one to every speaker and to each of the participants.

DISSEMINATING THE INSIGHTS GAINED FROM CONDUCTING A PROGRAM INCREASES SERVICE TO CLIENTS AND ADDS KNOWLEDGE TO THE FIELD

At the end of a program, whether one feels the exhilaration of a successful outcome or the pain of some missed opportunities—or a bit of each—one needs to document one's efforts. Also, the story should be told in all its stimulating and painful details. The articles one prepares, based on practical wisdom, produce the new hybrid seeds that keep services spreading and improving. Robert Shore, the social entrepreneur who founded Share Our Skills (1995), calls this process of telling one's story and sending it far and wide "centering an idea." He says that if organizations want to reach beyond their own territory, one of the most effective things they can do is develop a plan to make their idea available to others. He suggests that planners should build into their overall design some funds and time to disseminate strategies for replication and technical assistance.

When Kristen was doing the initial research to prepare her first set of classes, she found the literature on programs for young parents of diverse ethnic and economic backgrounds very limited. Therefore, when all the program details were at an end, she sat down at her computer and turned her creative energies to writing her own article. Experimenting with new program formats and content and then passing on what has been learned is a professional obligation. It is also a satisfying reward for the painstaking work of successful program development.

In the library at the college, Kristen found a reference book that lists virtually every journal in the social services and the type of material they accept for publication (Katz & Katz, 1995). She was surprised to discover how many journals there were that she had never heard of but whose readers might be interested in learning about LIFT House and its many small-scale programs. She sent her article to the four that sounded the most appropriate, promising herself that if she received rejection slips she would keep on trying.

Using the same article as a base, Kristen also offered to conduct a workshop or speak on a panel at the annual conference of two professional associations: The Human Service Providers of Tri-State, of which she was a member, and a conference sponsored by a consortium of groups concerned about child welfare titled, "Homeless Children: A Call to Action," which she learned about from a notice on the library bulletin board.

When Kristen first began attending professional conferences, she wondered how the organizers located speakers. She hoped that she would someday be asked to lead a session, but no one had come calling. She realized that most of the time, workers in a particular area of practice who think they have something to say put their names on the mailings of the groups in their area of practice. That way, they receive the requests for proposals for workshops that are usually sent out several months before the conference planners have finalized the program. Once again, she realized that one must reach out to get in!

The LIFT board members supported Kristen's efforts to disseminate their program strategies, realizing that increasing her professional competence and the reputation of the agency would result in better service to the LIFT residents. They also were keenly aware that funding for programs such as LIFT is precarious. An informed and supportive profession and public are the only bulwarks against the endless assaults of the budget cutters.

THE 5-MINUTE RECAP

- The task and time flowchart for an event often continues for several weeks or months after the program has officially ended.

- The reader follows the process of terminating a program and looking to the future by reading about the steps taken by Kristen after she completes a series of parenting workshops.

- Double checking each detail involved in returning the program site to its previous condition is a task often omitted by planners. Omission of a significant follow-through task can diminish an otherwise successful event.

- Key to ending an event and maintaining one's credibility for the next one is the preparation of an accurate, detailed financial accounting.

- If more money has been spent than was originally allocated, the planners need to find additional sources of funds and analyze the reasons for the shortfall so this kind of miscalculation can be avoided if the program is repeated.

- Every program should include a plan to reach out to those who did not attend, both to share the materials they missed and to learn about any barriers that might have kept them from participating.

- It is a basic rule of thumb in program development that one cannot give too many thank-yous for help received. When thanks are extended in creative and appropriate ways, planners increase the possibilities of future cooperation.

- Conducting a reasonably objective evaluation of how well a program worked is a complex but achievable goal. Evaluation begins at the inception of the planning process.

- Process or formative evaluation techniques create an ongoing flow of feedback that reshapes a program as it unfolds and provides insights that can improve the planning process if the program is repeated.

- Outcome or summative evaluation focuses on assessing the extent to which the program has met its initial objectives in a variety of dimensions.

- Programs that include training groups might use a pre- and posttest format to assess the extent of attitude or behavior change among non-participants after exposure to the program.

- In the two-group method (often referred to as the experimental method), the participants can be compared with a sample of similar participants who have not been exposed to a particular program.

- A comprehensive final report states the case for the allocation of time and resources and can spread the wisdom gained through the program process to the next set of planners.

- Program development and impact reports help improve service to clients while adding to the body of knowledge of social service practice.

- Social service workers can protect and expand the funding for their programs by enhancing the reputation of their agency through presentations at professional conferences and articles in professional journals.

PUTTING THEORY INTO PRACTICE

EXERCISE 1: REACHING OUT TO THOSE WHO DID NOT PARTICIPATE

You have just completed an open house for a community residence for developmentally delayed adults. There was much neighborhood resistance to the house, so this was an especially critical event. Brainstorm and then describe at least four activities to reach out to those neighbors (abutters) who did not show up for the event.

Example

I would write a letter to the editor of the local newspaper describing the event and thanking the people and groups who came and donated. This would let those who did not come see how successful it was and let them know that some people they might know did support the event.

EXERCISE 2: READING AND ASSESSING IMPACT REPORTS

Collect the annual reports and any program reports you can find from two or more social agencies either by simply asking for them or by networking through contacts. Read and analyze these reports, asking some of the following questions:

What appear to be the goals of this report (is it primarily a public relations piece, a fund-raising document, etc.)?

What did you learn from this report that could help you to mount a similar program if that was your assignment?

What specific changes, if any, does the author suggest and on what data do those suggestions rest?

To what extent do you think the report honestly grapples with the strengths and weaknesses of the program described?

If you were to work at that agency or were asked to repeat one of the programs, in what ways would this report give you specific direction?

What questions would you like to ask the authors of this report?

EXERCISE 3: ASSESSING PROFESSIONAL
ARTICLES ON PILOT PROGRAMS

Seek out a specialized professional journal in the field of your special interest. It might be a journal that deals with social casework, counseling, family therapy, social change, health promotion, recreation, and so on. By reviewing the table of contents of several issues, identify a few articles that describe and evaluate specific small-scale programs. Assess the usefulness of these articles to you by answering the kind of questions posed in Exercise 2 and adding your own.

CITATIONS AND SUGGESTIONS FOR FURTHER READING

Howe, F. (1991). *The board member's guide to fund raising: What every trustee needs to know about raising money.* San Francisco: Jossey-Bass.

WRITING AND DISSEMINATING PROGRAM REPORTS

Beebe, L. (Ed.). (1993). *Professional writing for the human services.* Washington, DC: NASW Press. This book is useful for preparing the program report in the most professional but readable style possible.

Katz, B., & Katz, L. S. (1995). *Magazines for libraries* (8th ed.). New Providence, NJ: Bowker.

Shore, W. H. (1995). *Revolution of the heart: A new strategy for creating wealth and meaningful change.* New York: Riverhead Books.

PREPARING AN EVALUATION

Abels, P., & Murphy, M. J. (1981). *Evaluation in the human services: A normative approach.* Englewood Cliffs, NJ: Prentice Hall.

Alter, C., & Evans, W. (1990). *Evaluating your practice: A guide to self-assessment.* New York: Springer. This book provides excellent case studies of program interventions in which careful monitoring and ongoing assessment were able to yield insights into the comparative effectiveness of differing program interventions.

Anspach, R. R. (1991, February). Everyday methods for assessing organizational effectiveness. *Social Problems, 38*(1), 1-19.

Bloom, M., & Fischer, J. (1982). *Evaluating practice: Guidelines for the accountable professional.* Englewood Cliffs, NJ: Prentice Hall.

Marlow, C. (1993). *Research methods for generalist social work.* Pacific Grove, CA: Brooks/Cole. This book provides a well laid-out text that helps one see the immediate relevance of a variety of research techniques to agency practice. It is particularly sensitive to tapping into cultural differences in the populations being studied. It offers many examples of both qualitative and quantitative research studies conducted in agencies that might suggest models.

Rossi, P. H., & Freeman, H. E. (1985). *Evaluation: A systematic approach* (3rd ed.). Beverly Hills, CA: Sage. This book provides an in-depth discussion and description of strategies for impact assessment for those who can put more sophisticated effort into the design and implementation of an evaluation research design for a program.

Smith, M. J. (1990). *Program evaluation in the human services.* New York: Springer. This book is a straightforward text that presents the essential elements in evaluation of social programs in a very readable and immediately useful form. It presents case examples of program evaluations.

PLANNING AND CONDUCTING GROUPS AND CLASSES

Corey, M. S., & Corey, G. (1992). *Groups, process and practice* (4th ed.). Pacific Grove, CA: Brooks/Cole. This book offers an introduction to the theoretical and practical considerations in planning educational and support groups similar to the parenting sessions described in this chapter. Part 3 offers several examples of groups formed around the special needs of populations or different ages exploring a variety of issues.

Jolles, R. L. (1993). *How to run seminars and workshops, presentation skills for consultants, trainers and teachers.* New York: John Wiley. This book would be very helpful to those planning workshops similar to the ones used to illustrate this phase of the planning process.

Nelson-Jones, R. (1992). *Group leadership, a training approach.* Pacific Grove, CA: Brooks/Cole. This book focuses on enhancing life skills training in a variety of settings. It takes a cognitive, behavioral, humanistic approach. It has particularly strong chapters on using structured activities such as coaching, behavior rehearsal, and role-playing.

RESOURCES FOR PARENTING CLASSES

Braun, L. A., Coplon, J. K., & Sonnenschein, P. C. (1994). *Helping parents in groups.* Boston: Resource Communications.

Families in Society: The Journal of Contemporary Human Services. (1993, January). (Issue on fathers)

Families in Society: The Journal of Contemporary Human Services. (1993, June). (Issue on teen pregnancy)

Kissman, K. (1992, April). Parent skills training: Expanding school-based services for adolescent mothers. *Research on Social Work Practice, 2*(2), 161-171.

Lee, J. A. B. (1994). No place to go: Homeless women. In A. Gitterman & L. Shulman (Eds.), *Mutual aid groups, vulnerable populations and the life cycle* (2nd ed.). New York: Columbia University Press.

Lee, J. A. B., & Swenson, C. (1994). The concept of mutual aid. In A. Gitterman & L. Shulman (Eds.), *Mutual aid groups, vulnerable populations and the life cycle* (2nd ed.). New York: Columbia University Press.

Rose, S. (1980, May). Teaching single parents to cope with stress through small group interventions. *Small Group Behavior, 20*(2), 259-269.

APPENDIX
A Sample Proposal

To: Maureen Cannel, Director of Corporate Giving for Centerville Bank

From: The Board of Directors of LIFT House, Inc., Anna Lee Chu, Chair

Re: Request for $31,000 for a 1-year pilot program titled the FATHER Project (Forging A Trusting, Healthy, Energetic Relationship), an outreach program of casework, support groups, and father-child activities intended to increase the current and ongoing bonding of young single fathers and their children.

"It takes only a moment, to 'father' a child, but it takes a life time to be a father to a child."

TABLE OF CONTENTS

220

INTRODUCTION

The members of the board of directors of LIFT House, a residence for young, previously homeless single women and their infant children (see brochure and annual report in Attachment A) are proud of their successful track record of working with new female-headed families. We have helped to create a safe and healthy environment for the babies and provided counseling that has helped the young mothers make realistic plans for their futures. All our residents are enrolled in programs that provide the training and education they need to become independent. We have, however, become increasingly concerned with our lack of progress in consistently and positively involving the fathers of the children who reside at the house.

A few of the fathers have come to visit fairly often, and a few have taken their children to their own homes or to their parents' homes for occasional visits. In most instances, however, the visits diminish after the first few months. Often the fathers' relationships with the mothers are so fraught with tension and anger that the mothers discourage contact between the child and father. Some of the mothers have lost track of the fathers' addresses, and in some cases the young mother has fled from the relationship because of concerns for her own or her child's safety.

The disengagement of the fathers from their children and from their children's mothers increases the financial pressures and emotional stress for the single-mother family. Disengagement from their fathering role can also create a legacy of guilt and shame for the young fathers, lessening the possibility of future involvement with the LIFT child and perhaps lessening the likelihood of their building a positive relationship with any other children they might father.

We do not believe that the disengagement of these young fathers from their children is inevitable. Also, we are not willing to "write off" these young fathers with the platitude, "boys will be boys." We reject the facile assumption that these fathers are not willing or able to care for and about their children. Rather, we are convinced that this disengagement is often the expression of—or the end result of—more far-ranging and complex problems in the lives of the young fathers and mothers. We believe that it is our role, as an agency committed to strengthening family life, to mount a frontal assault on these obstacles to fathering.

With the upheaval in welfare funding and the imposition of time limits on benefits, the urgency for this kind of outreach has been heightened.

STATEMENT OF THE PROBLEM

A review of the literature of successful programs for young fathers' and an in-depth survey we conducted of 16 fathers in four agencies that serve young single mothers (see Attachment B) point to the following several possible causes of the disengagement of young fathers:

- Denial or doubt about having "fathered" the child
- Feelings of inadequacy in taking on an unfamiliar, nurturing role, especially one that is not always accorded high status by the community or group
- Fear that by reaching out to their children they will be "entrapped" by the social service or legal system into financial support they cannot afford
- Crises or preoccupations in the fathers' lives that keep them from functioning in an appropriate or dependable way
- Tensions and conflict in the relationship with the mother of his child
- A feeling that they are not welcomed by the LIFT staff and residents or by the families of the young mothers

GOALS OF THE PROGRAM

The causes of disengagement point to possible strategies. Despite deep-seated suspicion and other negative feelings on the part of both the mothers and the fathers, we believe that many of these barriers to involvement might be *lessened* by a well-conceived, multipronged program. Toward this end, we propose the FATHER project, which will carefully reach out to the fathers of the residents of LIFT House. FATHER will welcome, teach, and empower them to assume a role in the lives of their children. We will be realistic in our goals and assess progress in small steps, understanding that from such steps bonding can take place that may brae fruit in the future. FATHER will undertake to:

1. locate each of the young fathers of LIFT residents, wherever possible, and create an individual action plan with him
2. teach and afford opportunities to practice basic parenting skills that will increase the self-confidence and skills of the young fathers
3. provide structured opportunities for interaction with the fathers' children in a manner tailored to the special needs of young fathers and their children
4. help young fathers understand and deal with the legal issues involved in their parenting responsibilities and to advocate for fair treatment
5. connect young fathers to those services and agencies that might help them cope with some of the crises in their personal lives that prevent them from parenting
6. provide a safe place for the mothers and fathers to ventilate negative feelings and find ways to share parenting information, decisions, and responsibilities
7. review each program to assess the ways in which fathers can be more positively integrated into LIFT House and to consistently evaluate and improve them

8. identify and train a few of the most able young fathers to work as part-time outreach and program aides

9. disseminate the wisdom we gain through this pilot project to other social service and community agencies

PROPOSED PROGRAM ACTIVITIES

1. *Individual casework* contacts will be made with the fathers of the children who currently live at LIFT and those who have graduated. To the extent possible, an action plan will be created by the father and the coordinator that will describe the services the father needs and the project activities he is willing to participate or take leadership in.

2. *A couple's discussion or support group,* focused around coparenting issues and conflicts, will be held each week with individual crisis intervention done with couples and individuals as needed.

3. *A six-session parenting course* in basic child maintenance and discipline skills for up to six fathers at a time will be repeated as needed.

4. *A weekly activity or outing* will be held at LIFT each weekend for up to five fathers and their children.

5. *Selected holiday and birthday celebrations* at the house will be organized to include the fathers and extended families in both the planning and participation.

6. *Dinner with Dads* will be held once each week (although fathers are welcome to see their children at dinnertime on other evenings).

STAFF REQUIRED

1. *FATHER coordinator:* A full-time position that reports to the program director of LIFT and consults with the FATHER advisory committee (see Attachment C for potential members and their affiliations) and a professional social worker.

   The person who fills this role should have had at least 3 years of experience in a group setting with some case management and program planning under professional supervision. Educational background beyond high school can vary, but college courses in child and adolescent development and excellent communication skills are helpful. Personal experience as a young father will also be very helpful.

2. *Consultant:* Centerville Mental Health Association will provide 2 hours each week for a social worker or counselor who will offer professional supervision to the FATHER coordinator and co-lead the couple's support and discussion group.

3. *Part-time program aide:* The coordinator will, as it becomes possible, hire one of the fathers as a program assistant with a small stipend.
4. *Program volunteers:* The LIFT program director will assign three experienced program volunteers to assist in FATHER activities.

BUDGET

	Requested	*Donated*[a]
Personnel:		
FATHER coordinator: 2/3 time	$23,000	
Fringe benefits, 22%	5,060	
Program aide		
$35 a week for 1 year	1,820	
Transportation:		
For program activities in house	200	
For van rentals, admissions, etc.	520	
Phone, stamps, and clerical		
(LIFT will absorb costs)		450
Refreshments:		
For meetings and celebrations		
LIFT will absorb dinner costs		500
Program materials:		
For classes and groups	300	
Admission fees, etc.	100	
Facility:		
LIFT will absorb space and utilities costs		
estimated at $300 per month		3,600
Consultation and evaluation:		
Centerville Mental Health Association will absorb costs		
104 hours at $50 per hour		5,200
Total cost of program for 1 year	$40,750	
Total requested from the Centerville Bank	$31,000	

a. Also called "in-kind" contributions.

EVALUATION

The FATHER Project will utilize the following materials in its ongoing and cumulative evaluation:

1. Weekly progress notes will be made on each action plan.
2. Program impact summaries will be written on each activity.
3. Participant feedback forms will be used for parenting classes and support groups.
4. Each advisory committee member will be asked to observe at least two activities and write an assessment.
5. Advisory board or staff retreat will assess progress at 6-month intervals.
6. Centerville Mental Health Association will prepare 6-month analysis of movement toward goals in each area and suggest changes based on client interviews, summaries, and advisory board feedback.

HIGHLIGHTS OF WORK PLAN
(* Continuing Activity)

Month #1   Orientation to house and individual interviews with LIFT residents
            Set up work space and forms
            Interviews with potential members of advisory committee
            Set date and arrangements for first meeting in Month #2

Month #2   Make contacts with LIFT alumni mothers*
            Create brochure and fact sheet
            Begin outreach to fathers*
            First Dinner with Dads night*·
            Initial advisory committee meeting

Month #3   First weekend activity*
            Begin couple's support group*
            First holiday celebration for families of mothers and fathers
            Preparation of first monthly newsletter*
            Report to LIFT board
            Preparation of written action plans for three fathers*

Month #4   Second advisory committee meeting

Arrangements of first six-session parenting class to begin in
Month #5

Follow-up activities on action plans*

Set date and arrangements for advisory committee retreat for
Month #6

Month #5   Begin first parenting class

Second holiday celebration

Prepare written action plans for three more fathers

Month #6   Finish first parenting class

Advisory committee retreat

Prepare midyear progress report and set goals for next half year

REFERENCES

Abels, P., & Murphy, M. J. (1981). *Evaluation in the human services: A normative approach.* Englewood Cliffs, NJ: Prentice Hall.

Adler, G. (1994). Community action and maximum feasible participation: An opportunity lost but not forgotten for expanding democracy at home. *Notre Dame Journal of Law, Ethics and Public Policy, 8*(2), 547-571.

Aldridge, T., Macy, H., & Walz, T. (1982). *Beyond management: Humanizing the administrative process.* Iowa City: University of Iowa Press.

Alter, C., & Evens, W. (1990). *Evaluating your practice: A guide to self-assessment.* New York: Springer.

Annual Registry of Grants Support. (1995). New Providence, NJ: Bowker.

Anspach, R. R. (1991, February). Everyday methods for assessing organizational effectiveness. *Social Problems, 38*(1), 1-19.

Axinn, & Levin, (1997). *Social welfare: A history of the American response to need* (4th ed.). White Plains, NY: Longman.

Bard, R. (1971). *Program and staff evaluation.* Washington, DC: Education Training & Research Sciences.

Beebe, L. (Ed.). (1993). *Professional writing for the human services.* Washington, DC: National Association of Social Workers Press.

Berrick, J. D. (1995). *Faces of poverty, portraits of women and children on welfare.* New York: Oxford University Press.

Bloom, M., & Fischer, J. (1982). *Evaluating practice: Guidelines for the accountable professional.* Englewood Cliffs, NJ: Prentice Hall.

Bobo, K., Kendall, J., & Max, S. (1991). *Organizing for social change, a manual for activists in the 1990's* (2nd ed.). Washington, DC: Seven Locks Press.

Boston Women's Health Book Collective. (1976). *Our bodies ourselves: A book by and for women.* New York: Simon & Schuster.

Boston Women's Health Book Collective. (1978). *Ourselves and our children: A book by and for parents.* New York: Random House.

Boston Women's Health Book Collective. (1992). *The new our bodies ourselves: A book by and for women.* New York: Simon & Schuster.

Brakeley, G. A., Jr. (1993). *Tested ways to successful fund raising.* Printed by University Microfilm International, 300 N. Zeeb Road, Ann Arbor, MI.

Braun, L. A., Coplon, J. K., & Sonnenschein, P. C. (1994). *Helping parents in groups.* Boston: Resource Communications.

Brawley, E. A. (1983). *Mass media and human services: Getting the message across.* Beverly Hills, CA: Sage.

Brody, R. (1993). *Effectively managing human service organizations.* Newbury Park, CA: Sage.

Brown, J. (1994). Agents of change: A group of women in a shelter. In A. Gitterman & L. Shulman (Eds.), *Mutual aid groups, vulnerable populations and the life cycle* (2nd ed., pp. 273). New York: Columbia University Press.

Christian, W. P., Hannah, G. T., & Glahn, T. J. (Eds.). (1984). *Programming effective human services: Strategies for institutional change and client transition.* New York: Plenum.

Clifton, R. L., & Dahms, A. M. (1993). *Grassroots organizations. A resource book for directors, staff and volunteers of small, community based nonprofit agencies* (2nd ed.). Prospect Heights, IL: Waveland.

Cloward, R. A., & Piven, F. F. (1971). *Regulating the poor.* New York: Random House.

Coley, M., Soraya, M., & Scheinberg, C. A. (1990). *Proposal writing.* Newbury Park, CA: Sage.

Conrad, W. R., Jr., & Glenn, W. E. (1983). *The effective voluntary board of directors.* Athens, OH: Swallow Press.

Coover, V., Deacon, C., Esser, R., & Moore, P. (1978). *Resource manual for a living revolution.* Philadelphia: New Society Press.

Corey, M. S., & Corey, G. (1992). *Groups, process and practice* (4th ed.). Pacific Grove, CA: Brooks/Cole.

Covey, S. R. (1990). *The 7 habits of highly effective people: Restoring the character ethic.* New York: Simon & Schuster.

Cox, F. M., Erlich, J. L., Rothman, J., & Tropman, J. E. (Eds.). (1987). *Strategies of community organization: Macro practice* (4th ed.). Itasca, IL: Peacock.

Dale, D., & Mitguy, N. (1978). *Planning for a change: A citizen's guide to creative planning and program development.* Amherst: University of Massachusetts, Citizen's Involvement Training Project.

Directory of grants. (1996). Phoenix, AZ: Oryx Press.

Dluhy, M. J. (with Kravitz, S. L.). (1990). *Building coalitions in the human services.* Newbury Park, CA: Sage.

Doress, P. B., & Siegel, D. L. (in cooperation with Boston Women's Health Book Collective). (1994). *The new ourselves growing older: Women aging with knowledge and power.* New York: Simon & Schuster.

Drucker, P. (1973). *Management: Tasks, responsibilities, practices.* New York: Harper & Row.

Drucker, P. F. (1985). *Innovation and entrepreneurship: Practice and principle.* New York: Harper & Row.

Duffy, T. K. (1995). The check-in and the go-rounds in group work: Guidelines for use. In L. Schulman (Ed.) (with Boston University School of Social Work Group Work Faculty), *Readings in differential social work practice with groups.* New York: American Heritage.

Dyckman, J. W. (1983). Social planning, social planners and planned societies. In R. Kramer & H. Specht (Eds.), *Readings in community organization practice* (3rd ed.). Englewood Cliffs, NJ: Prentice Hall.

Ecklein, J. L., & Lauffer, A. (1972). *Community organizers and social planners. A volume of case and illustrative materials.* New York: John Wiley/CSWE.

Ephross, P. H., & Vassil, T. V. (1988). *Groups that work.* New York: Columbia University Press.

Epstein, I., & Tripodi, T. (1977). *Research techniques for program planning, monitoring and evaluation.* New York: Columbia University Press.

Families in Society: The Journal of Contemporary Human Services. (1993, January). (Issue on fathers)

Families in Society: The Journal of Contemporary Human Services. (1993, June). (Issue on teen pregnancy)

Fatout, M., & Rose, S. (1995). *Task groups in the social services.* Thousand Oaks, CA: Sage.

Fischer, L. R., & Schaeffer, K. B. (1993). *Older volunteers: A guide to research and practice.* Newbury Park: Sage.

Forester, J. (1989). *Planning in the face of power.* Berkeley: University of California Press.

Fram, E. H. (with Brown, V.). (1994). *Policy vs. paper clips: Selling the corporate model to your non-profit board* (2nd ed.). WI: Families International.

Frame, D. J. (1995). *Managing projects in organizations: How to make the best use of time technique and people.* San Francisco: Jossey-Bass.

Freeman, J. (1972). The tyranny of structurelessness. In A. Koedt, E. Levine, & A. Rapone (Eds.), *Radical feminism* (pp. 285-299). New York: Quadrangle.

Gardner, H. (1995). *Frames of mind: The theory of multiple intelligences.* New York: Basic Books.

Gardner, J. W. (1964). *Self-renewal: The individual and the innovative society.* New York: Harper & Row.

Garland, J. A., Jones, H., & Kolodney, R. (1973). A model for stages of development in social work groups. In S. Bernstein (Ed.), *Explorations in group work.* Boston: Milford House.

Geever, J. C., & McNeill, P. (1995). *Guide to proposal writing.* New York: Foundation Center.

Gronbjerg, K. (1993). *Understanding nonprofit funding: Managing revenues in social services and community development organizations.* San Francisco: Jossey-Bass.

Gummer, B. (1990). *The politics of social administration: Managing organization politics in social agencies.* Englewood Cliffs, NJ: Prentice Hall.

Haines, B., & McKeachie, W. (1982). Cooperative versus competitive discussion methods in teaching introductory psychology. *Journal of Educational Psychology, 58,* 386-390.

Hare, A. P. (1976). *Handbook of small group research* (2nd ed.). New York: Free Press.

Henry, S. (1992). *Group skills in social work, A four-dimensional approach* (2nd ed.). Pacific Grove, CA: Brooks/Cole.

Horowitz, R. (1995). *Teen mothers: Citizens or dependents.* Chicago: University of Chicago Press.

Howe, F. (1991). *The board member's guide to fund raising: What every trustee needs to know about raising money.* San Francisco: Jossey-Bass.

Human Services Yellow Pages of Connecticut. (1996). Boston, MA: George D. Hall.

Human Services Yellow Pages of Massachusetts. (1996). Boston, MA: George D. Hall.

Human Services Yellow Pages of New York. (1996). Boston, MA: George D. Hall.

Human Services Yellow Pages of Rhode Island. (1996). Boston, MA: George D. Hall.

Ilsley, P., Jr. (1990). *Enhancing the volunteer experience: New insights on strengthening volunteer participation, learning and commitment.* San Francisco: Jossey-Bass.

Jansson, B. S., & Taylor, S. H. (1978, Summer). The planning contradiction in social agencies: Great expectations versus satisfaction with limited performance. *Administration in Social Work, 2,* 176.

Jencks, C. (1987). Who gives to what? In W. W. Powell (Ed.), *The non-profit sector: A research handbook.* New Haven, CT: Yale University Press.

Jolles, R. L. (1993). *How to run seminars and workshops, presentation skills for consultants, trainers and teachers.* New York: John Wiley.

Jorgenson, J. D., Scheier, I. H., & Fautsko, T. F. (1981). *Solving problems in meeting.* Chicago: Nelson-Hall.

Katz, B., & Katz, L. S. (1995). *Magazines for libraries* (8th ed.). New Providence, NJ: Bowker.

Kettner, P. M., Moroney, R. M., & Martin, L. L. (1990). *Designing and managing programs: An effectiveness-based approach.* Newbury Park, CA: Sage.

Kissman, K. (1992, April). Parent skills training: Expanding school-based services for adolescent mothers. *Research on Social Work Practice, 2*(2), 161-171.

Kotler, P. (1982). *Marketing for non-profit organizations* (2nd ed.). Englewood Cliffs, NJ: Prentice Hall.

Kouri, M. K. (1990). *Volunteerism and older adults: Choices and challenges.* Santa Barbara, CA: ABC CLIO.

Kramer, R., & Specht, H. (1983). *Readings in community organization practice* (3rd ed.). Englewood Cliffs, NJ: Prentice Hall.

Kretzmann, J. P., & McKnight, J. (1993). *Building community from the inside out, a path towards finding and mobilizing a community's assets.* Evanston, IL: Northwestern University, Neighborhood Innovation Network. (Distributed by ACTA Publications, 4848 N. Clark St., Chicago, IL 60640)

Lakien, A. (1974). *How to get control of your time and your life.* New York: New American Library.

Lauffer, A. (1978). *Social planning at the community level.* Englewood Cliffs, NJ: Prentice Hall.

Lauffer, A. (1982). *Assessment tools for practitioners, managers, and trainers.* Beverly Hills, CA: Sage.

Lauffer, A. (1983). *Grantsmanship* (2nd ed.). Beverly Hills, CA: Sage.

Lauffer, A. (1984). *Strategic planning for not-for-profit organizations and resource development.* New York: Free Press.

Lauffer, A. (1997). *Grants etc.* Thousand Oaks, CA: Sage.

Lee, J. A. B. (1994). No place to go: Homeless women. In A. Gitterman & L. Shulman (Eds.), *Mutual aid groups, vulnerable populations & the life cycle* (2nd ed.). New York: Columbia University Press.

Lee, J. A. B., & Swenson, C. (1994). The concept of mutual aid. In A. Gitterman & L. Shulman (Eds.), *Mutual aid groups, vulnerable populations and the life cycle* (2nd ed.). New York: Columbia University Press.

Lefferts, R. (1982). *Getting a grant: How to write successful grant proposals* (2nd ed.). Englewood Cliffs, NJ: Prentice Hall.

Leibert, E. R., & Sheldon, B. E. (1974). *Handbook of special events for non-profit organizations.* New York: Association Press.

Levine, H., & Levine, C. (1969). *Effective public relations for community groups.* New York: Association Press.

Lewis, J. A., Lewis, M. D., & Souflee, F., Jr. (1991). *Management of human service programs* (2nd ed.). Pacific Grove, CA: Brooks/Cole.

Lohmann, R. A. (1980). *Breaking even; Financial management in human service organizations.* Philadelphia: Temple University Press.

MacDonald, G. C. (1991). *Adolescent mother-infant dyads: Enhancing interactive reciprocy.* Unpublished master's thesis, Boston University.

MacGregor, D. (1965). *The human side of enterprise.* New York: McGraw-Hill.

Maguire, L. (1983). *Understanding social networks.* Beverly Hills, CA: Sage.

Marlow, C. (1993). *Research methods for generalist social work.* Pacific Grove, CA: Brooks/Cole.

Mendelsohn, H. N. (1987). *A guide to information sources for social work and the human services.* Phoenix, AZ: Oryx Press.

Moore, C. (1994). *Group techniques for idea building* (2nd ed.). Thousand Oaks, CA: Sage.

Moroney, R. M. (1977). Needs assessment for human services. In B. J. Friedan & M. J. Murphy (Eds.), *Managing human services.* Washington, DC: International City Management Association.

Nelson-Jones, R. (1992). *Group leadership, a training approach.* Pacific Grove, CA: Brooks/Cole.

O'Connell, B. (1976). *Effective leadership in voluntary organizations: How to make the greatest use of citizen service and influence.* New York: Association Press.

O'Connell, B. (1985). *The board member's book: Making a difference in voluntary organizations.* New York: Foundation Center.

Osborne, A. F. (1957). *Applied imagination* (Rev. ed.). New York: Scribner.

Ovrebo, B., Ryan, M., Jackson, K., & Hutchinson, K. (1994, Summer). The homeless prenatal program: A model for empowering homeless pregnant women. *Health Education Quarterly, 21*(2), 187-198.

Patti, R. J. (1983). *Social welfare administration: Managing social programs in a developmental context.* Englewood Cliffs, NJ: Prentice Hall.

Patton, M. Q. (1982). *Practical evaluations.* Beverly Hills, CA: Sage.

Patton, M. Q. (1987). *How to use qualitative methods in evaluation.* Newbury Park, CA: Sage.

Powell, M. C. (1994). On creativity and social change. *Journal of Creative Behavior, 28*(1), 21-32.

Powers, G. T., Meenaghan, T. M., & Toomey, B. G. (1985). *Practice focused research, integrating human service practice and research.* Englewood Cliffs, NJ: Prentice Hall.

Prince, R. A., & File, K. M. (1994). *The seven faces of philanthropy: A new approach to cultivating major donors.* San Francisco, CA: Jossey-Bass.

Raider, M. (1977, Fall). Installing management by objectives in social agencies. *Administration in Social Work, l.*

Robinson, A. (1995). *Grassroots grants, an activist's guide to proposal writing.* Berkeley, CA: Chardon Press.

Rose, S. (1980, May). Teaching single parents to cope with stress through small group interventions. *Small Group Behavior, 20*(2), 259-269.

Rossi, P. H., & Freeman, H. E. (1985). *Evaluation: A systematic approach* (3rd ed.). Beverly Hills, CA: Sage.

Rothman, J., Erlich, J. L., & Teresa, J. G. (1976). *Promoting innovation and change in organizations: A planning manual.* New York: John Wiley.

Rothman, J., Erlich, J. L., & Teresa, J. G. (1981). *Changing organizations and community programs* (Rev. ed.). New York: John Wiley.

Rubright, R., & MacDonald, D. (1981). *Marketing health and human services.* Rockville, MD: Aspen Systems.

Schaefer, M. (1987). *Implementing change in service programs, project planning, and management.* Newbury Park CA.: Sage.

Schram, B., & Mandell, B. R. (1997). *Introduction to human services policy and practice* (3nd ed.). Veedham, MA: Allyn & Bacon.

Schumacher, E. F. (1975). *Small is beautiful: Economics as if people mattered* (pp. 217). New York: Harper/Calaphone.

Seaman, D. F. (1981). *Working effectively with task-oriented groups.* New York: McGraw-Hill.

Shaw, S. C., & Taylor, M. A. (1995). *Reinventing fundraising: Realizing the potential of women's philanthropy.* San Francisco, CA: Jossey-Bass.

Shore, W. H. (1995). *Revolution of the heart: A new strategy for creating wealth and meaningful change.* New York: Riverhead Books.

Siefert, M. B. (1991, April). Skill building for effective intervention with homeless families. *Families in Society, 72*(4), 212-219.

Smith, M. J. (1990). *Program evaluation in the human services.* New York: Springer.

Soriano, F. I. (1995). *Conducting needs assessments, a multidisciplinary approach.* Thousand Oaks, CA: Sage.

Tropman, J. E. (1980). *Effective meetings, improving group decision making.* Beverly Hills, CA: Sage.

Ulshak, F. L., Nathanson, L., & Gillan, P. G. (1981). *Small group problem solving: An aid to organizational effectiveness.* Reading, MA: Addison-Wesley.

Upshur, C. C. (1982). *How to set up and operate a non-profit organization: Guidelines and procedures for incorporating, raising funds, writing grant proposals.* Englewood Cliffs, NJ: Prentice Hall.

Van Gundy, A. B. (1988). *Techniques of structured problem solving* (2nd ed.). New York: Van Nostrand Rienhold.

Walsh, M. E. (1992). *Moving to nowhere, children's stories of homelessness.* New York: Auburn House.

Wayne, J. (1995). Group work model to reach isolated mothers: Preventing child abuse. In L. Schulman (Ed.) (with Group Work Faculty, Boston University School of Social Work), *Readings in differential social work practice with groups.* New York: American Heritage.

Wayne, J., & Avery, N. (1979, January). Activities for group termination. *Social Work, 24*(1), 58-62.

Weinbach, R. (1994). *The social worker as manager, theory and practice* (2nd ed.). Needham, MA: Allyn & Bacon.

White, S. (1981). *Managing health and human service programs: A guide for managers.* New York: Free Press.

Who Cares Magazine, 1511 K St. NW, Suite 1042, Washington, DC, 20005, (202) 628-1691.

Winston, S. (1991). *Getting organized* (Rev. ed.). New York: Warner.

Wuthnow, R. (1994). *Sharing the journey: Support groups and America's new quest for community.* New York: Free Press.

INDEX

ABOUT THE AUTHOR

Barbara Schram has a Masters degree in Social Group Work from Columbia University and a doctorate in educational policy and administration from Harvard University. She has also been a long time organizer and activist in a variety of welfare rights and women's groups. She founded and now teaches in the Human Services Program at Northeastern University in Boston, MA.